For Barbara
&
Chuck
with love

[signature]

Voting with Dollars

Voting with Dollars

A New Paradigm for Campaign Finance

Bruce Ackerman and Ian Ayres

YALE UNIVERSITY PRESS   New Haven & London

Published with assistance from the foundation established in memory of Amasa Stone Mather of the Class of 1907, Yale College.

Set in Minion type by Achorn Graphic Services, Worcester, Massachusetts.
Printed in the United States of America by R. R. Donnelley and Sons, Harrisonburg, Virginia.

Library of Congress Cataloging-in-Publication Data

Ackerman, Bruce A.
Voting with dollars : a new paradigm for campaign finance / Bruce Ackerman and Ian Ayres.
    p.   cm.
Includes bibliographical references and index.
ISBN 0-300-09262-8 (cloth : alk. paper)
1. Campaign funds—United States.   I. Ayres, Ian.   II. Title.
JK1991   .A624   2002
324.7′8′0973—dc21
2001005370

A catalogue record for this book is available from the British Library.

The paper in this book meets the guidelines for permanence and durability of the Committee on Production Guidelines for Book Longevity of the Council on Library Resources.

10 9 8 7 6 5 4 3 2 1

For GUIDO CALABRESI, *trailblazer*

CONTENTS

FREE LUNCHES

There are lots of lunches behind this book. Ayres is especially indebted to a fateful lunch with Jeremy Bulow three years ago. Without Bulow's insights, he would never have been in a position to develop the notion of a secret donation booth.

The next crucial lunch was between Ayres and Ackerman, who had already been working on "patriot dollars." After a lot of munching and mulling, it began to seem that the two projects had a nonaccidental relation to one another. The "new paradigm" was on its way.

Enter Dan Berube—a successful lawyer from Memphis, Tennessee, whose academic ambitions got the better of him, propelling him to the doctoral program in Yale's political science department. Dan landed in Ackerman's seminar in theory and practice and took up the new paradigm with a vengeance. Given his legal skills, he was the perfect person to take the lead in writing a model statute. Our lunches were now trios—with Dan's probing questions forcing us to refine the broader project in many important ways.

As the book took shape, we passed it around and received valuable comments from Larry Alexander, Anne Alstott, Richard Briffault, Guido Calabresi, Jeffrey Gordon, Greg Klass, Sai Prakash, Andrzej Rapaczynski, and Fred Vars. Ayres tested it out in seminars at Columbia and San Diego; Ackerman at lectures at Princeton, Berkeley, Cardozo, and Brown. We came together for two insightful discussions at Yale Law School—one at the regular faculty seminar, another at Yale's annual global constitutionalism seminar attended by constitutional court judges from around the world.

We were also lucky to have found an incredibly dedicated group of Yale law students to serve as research assistants. Without them, we could never have mastered the details of current campaign finance regulation. Priya Aiyar, Bertrand-Marc Allen, Debajit Banerjee, Martina Caroni, Winter King, and Reshma Saujani spent seemingly countless hours trying to plug the infamous (and ever-expanding) master gaps list.

Thanks, finally, to our boss and friend, Tony Kronman, for footing the bill for this massive research effort.

I

The New Paradigm

1 Reforming Reform

Campaign finance lives in a time warp, untouched by the regulatory revolution of the past generation. Reformers suppose that they can adapt well-established models to fix the problem of big money in politics. But they are wrong. Real progress requires us to rethink the very foundations of the enterprise.

The old paradigm has three elements. The first confronts big money as if it raised a problem similar to the one posed by polluters dumping garbage into a waterway. The Environmental Protection Agency not only restricts the garbage each polluter can dump but places an overall limit on the amount of junk in the river. Why not do the same when big money pollutes democratic politics?

To be sure, the Supreme Court has resisted this analogy in the name of the First Amendment—repeatedly striking down efforts to restrict overall campaign spending. But judicial intervention manages only to precipitate predictable boos from the left, and cheers from the right, with no serious efforts at reappraisal from either side.

The debate is no less pre-scripted when we turn to a second basic remedy. Why not reduce or eliminate the flood of private money by providing for publicly subsidized campaigns? Reformers invariably understand the injection of "clean money" as a centralized process—replete with heavy-handed requirements that favor incumbents, entrench existing parties, and alienate citizens from funding decisions. Their basic proposal would serve just as well for farmers or arms exporters. Apparently, only minor modifications are required before politicians can join the feast at the federal trough.

For conservatives, the prospect of a political feeding frenzy heightens anxieties provoked by rigid command and control over private fund-raising.

But even their opposition wanes as they turn to the third reform plank. The reigning paradigm demands full publicity for all contributions. The public has a right to know who is paying whom when. With every deal open and aboveboard, let the voters decide whether a big gift or giver taints the candidate's integrity. This full-information plank has gained increasing prominence over the past decade. Even strict conservatives concede that secret transfers of cash look suspicious.[1] If the public keeps demanding reform, the best way to channel protest is by insisting on full information. Still more recently, leading liberals have been coming to the same conclusion as they despair when confronting the intractable difficulties of implementing other parts of the traditional paradigm.[2]

We challenge the organizing premise of this now-familiar debate. All three pathways to reform draw from a century-long argument about the regulation of the economy. Whenever a policy wonk confronts the widget market, it is second nature to ask whether widgets generate harms to third parties that require command and control regulation, whether widget producers need subsidizing to achieve optimal levels of production, and whether widget consumers require better information to make informed choices.

These standard responses systematically mislead when we turn to our present subject. Command and control, bureaucratic subsidies, and full information are part of the problem, not part of the solution. We reject a paradigm drawn from the regulation of widgets and build on a more democratic tradition centered on the franchise. When dealing with the ballot, Americans do not champion the virtues of full information. We make it a crime for anybody to penetrate the sanctity of the voting booth. Nor do we suppose that votes, like widgets, may be sold to the highest bidder. Each citizen expects his ballot to have equal weight in the final decision.

Why not think of campaign finance in similar ways? It isn't enough to count every vote equally on election day. The American citizen should also be given a more equal say in funding decisions. Just as he receives a ballot on election day, he should also receive a special credit card to finance his favorite candidate as she makes her case to the electorate. Call it a Patriot card, and suppose that Congress seeded every voter's account with fifty "patriot dollars." If the 100 million Americans who came to the polls in 2000 had also "voted" with their patriot cards during the campaign, their combined contributions would have amounted to $5 billion—overwhelming the

$3 billion provided by private donors.[3] Under this scenario, would George W. Bush and Al Gore—two heirs of political dynasties—have emerged as the leading candidates? If so, would they have made different issues central to their campaigns?

Our patriotic initiative avoids many of the difficulties associated with traditional "clean money" proposals. The old paradigm creates a special bureaucracy charged with the delicate task of doling out funds to qualifying candidates and parties. But the Patriot program does not keep ordinary Americans on the sidelines while bureaucrats give politicians handouts. Our new paradigm makes campaign finance into a new occasion for citizen sovereignty—encouraging Americans to vote with their dollars as well as their ballots, giving renewed vitality to their democratic commitments.

We have only begun to tap the potential of voting with dollars. Our paradigm also points in a new direction for the regulation of private contributions. Liberals and conservatives have increasingly converged on the "full information" plank of the traditional reform agenda—to the point where it is fast becoming a Motherhood issue. Who could possibly complain about requiring candidates to reveal who is bankrolling their campaigns, and how much they are giving?[4]

We do. Full publicity makes sense only under one assumption—that the candidates themselves know the identity of their contributors. Because candidates will naturally be grateful to big givers, shouldn't they be obliged to share this knowledge with the public? Otherwise, ordinary voters can't subject political rhetoric to a basic reality test—matching each politician's words against the list of contributors who will come around after election day to assert, however discreetly, their claims to official favor.

But this argument begs a big question—why *should* candidates know how much money their contributors have provided? When we are dealing with widgets, this kind of knowledge is a self-evidently good thing—if the widget producer doesn't know who is paying for his goods, and how much money is on the table, he won't be able to figure out whether to accept deals or reject them.

This point doesn't apply here. A victorious politician is guilty of corruption if he delivers the goods to his campaign contributors in too obvious a fashion. The analogy with the ballot box provides a sounder guide for policy. The secret ballot came to America only during the late nineteenth century.

Voters previously cast their ballots in full view of the contesting parties, who carefully monitored each decision. Within this framework, corrupt vote-buying was commonplace. Party hacks could readily determine whether they got what they were paying for. No voter could receive his election day turkey without casting his ballot before the watchful eyes of the turkey's provider.

It was the secret ballot, not some sudden burst of civic virtue, that transformed the situation. Once a voter could promise to vote one way, and actually vote another, it was no longer easy for him to sell his vote. Even if he sincerely intended to perform his side of the bargain, vote-buyers could no longer verify the credibility of his commitment. Suddenly, the promise of a voter to sell his franchise for money became worthless—and as a consequence, vote-buying declined dramatically.[5]

We use the same logic in dealing with private contributions. On analogy with the secret ballot, we propose the "secret donation booth." Contributors will be barred from giving money directly to candidates. They must instead pass their checks through a blind trust. Candidates will get access to all money deposited in their account with the blind trust. But we will take steps to assure that they won't be able to identify who provided the funds. To be sure, lots of people will come up to the candidate and say they have given vast sums of money. And yet none of them will be able to prove it. As a consequence, lots of people who *didn't* give gifts will also claim to have provided millions of dollars.

The resulting situation will be structurally similar to the one created by the secret ballot. Protected by the privacy of the voting booth, you are free to go up to George W. Bush and tell him that you voted for him enthusiastically in 2000 even though you actually voted for Al Gore. Knowing this, neither the president nor you will be prone to take such protestations seriously.

The same "cheap talk" regime will disrupt the special-interest dealing we now take for granted. Just as the secret ballot makes it more difficult for candidates to *buy* votes, a secret donation booth makes it harder for candidates to *sell* access or influence. The voting booth disrupts vote-buying because candidates are uncertain how a citizen actually voted; anonymous donations disrupt influence peddling because candidates are uncertain whether givers actually gave what they say they gave. Just as vote-buying plummeted with the secret ballot, campaign contributions would sink with the secret donation booth.

But not to zero. There are lots of reasons for contributing to campaigns, and the new regime undercuts only one of them—the desire to obtain a quid pro quo from a victorious candidate. It would no longer make much business sense for a group of trial lawyers or oil barons to contribute big bucks to a candidate to encourage special-interest legislation. But the secret donation booth will not deter gifts from citizens who simply wish to express their ideological commitment to a candidate's causes without any expectation of special access or influence. These ideological gifts may well be very substantial, depending on the candidate's charisma and the attractiveness of her positions.[6] Nevertheless, the overall volume of private donations will generally be much lower.

Especially when Patriot is taken into account. Each voter already has 50 Patriot dollars at his disposal to support candidates and political organizations during the campaign. Only those who find this sum inadequate to express their convictions will dip into their private funds. Cumulating our two initiatives, it seems safe to predict that our new paradigm will generate a big change in the prevailing public-private mix of financing. During the last campaign more than $3 billion flowed into the campaign coffers of all aspirants for federal office, but we would be surprised if half this sum were generated under the new regime; in contrast, $5 billion or so would be coming into the campaign through the patriotic system. On conservative assumptions, public funds would dominate by a ratio of 2 to 1, and probably much more. At the same time, the total resources available for political speech would be much greater under the reformed system—in contrast to the $3-plus billion under the ancien régime, politicians would have more than $6 billion with which to engage the voters. The new paradigm, in short, promises an effective increase in both political equality *and* political expression. It achieves this result without compromising any of the basic liberties of citizens—even the freedom to give private contributions. As long as givers channel money through blind trusts, they should be free to give substantial amounts to the causes they favor.

This conclusion leads us to distance ourselves from the final, and most important, remedy in the traditional reform repertoire. Above all else, the great progressive goal has been to limit the amount of private money flowing into campaigns. Ever-more-rigorous restrictions are pursued on two levels: First, reduce the amount any particular giver can donate; second, reduce the total amount any candidate can spend. The reform legislation sponsored by

Senators John McCain and Russell Feingold is the best known recent example, but we have been through cycles of restriction before, and the results have consistently disappointed expectations.

The dismal cycle looks like this. Phase one: Legislators impose limitations in response to popular disgust at the role of big money in politics; phase two: Big givers devise legal loopholes enabling them to continue giving large sums; phase three: Reformers mobilize another wave of popular disgust, and we return to phase one.

The seemingly remorseless character of this cycle has greatly impressed liberal academics of late—leading them to question the efficacy of the traditional emphasis on command and control. According to this increasingly fashionable view, controlling the flow of campaign funds is like the effort to dam the Mississippi. You may stop the river from overflowing its banks at one point, but this triumph will lead to unexpected inundations elsewhere. Like water seeking its own level, private money will inexorably flow around reformist barriers to overwhelm the political process. Rather than damming the flow, sober reformers should simply inform the public about its true extent. Speaking broadly, the new "hydraulicists" urge the reform movement to reject its previous fixation on command and control and to make full information their first priority.[7]

We have already explained why the hydraulicist emphasis on full information is mistaken. We also think that these academics' despairing diagnosis of command and control is exaggerated. Direct control *can* sometimes be effective, and we shall be making strategic use of this tool. Nevertheless, there is a Sisyphean aspect to the struggle for ever-more-stringent and comprehensive controls. Restrictive command and control should no longer be the first priority of reform. It should function as a technique of last resort, filling in gaps left by structural measures like the secret donation booth. Requiring a blind trust doesn't place substantive limits on private fund-raising, but it does purge the practice of some of its worst features. We should consider additional restrictions only after assessing the dangers that remain even after special-interest deals are disrupted by the secret donation process mandated by the new paradigm. As long as a patriotic finance initiative assures the dominance of citizen funding in the overall mix, we believe that only very selective controls—targeted only at the very biggest givers—will seem sensible.

To sum up the new paradigm: We reject centralized campaign subsidies in favor of massive democratization through Patriot dollars; we reject full disclosure of private contributions in favor of the secret donation booth; we reject comprehensive controls on private money in favor of selective restrictions imposed only as a last resort.

We call this "voting with dollars" because it mimics two core attributes of the franchise: Citizens are given equal voting power, but they must exercise this power anonymously. The basic equality of citizens is expressed by their equal access to Patriot dollars. The secrecy of the ballot box is expanded to disrupt special-interest dealing in campaign finance.

We refuse, in short, to view the problem of campaign finance as if it represents the all-or-nothing choice of suppressing private contributions or leaving them unregulated. Our new paradigm uses anonymity to cleanse private giving of its worst abuses while allowing it to serve as a valuable supplementary support to the robust public debate fostered by billions of Patriot dollars allocated by millions of concerned citizens.

In the remainder of Part I we shall scrutinize these basic issues at greater length: What is really at stake in the choice between new and old reform paradigms? How do the different components of the new agenda fit—or fail to fit—together?

In Part II we begin the hard work required to convince traditional reformers, and ultimately ordinary citizens, to take the new paradigm seriously. Whatever the weaknesses of the old agenda, it is now a familiar part of the established debate. Reformers and legislators find it "natural" to argue about statutory details surrounding command and control, centralized subsidy, and "improved" information. Newfangled notions like Patriot dollars and secret donation booths won't stand a chance unless they achieve practical form in the shape of proposed legislation. We move down this path from theory to practice by considering key questions of statutory design: How to safeguard against massive corruption by sleazy types who offer to buy 50 Patriot dollars for 10 greenbacks? Who should qualify for a Patriot account? Who should be authorized to receive the money? When a patriot cardholder goes to her neighborhood automated teller machine, should she be able to spend all her money on any campaign she likes, or should the $50 be broken into subaccounts for presidential, Senate, and House races?

Similar questions arise in organizing the secret donation booth. Imagine, for example, that a big donor deposits a check for $100,000 into the booth and directs it toward a particular candidate. When the grateful politician receives word that his campaign balance has increased by this whopping sum, won't he make every effort to identify the big donor with precision? Isn't it naive to suppose that some clever bit of institutional engineering will stop the big donor from establishing that he was in fact the guy who forked over the dough?

Finally, it is essential to design adequate institutions to manage the new system. We take on this task in Chapter 9. The current Federal Election Commission is an icon of ineffectiveness. How might a new commission be organized to withstand the enormous political pressures generated by the joint operation of patriotic currency and the secret donation booth?

Our solution places central responsibility on a new five-member FEC consisting entirely of retired members of the judiciary. We do not suppose that these senior jurists can properly be placed entirely above politics—like all other major officials, they should be nominated by the sitting president and confirmed by the Senate. But once they have assumed office for a ten-year term, they should be given primary responsibility for making the appointments, and approving the regulations, required for the effective operation of the new paradigm.

If we can't provide plausible answers to these and similar design questions, we might as well fold our tents and return to the ivory tower. But even if we respond with realistic solutions, we are not home free. Although we may persuade you that the new paradigm can be transformed into an operational reality, we must still defend its constitutionality.

Since its epochal decision in *Buckley v. Valeo*, the Supreme Court has proved a formidable obstacle to reform under the old paradigm. Traditional reformers have responded in kind by casting the Court as Public Enemy Number One. In this familiar morality play, "real" reform must wait until the Court comes to its senses and overrules *Buckley*. Until this great moment of judicial redemption, realists can hope only for interstitial reforms—mere Band-Aids that barely patch over the diseases of the body politic.

In Chapter 10 we challenge this reformist apologia. By framing our proposals to comply strictly with all existing constitutional requirements, we establish that the new paradigm authorizes massive change *now*, and that activists need not content themselves with marginal improvements until the dawning of the day of judicial repentance. Indeed, it is a mistake even to yearn for *Buckley*'s total repudiation. The case contains some principles of enduring importance.

We conclude our reflections with a model statute, accompanied by technocratic appendixes clarifying the operational dynamics of the new system. These operational matters need much technical improvement. But the only way forward is to expose the plan to more general scrutiny, encouraging sharp minds to plug loopholes and find problems that we have not yet glimpsed, let alone resolved.

We completed work on this book on August 10, 2001—at a time when the McCain-Feingold bill had passed the Senate but had not yet been considered in the House or conference committee. If the Senate bill makes it into law, there will be many textual changes. But we would be surprised if any will require a revision of our overall assessment of the legislation.

2 | Patriot

Liberal democracy requires an awkward balance between two spheres of life. Within the sphere of democratic politics, we confront each other as moral equals, and we deliberate about our collective future. It is not good enough to say "I want it!" We must make a good-faith effort to justify public decisions as serving the public good. This is what responsible citizenship is all about.

The organizing principles of a liberal market are different. We come to the table with unequal assets, often vastly unequal. We bargain to further our private interest, without trying to justify our deals in terms of the greater public interest. It *is* good enough to say "I want it": That's what freedom is all about!

Our collective anxiety about campaign finance testifies to the uneasy co-existence of the spheres. Consider how Americans commonly try to reconcile liberal markets with democratic equality. The standard reconciliation, as we shall call it, is a straightforward two-step argument. Step one begins by conceding that the single-minded pursuit of self-interest may generate pervasive inequalities and inefficiencies. But if these prove unacceptable, we can always move to step two: It's our job as citizens to deliberate together and take corrective action—redistributing wealth from rich to poor and taking regulatory actions when markets fail.

This two-step, in turn, promises instant relief from tension. We can have our cake and eat it too by reminding ourselves that the market is ultimately under the control of democratic citizens—who can alter economic outcomes whenever they find them seriously deviating from their ideals of social justice.

All this is vaguely familiar from high school civics, but familiarity breeds anxiety. When Americans contemplate the present state of campaign finance, there is a pervasive recognition that big money threatens to undermine the standard reconciliation.

The problem is obvious. If the deliberations of democratic citizens are crucial in the legitimation of market inequality, we cannot allow market inequalities to have an overwhelming impact on these deliberations. If this happens, we can no longer say that we, as citizens, have authorized the pervasive inequalities we experience as market actors. Politics will have been transformed into a forum in which big money praises itself.

Call this the circularity problem, which leads to a basic conclusion: The insulation of democratic politics from the rule of big money is, under the standard reconciliation, a necessary condition for the legitimation of big money in the marketplace itself.

This conclusion provides a distinctive rationale for distributing votes and money on a different basis. If each citizen received the same number of votes as he had dollars, a majority vote in favor of a tax scheme that placed a heavy burden on the poor would not serve to legitimate the resulting distribution of wealth. But when each citizen gets one vote, a majority vote in favor of a regressive tax scheme may represent something different—a judgment by the majority, after due deliberation, that the present distribution of wealth is too equal and that the public good may be served by making it more unequal.

Campaign finance reform continues the concern with circularity beyond the formal commitment to one person, one vote. Even when our votes count equally, inequality of private wealth may distort public deliberation in ways that are inconsistent with our mutual recognition as equal citizens. Although this concern motivates all reform work, we propose to translate its practical policy implications in a different way.

Our principal target is a logical flaw that lies at the heart of the traditional reform agenda. This familiar view links diagnosis to reform in a natural, but ultimately misleading, fashion.

Diagnosis: The problem requiring reform is the power of big money
    to undermine free and equal democratic deliberation.
Conclusion: Because private property is the problem, we should seek
    a regulatory solution that looks as unproperty-like as possible.

This is a non sequitur. Big money *is* the problem, but the best solution may still involve creative adaptations of the very institution that created the problem.

This is the guiding thought shaping the new paradigm. We place a high value on the decentralization, flexibility, and individual choice that a market system makes possible. The traditional embrace of centralized bureaucratic solutions sacrifices these values needlessly. The right response is to reshape the political marketplace and enable it to become more responsive to the judgments of equal citizens than to the preferences of unequal property owners.

Consider how Patriot retains many of the virtues of a private property/ free market system. While private markets allow for the broad exercise of consumer sovereignty, Patriot does the same for citizen sovereignty— as a result of two structural modifications in the ordinary private-money system.

The first involves the principle of distribution. Patriot distributes dollars on the same egalitarian basis as the vote. Each American obtains a Patriot account in her capacity as an equal citizen, and it is up to her to decide how best to spend the new patriotic currency. Fifty dollars may not seem like much. But as millions of citizens vote their Patriots, they will have a big impact on the political marketplace.

It is hard to guess how many Americans will take advantage of their new patriotic opportunity. But as a thought experiment, suppose that it is the same as the number of voters on election day—this means 100 million Americans will contribute 5 billion Patriot dollars during the year when the presidency is up for grabs. What will be the consequences of this enormous infusion of cash?

Begin with a minimalist scenario—under which the $5 billion flows to the same actors in the same proportions as under the present system. If Candidate X gets 2 percent of all private money today, he would receive 2 percent of the total fund—consisting of both patriotic and private dollars— under the new paradigm. X would be getting more money when measured in absolute terms—for the total fund would be much larger than the three billion private dollars contributed to federal campaigns in the most recent campaign cycle.[1] But the relative financial standing of candidates and political organizations would not change. This outcome seems unlikely, but it raises a useful analytic question—should Patriot be considered a policy failure if it generated the minimalist outcome?

We do not think so, because the experience of political life in the patriotic world would be different. When Americans encounter a barrage of political advertisements on television today, they think of themselves as passive consumers—just as they do when viewing advertisements commending fancy cars or prescription medicines. But political advertising in the patriotic world will carry a different social meaning. Turning on the TV will become an occasion for citizens to reflect on their own communicative choices—should I send my Patriot dollars to insurgent X or political party Y? In turn, these questions will prompt millions of informal conversations as countless face-to-face groups consider their options together.

Nowadays, electioneering prompts affirmative activity from most citizens only on election day, when they spend the half-hour or so going to the polls. But the democratization of campaign finance will invite millions to take a small but active role throughout the election campaign. By casting their patriotic dollars, Americans will be giving renewed social meaning to their self-understanding as free and equal citizens, engaging in democratic deliberation.

The generation of social meaning is important in itself. The American republic is nothing other than a vast collection of human beings who take the trouble to take their common citizenship seriously, and on a regular basis. The millions of conversations and small decisions surrounding patriotic expenditure will provide an important new social context in which Americans will reaffirm their relationship as citizens, charged with the responsibility of steering the republic on a sound course.[2]

Call this the citizenship effect, and, so far as we are concerned, it seems worth a few billion dollars. But the minimalist scenario greatly understates Patriot's promise. Even assuming no change in the existing system of private finance, candidates and political organizations will soon learn that they need not rely on the small elite of private-money donors but can finance themselves through broad-based appeals to the patriotic citizenry. Given the dramatic change in the distribution in the supply of campaign funds, political entrepreneurs and organizations will enter the market to fill previously unexpressed forms of political demand. Call this the agenda effect.

We shall speculate later about the way the patriotic marketplace will reward some groups at the expense of others. At this point, it is enough to emphasize that the shifting supply of funds will not necessarily favor political liberals or conservatives. That will depend on the evolving beliefs of the general citizenry, and the vigor and imagination with which established and insurgent politicians and parties compete. The beauty of the patriotic marketplace is that it diminishes the importance of existing links between establishment politicians and established funding sources, instead requiring incumbents to be forever responsive to rising tendencies in public opinion. Incumbents who insulate themselves from their constituents will see rivals gaining a decisive advantage in patriotic fund-raising. The predictable result, in short, is not only the activation of the citizenship effect, but an ongoing demonstration of the power of citizen sovereignty to shape the parameters of representative government.

We have been ruminating upon one simple point that distinguishes patriotic dollars from private dollars: Voters possess 50 Patriots each, but vastly different numbers of private dollars. But our focus on the effective exercise of citizen sovereignty paves the way for a second basic difference, involving restrictions on alienability. We sometimes speak as if economic agents can spend private money for anything they like, but this is an exaggeration. One restriction is particularly noteworthy: Every democratic system makes it a crime for private-money holders to buy votes, even at prices that poor people would accept. This restriction expresses a foundational commitment to the standard reconciliation: Market inequality is legitimate only when it gains the deliberate assent of free and equal citizens, and so vote-buying threatens not only the reality of democratic deliberation but the very legitimacy of the distribution of property itself.

Symmetrical reasoning generates an equal but opposite restriction on the alienability of Patriot dollars. Just as an American cannot sell his vote for fifty private dollars, he should not be permitted to sell his Patriot account for fifty private dollars. We are not creating the new currency to enable Americans to spend an extra night at the movies or the ballpark. The aim is to break the circularity problem by enhancing the ability of Americans to act effectively in their capacity as free and equal citizens. It is a serious mistake to suppose that Patriot dollars can be treated by their recipients as if it were a grant of power over ordinary consumption goods. To the contrary, the purpose of Patriot is to allow citizens to decide, under appropriate conditions, whether American democracy should make an effort to redistribute private dollars, and if so, how many and in what ways.

Many will balk at any type of public finance. The idea that the government would simply give people $50 on the basis of their citizenship is abhorrent to their conception of small government. But notice that we are already doing the same thing with regard to another political asset—the vote. Just imagine how much the government could generate in revenue if it auctioned voting rights to the highest bidder. A lot more than the cost of the Patriot system! But our system forgoes these potential revenues in favor of political equality. Patriot merely expands this equal voting principle into the domain of public discourse—giving citizens more nearly equal power to have their ideas expressed in the preelection debate that frames the crucial issues for electoral decision.

Many Americans may reject the invitation to citizenship proffered by their Patriot accounts and simply let the $50 go untouched. Some may even deride the very idea of participating with their fellow citizens in the project of democratic self-government. If everybody felt that way, the republic would be on its deathbed. But we have not (yet) come to such a pass, and we should not allow skeptics to demoralize the rest of the citizenry by trading their Patriot accounts, or their votes, for a night at the racetrack. If they don't want to use their Patriot dollars to enhance public debate, these funds should simply expire at the end of the electoral campaign.

This is what happens with the vote—either you use it or you lose it. And for the very same reason—within the constitutional framework of American democracy, the vote is a vehicle through which citizens express their judgments about the public good.[3] Votes can't be "saved up," like private money, for private consumption at some future date. Either a citizen is sufficiently motivated by the project of self-government to go to the polls (in which case his vote should count on equal terms with the rest of us), or he is so apathetic that he fails to show up on election day (in which case his apathy should not give him the privilege of saving his vote for future use).

Although we base these restrictions on foundational democratic principles, they immediately generate a practical problem: What is to stop millions of cynical citizens from cashing in their Patriot dollars in "black market" transactions with corrupt politicians: "Psst, Joe American, how about selling me your fifty Patriots for ten privates! Both of us will be better off: You get to go the movies, and I get a head start on my less cynical opponents—if any of these innocents survive the first round of fund-raising competition!"

The problem isn't new. During the nineteenth century, Americans confronted a massive black market for votes—with machine politicians buying tons of ballots from the poor and ignorant at bargain prices. During this entire period, vote-buying was strictly illegal, but the threat of criminal prosecution was hollow. The practice was so common that it overwhelmed public prosecutors, who were easily diverted by sitting politicians to the investigation of other, "more serious," crimes.

Then some clever Australians hit upon a solution, which now strikes us as obvious but which represents one of the great leaps forward in the history of modern democracy. By creating a secret ballot, they drew a curtain between corrupt politicians and the voters, disrupting potential black-market transactions.[4] This elegant change in informational conditions accomplished something that the threat of criminal prosecution never achieved. Honest elections became a real possibility in the Western world. By disrupting the black market for votes, the secret ballot became the foundation for the construction of a parallel sphere of life—in which equal citizens, rather than unequal property owners, express their political judgments.

We propose an analogous measure to safeguard the integrity of Patriot dollars. Thanks to modern technology, citizens need not go to their voting precinct and draw a curtain before sending their Patriot dollars to candidates or political organizations. A trip to their neighborhood ATMs, or eventually a click of their mouse on the Internet, will suffice to allow citizens to vote their dollars in secrecy.

We shall defer these (crucial) details until Part II and instead focus here on the basic choices posed by our proposal. In particular, how does it compare with more traditional efforts to inject "clean money" into the political process?

Old vs. New

The old reform agenda seeks not to channel markets but to replace them. Rather than distributing Patriot dollars to citizens, and allowing them to choose the candidates and organizations most worthy of support, the old reform agenda hands a pot of money to bureaucrats, who are supposed to dole it out by referring to criteria established by a statute.

This basic schema predictably generates a rush of aspiring politicos toward the till. Politicians are not shy, and if large bundles of free cash are in prospect, why not announce that you are running for the presidency? Even if you have no chance of winning, you will gain the precious opportunity for free publicity that may help you out in your next race for alderman.

Patriot solves this basic problem in the manner of other markets: Candidates compete with one another for scarce Patriot dollars, and those who can't persuade citizens to give will quickly fall by the wayside. But the old agenda does not have this simple solution available and must construct other criteria to separate serious from frivolous candidacies, lest "campaign reform" become a synonym for raids on the treasury by egomaniacal publicity hounds.

Call this the threshold problem—and it invites a series of trade-offs, all of them unsatisfactory compared to the patriotic alternative. The most basic involves the level of the threshold. A high threshold means that few candidates get money but that those who do all have a significant chance to win, and hence that the public will support a relatively large grant of public funds to subsidize these serious campaigns. Lowering the threshold encourages more insurgencies, but also more silly candidates, whose use of public funds for self-promotion may discredit the system, and who, in any event, serve as an excuse for underfunding all campaigns. After all, there is a limit to the amount of public money that should be spent on electioneering—the more candidates, the more money pouring out of the treasury. There is no way to repeal the iron law of the multiplication table, legislators will soberly explain to their constituents clamoring for reform.

But incumbents fail to mention that they are interested parties in the affair. They have a natural tendency to favor high thresholds—because most of them will be running for reelection, and won't be enthusiastic at the prospect of insurgents making life difficult. They also have an incentive to keep subsidies low—because they are already well known and established, while most challengers need lots more cash to get their names across.

Reform leaders who aren't legislators will predictably favor lower thresholds and higher subsidies, but even they can't avoid the basic mathematics of the situation—the more candidates, the more costly the subsidy, and the greater the tendency to starve the most serious candidates in order to free resources for the odd insurgency.

The basic threshold problem generates a host of other difficulties. One obvious way of filtering for serious candidacies is to give a favored position to the major parties, which have established track records of substantial voter support. Any candidate gaining the endorsement of the Democratic or Republican parties obviously has a lot better chance of winning at the polls than any candidate marching under the banner of the Natural Law Party. Although only a Martian would find this point problematic, it offends democratic principles to allow the major parties to feed too ostentatiously at the public trough while excluding others by the force of law—which they have every incentive to do, since they are the folks writing the reform legislation in the first place.

For decorum's sake, and to avoid constitutional challenge, the majors tend to offer third parties half a loaf. Minor parties that meet a lowish threshold get some money—but much less than the sums flowing to major-party candidates.[5]

A quick contrast to Patriot suggests that these epicycles are a product of the old agenda's central misconception—its fondness for bureaucratic solutions to the resource allocation problem. There is no need to design different thresholds for different parties. Simply leave it up to citizens: If they think a particular third party is worthy, they will have no problem marching up to the ATM and beaming it patriotic resources.

Better yet, Patriot provides a neat solution to another important problem. Even successful third parties lose political momentum over time, as the majors steal their issues or their complaints are made irrelevant by changes in the world. This means that a third party meeting statutory funding thresholds during one electoral cycle may encounter an embarrassment of riches during the next cycle. Consider the tragicomic situation of the Reform Party during the 2000 election. Because Ross Perot won more than 5 percent of the presidential vote in 1996, his party qualified for a subsidy of $12.5 million for 2000. But because the party was a creation of Perot, it confronted a crisis when the billionaire refused to run again—leaving the $12.5 million for any political entrepreneur ambitious enough to seize the prize. In this case, Pat Buchanan turned out to be the winner—despite his problematic relation to the ideology that drew millions to the Reform Party in the first place.[6]

Unsurprisingly, his success in gaining the party's nomination was accompanied by vicious infighting and the demoralization of thousands of Reform partisans who saw Buchanan stealing the party from them.

All this infighting and alienation is the predictable consequence of the traditional paradigm. Under Patriot, Buchanan would have had much less incentive to take over an ideologically uncongenial third party—both because Reform would no longer be guaranteed a pot of money on the basis of its past performance and because Buchanan could raise Patriot dollars from his hard-core supporters even when running as an independent. By the same token, Patriot would have squarely forced Perot's partisans to face up to their dilemma: Given Perot's departure from the scene, they must either generate a credible leader committed to Reform ideals or fail to raise patriotic contributions from the millions of voters who had formerly flocked to the Perot banner.

The threshold problem is even more intractable when it comes to funding primary races. The filtering mechanism provided by political parties during the final election is, by definition, unavailable. But some mechanism must be found to resolve the trade-offs required in determining the height of the threshold.[7] Consider the solution advanced by a citizen's movement now agitating for campaign reform at the state level. The Clean Money Initiative has recently scored stunning successes by taking a detour around state legislatures and appealing to the people through referenda. Maine's voters, for example, approved a clean money program that set the threshold at a level far lower than most sitting legislators would find comfortable. A candidate for governor, for example, must raise contributions of at least $5 from only 1,500 residents (out of 1.25 million in the state) to qualify for public money, and aspirants to the state legislature must satisfy even lower thresholds.[8] But low thresholds mean that states must limit the size of their subsidies or risk a run on the state treasury by a host of marginal candidates. In races involving larger constituencies, and more intense use of mass media, the trade-offs between level of threshold and size of subsidy quickly become forbidding.[9]

Nonetheless, we applaud Clean Money's embrace of market signals as a solution to its threshold problem. The reformers' statute requires prospective candidates to establish their democratic credibility by generating a broad base of support from small contributors of private money. When viewed from one angle, Patriot simply generalizes Clean Money's threshold mechanism into a comprehensive solution to the entire problem. Rather than using private money as a stepping stone to bureaucratic funding, it invites candidates to appeal to citizens for patriotic money on an ongoing basis. Rather than allow the proliferation and partisan exploitation of bureaucratic rigidities, Patriot invites the candidates, and their parties, to compete endlessly for citizen support in the patriotic marketplace.

Problems with Patriot?

Is Patriot's dynamic responsiveness to the citizenry an unalloyed good?

Perhaps not, or so a sophisticated defender of the bureaucratic approach may suggest. For all the populist complaint, the two-party system has served America well over the long haul. Won't Patriot encourage its replacement by the fragmented multiparty systems of Europe and Latin America?

America's two-party system has sustained itself for centuries, despite many changes in campaign finance and organization. As Maurice Duverger suggested, and later political scientists have confirmed, the secret of its staying power is the Anglo-American system of single-member geographic constituencies—where victory goes to the plurality winner without the need for a runoff if nobody gets a majority.[10] This "first past the post" system gives a third party overwhelming incentives to join forces with the major party closest to it. Otherwise, the more antagonistic major party will continually win elections with minority support simply because the opposition is splitting its majority between two or more parties. European systems of proportional representation do not impose this severe penalty—if a third party wins 20 percent of the vote, it gets 20 percent of the seats, rather than losing almost everywhere, as in Britain or the United States. This basic point accounts for multiparty systems in Europe and their relative absence in English-speaking countries. Even far-reaching changes in campaign finance will not repeal the basic electoral logic that generates two major parties.

Patriot will only make it harder for established party leaders to take their subsidies for granted. Rather than applying to a bureaucrat, they will be constantly obliged to appeal to citizens and compete for funds against insurgents. But it is a mistake to confuse the fate of particular party leaders with the fate of the two-party system.

A related critique has more bite. Under the old paradigm, major party candidates get equal subsidies even if one party obtained 60 percent of the vote in the previous election while the other gained 40 percent. Interparty parity is not guaranteed under Patriot. Candidates and parties popular early in the campaign will succeed in gaining more patriotic funds, and may then parlay their early advantage into further gains in popularity and patriotic support. This snowball effect is constrained by the bureaucratic system, which gives more resources to the less popular major-party candidate and thereby enhances her chance to appeal to the citizenry to reconsider their current inclinations.

We agree that snowballs can sometimes become a problem. But not often. Indeed, the objection does not even apply to primary contests. To the contrary, snowballs would have a salutary effect during this first campaign phase. Under Patriot, for example, John McCain's early successes on the campaign trail would have generated an enormous snowball of Patriot dollars, and rightly so: *shouldn't* early successes be rewarded by enabling the frontrunners to define the terms of the competition while others stand in the shadows?

In contrast, bureaucrats under the old paradigm cannot respond to these groundswells of public opinion. They simply dole out equal chunks of cash to all politicians satisfying a threshold test of seriousness. Snowballs of patriotic cash serve as a much more efficient and responsive mechanism for identifying serious primary contenders. Rather than a problem, the snowball effect is a solution to the problem of narrowing the primary field to a few serious candidates.

And even during the general election campaign, the problem can be easily exaggerated. By this point, both major party candidates will have already established a substantial presence in the political arena. Given their prominence, they should not be allowed to blame the system if they fail to sustain their political momentum in the patriotic marketplace. It is up to them to figure out themes that will appeal to the patriotic public. They should not have a right to demand bureaucratic grants of public funds to compensate them for failures of outreach and political imagination.

Consider that only half of eligible Americans go to the polls during presidential elections and only one-third vote during "off-year" congressional elections.[11] Patriot will give candidates a tremendous new incentive to reach out to the "silent majority" currently disconnected from the entire demo-cratic process. If one candidate succeeds in reaching out to millions of these citizens, and thereby obtains a significant fund-raising advantage over her competitor, this should be scored as a big plus for the new agenda over its bureaucratic alternative.

We concede, of course, that one of the major parties may, from time to time, select such a bad candidate that he will be snowballed under a landslide of patriotic dollars for his opponent—and that a bureaucratized alternative would allow him to disguise the demoralization of his campaign by the guar-anteed injection of public funds. While a truly crushing defeat may be bad for democracy in the short run, it is probably healthy in the longer run—as the debacle prompts massive soul-searching and the rise of new leader-ship. As long as patriotic finance is available to more attractive leaders in the future, the defeated party will rise again.

Even in the short run, the new paradigm contains additional resources that will ameliorate the disaster. As we suggest in the next chapter, our sec-ond major reform—the secret donation booth—will encourage party loyal-ists to prop up unpopular campaigns with private money when candidates are doing especially poorly in the patriotic marketplace. In this and other ways, our two reforms function as parts of an interacting agenda. Our aim is to build a whole that is more than the sum of its parts.

3 | The Donation Booth

New Haven is the home of Connecticut's Experimental Agricultural Station—give them two breeds of apple, and they will try to come up with a juicier and more robust hybrid. Only a couple of miles down the road is the Yale Law School, where we are in the same business. We are searching for policy hybrids that combine the best features of previously distinct breeds of social power: the electoral system and the market system.

In structuring the injection of "clean money" into political campaigns, we sought to marry the egalitarian ideals of the ballot box and the flexible response of the marketplace. Patriot emerged as the policy hybrid. We approach the problem of private contributions in a similar spirit. On the one hand, we argue against traditional reformers who aim for the complete elimination of private money from political campaigns. On the other, we reject the fashionable notion that full information can play the same cleansing role in politics that it plays in the marketplace. We propose a policy hybrid that channels private giving in publicly constructive directions.

The secret donation booth promises the effective control of existing pathologies without eliminating the positive features of private choice. By greatly reducing—if not entirely eliminating—the special-interest dealing and gross inequalities that scar the present reality, the new paradigm will enable Americans to create a culture of publicly responsible private giving that is worthy in its own right.

What is more, and as we have already begun to notice, Patriot isn't perfect. Like everything else in life, it has its problems—ones usefully addressed by the private giving that will continue to flow through the secret donation booth.

We offer a critique of two planks of the traditional reform agenda. We first take aim at the full information plank, and explain why the secret donation booth provides a better solution to the problem of private giving. We then explain why it is a mistake to replace private giving entirely with public funding. As long as Patriot dollars play the predominant role, the system will be strengthened by the addition of socially responsible private giving to the mix.

The Anonymity Tool

The case for full information is pretty straightforward in the marketplace.[1] When consumers and producers are ignorant about their options, they cannot identify the best deals available. Ignorantly supposing that the offer on the table is the best available, a seller or buyer makes a deal without recognizing that somebody else can maximize value at a lower price.

This straightforward point doesn't carry over to campaign finance. When I enter the market for a new car, I will naturally pay a lot of attention when somebody offers me accurate information on the relative attributes of Fords and Toyotas—if I buy a lemon, I will bear directly the brunt of the costs of my ignorance.

But when I act as a citizen, this is no longer true. My vote is only one of millions, and the chances of my deciding the outcome of a national election are tiny. Even the Bush-Gore election wasn't decided by a single vote—though it came pretty close! And in most national contests, the odds of tipping the balance are vanishingly small.

This does not make my vote meaningless. In going to the polls, I am affirming my equal standing as a citizen, and contributing my opinion as to the right course for the nation. Although my opinion may not decide the outcome, the republic would die without lots of citizens going to the polls; and that is enough to impose a duty on all citizens to join their fellow Americans in maintaining a crucial democratic institution.

Nevertheless, duty is a weaker motivator than self-interest, and this means that most voters will not be as well informed about the choice between Gore and Bush as they are, say, when deciding between Ford and Toyota. This basic point makes campaign finance important: If all voters responded to the dictates of duty by informing themselves thoroughly, then it would be relatively unimportant how much money a candidate spent for campaign commercials. It is precisely because most Americans aren't inclined to spend much time and energy on political learning that campaign finance becomes important: The more money a candidate has, the greater his chance to transcend the knowledge barrier. At the same time, low voter motivation makes a full-information remedy a profoundly problematic aspect of the old reform paradigm.

Quite simply, if most voters pay scant attention to politics, they won't take the time to go through the lengthy lists of donors published in the name of "full information." Each side, in its political advertisements, will seek to exploit embarrassing donations to the other—and politicians will consider this cost when accepting money from notorious groups. But they will also consider that big gifts permit them to buy a lot more advertising and overwhelm any negative publicity with another round of positive ads or counterattacks. Dirty money is better than no money. Although a few informed citizens may punish a candidate by voting for someone else, tainted money gains more votes than it loses.[2]

If this weren't true, candidates and parties would voluntarily turn down large tainted gifts. But this doesn't happen.[3] Indeed, if full information were a powerful remedy, we should expect interests to contribute to candidates they actually oppose—and thereby induce appalled voters to abandon the tainted candidate! But does anyone think that the trial lawyers who gave millions to Gore were trying to scare voters in Bush's direction or that the large gifts given by drug companies to Bush were an effort to secure the White House for Gore?

"Full disclosure" is an attractive sound bite, but it simply doesn't change the basic political incentives that encourage politicians to accept big money from special interests. Nor does it do much to expose contributors to criminal liability for bribery. The kinds of deals that are provable (money for access) are not illegal, and the kinds of deals that are illegal (money for influence) are not provable. At the end of the day, mandated disclosure may make us feel good about ourselves but it does little to insulate the political sphere from the corrupting influence of unequal wealth.

The secret donation booth gets to the heart of the problem. A candidate is less likely to sell access or influence if he can't be sure that the buyer has actually paid the price. At the same time, a giver will be sorely tempted to say that she has given a large sum, then chisel on the deal. After all, if the candidate believes her, she will achieve her aim of special influence without paying the price; and if the candidate doesn't find her credible, any actual donation will have been spent for nothing.

Talk is cheap. And it is possible that the secret donation booth will generate enormous amounts of hot air. Thousands may flock to the candidate to promise gargantuan sums which never arrive through the blind trust— increasing candidate skepticism and making it harder and harder for special interests to buy special access and influence. To be sure, special interests may respond to their new credibility problem by inviting candidates to watch them deposit their gifts into the secret donation booth or by waving canceled checks returned from the blind trust. We will consider how to undercut these efforts in Chapter 8. But for now, it is sufficient to emphasize the distinctive aspect of our strategy: Rather than prohibiting true donors from speaking or sending ancillary signals, our system permits faux donors to send the same signals, and thereby create a regime of cheap talk that makes indisputable gift-giving impossible.

Another way to characterize cheap talk is "lying." And some may oppose our reform on the ground that it is simply wrong for the government to promote or encourage lying in any form. This is a case of misplaced moralism. Recall the (possibly apocryphal) story of the Danish king wearing— and urging other Christians to wear—the yellow star during Nazi occupation. Was it wrong to present oneself as a Jew, and thereby make it more difficult for the Nazis to identify their victims? A more modern example: Suppose that the heterosexual neighbors of a harassed gay resident raise the rainbow flag in front of their homes—even though this might subject them to physical harm.[4] Should this act of social solidarity be condemned merely because it creates a false impression among the harassers?

To be sure, our faux donors will not be acting from admirable motives. By hypothesis, they will be seeking to gain special advantage or influence. Nonetheless, their cheap talk will operate in precisely the same way as these more noble enterprises. Just as the Danish king sought "to ambiguate" the social meaning of the yellow star, the faux donors will ambiguate the social meaning of the sentence "I'm sending you a check for $10,000."[5] If the Danish king had been successful, the star would no longer have stood for "Jew," but for "Jew or Gentile." By the same token, everybody will know that nobody can credibly establish his gift under the new paradigm, and as a consequence, the claim about the $10,000 check will no longer be taken as a statement of fact but as a metaphor: "The check may or may not have been deposited in the donation booth, but I heartily approve of your candidacy!"

Given the changed social context, we would urge our moralizing critics to consider whether they are indulging in rhetorical overkill in characterizing the cheap-talk regime as involving "lying" at all. We are dealing with a context in which puffing and exaggeration is socially expected and the very notion of "lying" doesn't have much traction. At the very worst, we are dealing with "white lies" which cannot seriously mislead anybody but a fool.

And politicians are anything but fools. They are already dealing with similar statements on a continuing basis. A day does not pass without a constituent saying that he voted for the politician at the last election. If all such protestations were believed, successful politicians would suppose they had won unanimously! But because the voter cast his ballot behind a curtain, no politician takes such protestations as anything more than metaphorical statements of support—which is precisely the way they will interpret remarks about contributions under the new paradigm. We doubt that even the most rigorous moralist will challenge the secret ballot on the grounds that it promotes "lying"; but if this is true, it is only the novelty of the secret donation booth that provokes a similar response.

We also challenge a second premise of the moralist's critique. Not only is it wrong to equate "cheap talk" with "lying"; it is also wrong to say that, by enacting the new paradigm into law, the state *endorses* lying. The system will work just as well if donors respond to the secret donation booth by creating a norm of silence—under which it is deemed improper to inquire or divulge how much one has given to particular candidates. This is the way most Americans have responded to the institution of the secret ballot. Nowadays it is a no-no to ask somebody how she voted—except for very close friends and family, such a question intrudes on one's freedom, as a citizen, to cast one's ballot without coercive oversight. Similarly, many people think it inappropriate to make a public declaration about their secret vote, except under special circumstances. It would be entirely proper for donors to adopt the same norm in a world of the secret donation booth. Such conscientious folk would be free, of course, to endorse candidates and positions with enthusiasm, and proudly declare that they have made a contribution. But in deference to the system of campaign finance established by their fellow citizens, they refrain from saying how much they have given. If the state endorses anything, *this* is the position implied by the enactment of the new paradigm.

The moralist's critique may serve as a debater's point, but this is a dog that will not hunt. In enacting the new paradigm, the state does not endorse the efforts of citizens to exaggerate their gifts; if somebody wishes to break his silence and brag about his giving, it is he—not the state—who should take responsibility. And even if he chooses to exaggerate the extent of his gift, the braggart hasn't done something awful. While self-promotion isn't precisely admirable, since when has it become un-American? Especially when exaggerated claims won't mislead serious politicians, who are perfectly aware of the difference between cheap talk and cold cash.

We do insist on drawing a line that cannot be crossed. But this line distinguishes between cheap talk and decisive action, not between silence and speech. Under the new paradigm, no donor is allowed to attempt an end run around the secret donation booth by handing his favorite politician a bagful of cash or a personal check. Such direct transfers will be criminal felonies equivalent to the bribery of a high state official. But we reserve such severe sanctions for the small number of sociopaths intent on subverting the system by direct transfers of cash, not the large number of idle chatterers.

Anonymity and Inequality

We have been exploring how the secret donation booth disrupts the special-interest dealing that corrupts existing politics. Our reform will also make a major contribution to the underlying problem of inequality in the provision of campaign funds. The donation booth will predictably reduce the total amount of private dollar contributions. (The secret ballot has been estimated to have decreased voter turnout by about 12 percent.[6]) And it will have a particularly powerful impact on the frequency of six- and seven-figure donations. Only the richest and most ideological Americans would seriously consider giving a million dollars to a candidate if the gift did not buy special access and influence—or even allow for the fleeting fame produced by newspaper articles listing the biggest givers![7]

The impact on big giving will be especially dramatic in a patriotic world with millions of citizens adding their mites of $50. With 5 billion Patriot dollars already in the pool, large private-dollar donations are likely to be less pivotal in winning elections—and therefore less valuable to politicians, especially if their solicitation requires actions that will alienate large numbers of patriotic donors.

The reduction in big gifts means that small gifts will bulk larger within the overall mix of private contributions. Under the current system, somewhere between 4 and 12 percent of registered voters contribute something to federal campaigns, but only one-tenth of 1 percent give $1,000 or more.[8] During the 1996 cycle this amounted to 235,000 voters—who nonetheless contributed about one-half of the total.[9] Unsurprisingly, the vast majority of big givers are rich—81 percent earned more than $100,000 a year.[10]

Concentration ratios of this kind will decline under the new regime—though we will still be a long way from equality in private giving. Except for the most devoted ideologues, the average voter will have better things to do with her $30,000 to $40,000 a year than make anonymous gifts to politicians. And the tens of millions who earn $20,000 or less will be even more emphatically underrepresented.

Which leads to an obvious question. Even if big private gifts drop by 50 percent or more under the new regime, why not set an even more ambitious goal? Why not abolish all forms of private giving?

The abolitionist arguments are straightforward. Americans don't have the right to buy extra votes on election day—we insist instead on the principle of one person, one vote. By the same token, our commitment to equal citizenship should extend to the distribution of Patriot dollars—"one person, fifty Patriots." If everybody is treated as an equal citizen at the ballot box, why shouldn't his claim to equal citizenship be respected during the election campaign?

This egalitarian point is not merely symbolic—though we hardly wish to trivialize the expressive dimensions of citizenship. Because most private funding will invariably come from the upper reaches of society, anything short of abolition will skew outcomes in favor of the rich. Granted, there are "limousine liberals" as well as "dirt-poor conservatives." But these are exceptions to the general law linking class with political opinions. So private funding violates equality and favors the rich.

Let's get rid of it. It's as simple as that.

We don't think it *is* that simple, but we don't wish to belittle the basic anxieties that fuel the abolitionist argument. To the contrary, they go to the root of the circularity problem that fuels our own reformist concerns. No less than the abolitionists, we envision democratic politics as a distinct sphere of equal citizenship, which should never be reduced to a reflex of the surrounding system of economic privilege. When this vital insulation is stripped away—as is happening today—it is not only the political system that suffers a dramatic loss in democratic legitimacy but the economic system as well. The question is whether the substantial steps we have already proposed suffice to break the grip of circularity and allow space for a vibrant politics of equal citizenship; or whether, as the abolitionist suggests, even more must be done.

This is, we are happy to admit, a question open to good-faith disagreement. But a host of countervailing factors incline us against the abolitionist view—beginning with a realist caution. Even if the abolitionist proposal were adopted, there would be many other ways for the rich to project their influence. Owners of newspapers and Web sites are also much richer than average; yet surely a free press is absolutely central to the workings of a democratic society. The rich and powerful will always manage somehow to gain undue prominence for their opinions; the question is whether we can design a system of countervailing power to keep this tendency under control.

Our point, it should be emphasized, applies not only to capitalist economies. The twentieth century has taught us that socialist systems have an even harder time preventing the bosses of nationalized industries from dominating public policy. It is a mistake, then, to look upon abolitionism as if it were a great leap forward to a Utopia where democratic politics is, at long last, perfectly insulated from the unequal economic system within which it is embedded. Abolitionism simply drives wealth into the remaining channels of political influence—ranging from think tanks to television stations, from traditional newspapers to the latest Web page gimmick. These extra investments will give the wealthy less bang for their buck than political contributions (otherwise they would be making them today). The question posed by abolitionism is whether this marginal diminution of inegalitarian influence is offset by other factors of greater importance.

The Case for a Mixed System

We stand before you as unrepentant social engineers—minor-league players in a vast squad of structural reformers stretching back to 1787, when a few men in Philadelphia had the nerve to propose an untested scheme of government for a vast continent. The Founding Fathers mixed their Enlightenment faith in the science of institutional design with a sober appreciation of its ultimate limitations. We hope to follow them down this path as well—and these reflections lead us to recommend a mixed system, rather than one that relies exclusively on public finance through Patriot Co.

Begin by considering that Patriot is simply an enabling measure. It is up to each American to decide whether she will take the time and trouble required to use her Patriot account and to engage the issues and personalities thrown up by the campaign. She is free to ignore the whole affair, dismiss the campaign's sound and fury as meaningless noise, and let her $50 account lapse unspent on election day. To be sure, the republic would be on its deathbed if all Americans took this tack. But this only makes the basic point: Patriot may empower citizens, but it cannot create them. Americans become citizens only through engagement in a much broader cultural enterprise—through which they encourage one another to participate in the democratic process on an ongoing basis. Every dinner table debate about politics, as well as every march on Washington, is part of this culture of active citizenship.[11] Patriot makes sense only as long as this culture is alive and well—offering Americans a new tool to revitalize their faith in democratic politics. But the tool should not be mistaken for the larger culture which it enables.

These Tocquevillean banalities, we suppose, will seem uncontroversial—but how do they help make a case for a mixed system of campaign finance?

To see our point, put yourself in the position of a modestly active citizen—the millions of men and women who do not scoff when the question of Gore or Bush comes up at the dinner table or around the water cooler but engage in good-faith debates over who the better candidate is; who do not immediately turn to the sports channel or the movie reviews when the campaign bulks large on television talk shows or newspaper front pages. Imagine next that you get a little more involved in the personalities and issues of the campaign—to the point that you want to do more than simply defend your favored cause and candidate in casual conversation and vote for him on election day. What more could you do?

Go to a meeting, knock on some doors, write a letter to the editor, get on the Internet, and lots of other things—like giving $100 to your side of the ongoing political debate. It is through activities like this that the culture of active citizenship reproduces itself. Without some people staying in active gear all of the time, and lots of people moving into gear some of the time, our civic culture will gradually disintegrate.

We do not wish to exaggerate the role of the $100 contribution in sustaining this culture. It is simply one of many ways Americans show that they care about the fate of the country, and thereby encourage others to engage in the enterprise of active citizenship. But it *is* one way, and one not to be despised. Indeed, political gift-giving has become an increasingly important way in which Americans manifest their civic concern.[12]

Flatly prohibiting private campaign contributions would be a real loss to the civic culture—especially when we consider how the social meaning of small gifts will change within the new regime of campaign finance. Nowadays the entire practice of campaign contributions has been put under a cloud as a result of its notorious abuse by big money. Once the secret donation booth purges the practice of special dealing, its social meaning as an act of citizenship will be further enhanced.

To see our point, place yourself in the position of a hypothetical citizen in proud possession of her Patriot card. Early in the campaign, she goes to her ATM and votes $50 for her favorite candidates. But as the campaign proceeds, she gets increasingly interested, and wants to contribute further: "My Patriot account may be empty, but this campaign is really important—and I want to put my *own* money where my mouth is!"

Thanks to the donation booth, she has no fear that her extra gift can be disparaged as an effort at pursuing her self-interest. The context makes it clear that she is making a genuine gesture of concern for the fate of her country. Indeed, her gift might inspire others to take the country a little bit more seriously in their own deliberations. It is by countless small acts that a culture of active citizenship re-creates itself over the generations.

When we put a concrete proposal on the table later in the book, we shall try to enhance further this citizenship effect. Our model statute will not insist on a strict regime of anonymity. If givers choose, they may authorize the trust to record their name on a list of contributors and publish it to the world. There is only one thing that the trust *must* keep secret: the amount of their contribution in excess of $200. This will make it possible for givers to stand up and be counted in public, and credibly state the precise amount of their small gifts—while making it impossible for candidates to identify how much big givers are giving.

We defer details until later, lest they divert attention from the main point: You don't have to be a modern Tocqueville to note that our civic culture isn't in the best of shape. Every act of civic engagement left undone—including private gifts when purged of the taint of special interest—is therefore a genuine loss, whose sacrifice should not be taken lightly.

To restate the point in more general terms: Within the new paradigm, voting with private dollars should count as a legitimate act of citizenship, as long as steps have been taken to enable citizens to vote with Patriot dollars as well. This conclusion, in turn, sets the stage for a more complicated defense of a mixed system of campaign finance.

Half of this argument consists of a series of critical appraisals of Patriot itself. In introducing the initiative, we have naturally emphasized the positive aspects of its promise of citizen sovereignty. But like all other good things in life, Patriot has its problems. The second half of the argument considers whether private giving, filtered by the donation booth, can help solve these problems. If the answer is yes, the mixed system of voting with public and private dollars yields a whole that is bigger and better than the sum of its parts.

The answer is yes.

Patriot has many weaknesses, but the ones we consider have a distinctive structure. All of them are inextricably intertwined with the good things about the program—they are the characteristic vices, as it were, of Patriot's characteristic virtues. Given this intimate relationship, they are especially worthy of analysis—because there can be no hope of eliminating them within the patriotic framework, it would be especially heartening to discover that private giving through the donation booth can serve to compensate for vices that would otherwise be irremediable.

Let us begin, then, with one of Patriot's greatest virtues—the way it encourages Americans to become more active citizens during the campaign as they deliberate with one another on the best way to vote their Patriot dollars. But there is a vice associated with this great virtue—what happens if most Americans fail this test of civic virtue and ignore the candidates?

The problem is especially acute during the earliest stages of the campaign. The overwhelming majority of Americans don't pay attention to the upcoming election before the primaries begin. Yet it is precisely at this time when the candidates will be urgently needing start-up funds. If they can manage to sustain themselves financially during these early months, some of their campaigns will take off by the time more Americans start paying attention and respond by showering patriotic dollars into their campaign chests. Call this the problem of selective attention.

How does private giving provide a solution? The donation booth is a means for more active citizens to put their money where their mouth is. Given their greater political involvement, they will appreciate the importance of an early gift in keeping promising candidacies afloat.[13]

Private giving won't be a perfect solution. It obviously favors candidates appealing to the rich, who can indulge the luxury of giving more readily. But this distributional point does not weigh so heavily in the start-up phases of the campaign, where costs are lower than those incurred in more intense campaigning. As long as candidates can find a smallish number of private givers to supplement the early trickle of patriotic contributions, they may stay alive long enough to reap a richer harvest.

The question of distributive justice becomes more complex when we focus on another vice-of-virtue problem. By flooding the system with citizen dollars, Patriot introduces a much-needed egalitarian counterweight into an increasingly plutocratic system of finance. But if we follow the path of abolitionism, and eliminate all private contributions, this renewed egalitarianism has its drawbacks.

Most Patriot dollars will be spent in support of candidacies that appeal to very broad constituencies, leaving minoritarian parties and candidates with fewer patriotic resources to push their programs. In the grand scheme of things, this is as it should be—political campaigns in a democracy are, first and foremost, contests for majority support, and the worst charge against a finance system is that it allows a moneyed minority to dominate the interests and ideals of a popular majority. Nevertheless, we believe that the majoritarian tendencies of Patriot can also be viewed as a vice—especially during the early phases of a campaign.

The primary season is a time when the vibrant expression of minoritarian positions and candidacies can play an especially constructive role in democratic politics. Even within the short term, they prod broader publics in new directions, leading major candidates to embrace positions they had previously believed beyond the pale. And in the longer run, the ideals voiced by minority candidates have regularly transformed themselves into mainstream beliefs.

Call this the minoritarian difficulty; the question is whether private giving, mediated by the donation booth, can compensate for this patriotic deficiency. The case for a mixed system looks good because, as we have noted, one should expect private-money contributions to be relatively important early in the season. But one further condition must be realized before we are home free—the distribution of private donations, as compared with that of early Patriot dollars, must be skewed to the minoritarian extremes away from the majoritarian center.

Speaking broadly, this condition won't be hard to satisfy. The secret donation booth tends to filter out self-interested contributions, while allowing an unimpeded flow of ideological gifts. Operationally speaking, the decisive question is: Will ideological contributions be skewed toward the extremes of public opinion?

Very likely. Although it is possible to imagine a world dominated by passionate centrists, twentieth-century politics has proliferated ideologies of the right and left in much greater abundance. The minoritarian case for a mixed system seems empirically well grounded.[14]

This same ideological skew is central to our final vice-of-virtue argument. This potential pathology arises toward the end of the campaign. From time to time, a major party may be captured by an ideological faction that nominates an extreme candidate who fails to attract broad support in the center. Patriotic contributions plummet, leaving the "major party" no choice but to launch a minor-league effort.

As we explained in Chapter 2, this snowball effect is a vice of one of Patriot's principal virtues—its commitment to citizen sovereignty, not bureaucratic centralization, as the organizing principle of campaign finance. It won't be easy to eliminate the problem entirely, but the ideological character of private donations helps ameliorate concern. An extremist takeover will predictably inspire right- or left-wing ideologues to step up their private giving in an effort to make the best use of their moment of major-party domination. To be sure, this compensating effect will give an advantage to right-wing over left-wing ideologues—because the leftists will typically have less money to spare for private gifts. Worse yet, and in contrast to the first two vice-of-virtue problems, the snowball problem occurs at a late stage of the campaign, when costs are high. Although left-wing ideologues may be rich enough to compensate for selective-attention problems and minoritarian difficulties at the beginning of campaigns, they may have a harder time bankrolling a campaign experiencing powerful snowball effects. This will be easier for right-wing ideologues.

The structural disparity is unfortunate, but we need not claim that our mixed system is perfect—only that it is better than an abolitionist alternative banning private funding and relying exclusively on "clean money" distributed through the patriotic decisions of the general citizenry.

Our first argument for a mixed system emphasized the positive role that private giving plays in the American culture of active citizenship. Our second considered how the relatively active portion of the citizenry might use the private donation booth to compensate for some characteristic deficiencies in patriotic finance. Our final argument invites you to shift focus—from the acts of citizens to the incentives of legislators. How does the choice between a mixed system and an abolitionist approach change the incentives of these crucial decisionmakers?

Consider that sitting legislators already have great advantages over their potential electoral challengers. They have been working for a long time—some for a very long time—getting their names and opinions before the public. And by definition, they have been successful enough to win the prize of office. To make up for this long-term deficit in "informational capital," challengers need lots of money.[15] Worse yet, they have a tougher time getting on television for free. Sitting legislators constantly use the power of their office to make "news"—announcing local projects, voting on popular measures—and thereby appear on nightly newscasts while likely opponents smile grimly on the sidelines.[16]

Incumbents have more than informational capital going for them as they confront prospective opponents. They also find it easier to raise money—using their office to reward big donors and punish those who haven't put money into the till. As a consequence, incumbents are unlikely to disturb the existing system—unless, that is, a reform movement gains powerful support among ordinary citizens who are willing to punish incumbents at the ballot box for their fealty to the status quo.

Such a movement already exists, of course, but assume that it gains momentum over the next decade, and that its focus gradually shifts away from the old to the new reform paradigm—a big assumption! Confronting an aroused public, legislators find their maneuvering room restricted to two choices—either a mixed system or an abolitionist system relying exclusively on patriotic finance. If they seek to further their narrow self-interest as incumbents, which option will they prefer?

Our answer will seem counterintuitive, given the notorious reluctance of contemporary politicians to cut themselves off from private funding. But if you are willing to suspend disbelief long enough to countenance our hypothetical scenario, it will become clear that most self-interested incumbents would suddenly wish to abolish private giving entirely rather than endorse a mixed system. Consider that the secret donation booth will eliminate the incumbents' main advantage in the private fund-raising business—they can no longer reward big donors, for they will no longer be able to identify them. And so far as ideological gifts are concerned, their opponents might often be in a position to compete effectively for money. By abolishing all private gifts, incumbents close off this threat, and can rely upon their superiority in informational capital to carry them to victory.

Once Patriot is made the exclusive source of campaign funding, an incumbent has another ace up his sleeve. Our model statute provides generous funding for Patriot accounts, but there is no reason for incumbents to agree—instead of seeding each voter's account with $50, why not "save some money" and appropriate only $5?

This money-saving measure may or may not be popular with the voters, but one thing is clear—it will vastly reduce the chance that an electoral opponent will raise enough money to launch an effective challenge. For self-interested incumbents, the election-maximizing logic is clear—first deny challengers access to ideological gifts from the private sector; then starve them by underfunding Patriot.

But what makes sense for incumbents doesn't make sense for the rest of us. There is a very real danger that politicians might, in response to the next wave of reformist agitation, use abolitionist demands for the elimination of private funding as a convenient fig leaf to transform Patriot into an insurance policy for incumbents. Opponents of this scheme might eventually convince the Supreme Court to strike it down as unconstitutional. But then again, they might fail in this effort, and in any event, serious damage may be done in the interim.

Rather than relying on the Court, new paradigmers should avoid the temptations of abolitionism in the first place. By using the donation booth to purge private giving of its taint, reformers deprive incumbents of their present fund-raising advantage with big givers, and give challengers a real chance to raise enough private money to offset the remaining incumbents' advantage in informational capital. The mixed system will also serve as a check on legislative incentives to starve Patriot. With private money still flowing through the donation booth, incumbents who don't expect to get much will have an incentive to oppose efforts to drive the patriotic allocation below $50—for they will have to rely on patriotic finance for more of their resources.[17]

In drafting our model statute, we shall be making further efforts to deal with the underfunding problem. But even without them, the mixed system plays a key role in limiting the possibilities of abuse. Public and private components operate to check and balance the worst evils of either system functioning alone.

Competing Mixtures?

There are many ways of mixing public and private finance. Even supposing that a mixed system is best, why choose our particular combination?

A thought experiment will usefully illuminate the critical design issues. Consider an alternative that rejects Patriot and relies on a system of matching grants for private donations. This approach seeks to equalize financial resources through a progressive matching formula: If Jane Poor gives $100, her favorite candidate will find his blind trust enriched, say, by $300, but $100 coming from Joe Bourgeois would generate only $200, and the same amount from Bill Gates would yield the candidate $100 (or maybe less). Compared with this familiar design option, our mixed system has two distinctive features. The first is unconditionality: Each American gets 50 Patriot dollars simply by registering to vote. In contrast, a matching-grant scheme requires a citizen to sacrifice some of her private money in order to gain access to public funding. If Jane Poor gives zero dollars under a matching system, her favorite candidate gets nothing; but under our alternative, she is still free to give 50 Patriots even if she spends all her private dollars on food, rent, and clothing.

But of course, the unconditional character of the basic $50 grant comes at a cost—especially to those who would have given anyway. Under a matching system, a private gift of $100 or $200 might generate a substantial subsidy, especially if it came from Ms. Poor. But under our scheme, there is no progressivity for private dollars: If anybody wants to spend more than 50 Patriots, all dollars count equally, and none are subsidized. Call this the no-subsidy principle.

The choice between the two systems comes down to this: What's so great about unconditionality and no-subsidy?

These two ideas have very different standing. Unconditionality is based on a basic political principle, while no-subsidy is based on a series of prudential considerations that seem compelling but are not on the same moral level.

Begin on the prudential side. To narrow our focus to the no-subsidy question, suppose that in addition to granting each voter 50 Patriot dollars, a progressive subsidy was provided for all private gifts—large for Jane Poor, nonexistent for Bill Gates. If we lived in an ideal world, we would not object to such a scheme. To the contrary, it would usefully ameliorate the pro-rich bias of our existing mixed proposal.

Nevertheless, you may have noticed that our world falls sadly short of the ideal, and we are reluctant to invite real-world politicians into this particular briar patch. Even if a consensus were reached on the proposition that the poor should be subsidized more than the rich, specifying the precise formula would provoke a partisan battle royal—with Democrats and Republicans fiercely manipulating the subsidy schedule to their partisan advantage. Even after they arrived at a statutory solution, the parties would be tempted to revisit the issue and rejigger the formula constantly to reflect changes in the political balance of forces.

One of our principal goals is to design a system that reduces such temptations. Campaign finance is an exquisitely sensitive matter to politicians, and every time they get involved in statutory revision, they may easily go on a partisan rampage, wreaking havoc on the entire structure. The best response is prevention: Eliminate alluring statutory "solutions" before they generate endless partisan squabbling. In this particular case, abstinence comes at a price in terms of equal citizenship—after all, a progressive matching formula would indeed ameliorate the inequality problem that remains even after we have introduced 5 billion Patriot dollars into the mixed system. Nonetheless, it does so only at an unacceptable cost in politicization.

A progressive matching formula is also incompatible with a second objective: to design a system that is relatively simple for Americans to understand and for bureaucrats to operate. Progressive matching inevitably makes the administration of the donation booth a cumbersome affair, because donors must somehow establish their annual income to qualify their gift for the proper matching sum. Such a scheme not only is expensive to operate. It will strain the system in other ways—making it more difficult both to preserve donor anonymity and to safeguard against fraud.

Finally, any matching scheme will cost billions of additional dollars and compete with our first fiscal priority—which is to fund Patriot, a program that will cost $5 billion, or more, during presidential election years. It seems smart to put first things first, and make Patriot our overriding fiscal goal. Subsidized private giving will have to wait, probably indefinitely.

This conclusion is entirely prudential—but no less compelling for that! In contrast, our decision to grant Patriot dollars unconditionally is based on basic—albeit controversial—political principles. To define the relevant questions, we continue our comparison with the matching-grant alternative—waiving all prudential objections for purposes of clarifying the moral issue at stake.

Suppose that somebody proposes to scrap our Patriot scheme entirely and replace it with a thoroughgoing matching-grant alternative. Because this eliminates our $5 billion plus program, our rival can become more generous in his provision of progressive subsidies—perhaps a gift of $10 from Jane Poor will now net her favorite candidate $50 or even more. Nevertheless, the scheme remains conditional. It is not enough for a citizen to register to vote. She must also sacrifice some of her private income to gain access to a share of campaign finance funds: If Jane gives zero, the candidate still gets zero. Under our proposal, Jane can give 50 Patriot dollars even if she gives zero private dollars. Is this a morally significant difference?

The question is less novel than it may seem at first glance. When we move back in time, a similar issue was raised in connection with the right to vote. Advocates of poll taxes traditionally argued that it was not enough for Americans to register to vote or pass a literacy test. They should also be required to pay a special tax before gaining access to the ballot box. On this view, the sacrifice of some cash was required before an American could establish that he merited the franchise.[18]

But the nation has decisively rejected such reasoning.[19] The right to vote is not something that must be purchased. An American may decide that her private needs are so pressing that she can't afford to pay the $10 poll tax, but this should not bar her from the ballot box. The choices she makes as a private consumer do not disqualify her from making choices as a private citizen. To the contrary: Americans are citizens before they are consumers, and their basic citizenship rights depend neither on their wealth nor the intensity of their private desires. But if this is true on election day, shouldn't it also be true during the election campaign?

This is the point of the unconditional grant of Patriot dollars. Under modern conditions, it is wrong to treat campaign funding as a frill. Unless we find a way to democratize campaign finance, the right to vote will become mere shadow play. Within this setting, Patriot dollars are a form of citizenship power no less fundamental than the vote itself. Just as Americans no longer have to sacrifice private goods to gain access to the vote, they should not be required to sacrifice private goods to gain access to Patriot dollars. Only by combining votes and Patriot dollars can citizens regain a semblance of popular sovereignty in today's world—and they should be satisfied with nothing less.

This is, at least, the moral foundation of our initiative, and our ultimate reason for rejecting alternative mixed systems. What is more, matching-grant proposals make a hash out of the political, bureaucratic, and budgetary realities.[20] Sound democratic morality is perfectly compatible, in this case at least, with plain old common sense.

We have been fighting a two-front war—on one front, defending the secret donation booth against the traditional reformist prejudice in favor of full information; on the other, defending it against abolitionists who would eliminate private giving entirely. How much progress have we made?

It is premature to declare victory on the first front. We have explained why full information won't accomplish very much (other than inviting us to feel good about ourselves). But we have not refuted all the serious objections to our own proposal. Most obviously, big donors and ambitious politicians will have powerful incentives to destroy the integrity of the secret donation booth, and will design clever ways to determine the precise identity of the donors who are depositing big checks into the blind trust. Unless we can credibly secure the system against sabotage, the case for the donation booth remains incomplete. Even if full information generates only small gains, this is better than a splashy proposal that looks good on paper but flops in practice. We shall take up this operational challenge in Part II.

We have accomplished more on the second front. Creative abolitionists may well design clever responses to one or another of our arguments for a mixed system. But we doubt that they can counter all of them. Voting with both public and private dollars not only promises to enhance the existing culture of active citizenship. It will also significantly improve on the operation of a purely patriotic system of campaign finance. Private dollars flowing through the donation booth will ameliorate problems that otherwise would be generated by the selective attention of most citizens, the tendency of Patriot dollars to starve minoritarian opinions, and the risk of the occasional snowball effect. No less important, it will check and balance tendencies by sitting politicians to starve their electoral opponents by underfunding Patriot.

All of these factors are significant. Together they add up to a very strong case.

But not open-and-shut. The abolitionist *can* respond to our cascade of arguments by recalling the intrinsic appeal of abstract principles of equality. Recall the simple analogy to the ballot box with which we began the argument: We do not give anybody the right to buy extra votes on election day merely because he is willing to pay for them. But if one person, one vote is the right way to proceed on election day, why not insist on one person, 50 Patriots during the preelection debate?

We do not deny the symbolic force of this question.[21] But at the end of the day, we do not think it outweighs the prospect of a more vigorous and secure democracy offered by a mixed system.

4 Regulations of Last Resort

We have been pursuing a structural approach. Rather than telling people how much they can give, we have been reorganizing the process of giving. This structural emphasis contrasts sharply with the transactional focus of the old paradigm: Under existing federal law, for example, nobody can give any candidate more than $1,000 during a particular campaign.[1]

This focus on specific transactions is the product of generations of reform effort. Although activists certainly recognize the importance of (centralized) subsidies and (full) information in their overall strategy, they reserve their greatest passion for the effort to purge big gifts from politics. Senator John McCain's recent meteoric rise testifies to the power of this appeal—which made him a serious presidential candidate.

The old paradigm's transactional focus has had predictable consequences. As reformers succeed in abolishing one or another suspect transaction, donors and politicians respond by skirting the new law and designing new forms of dealing that permit business as usual. The current campaign against soft-money contributions provides an apt illustration. Existing law bans big contributions to candidates but permits big gifts to political parties. So big givers take advantage of this loophole to channel vast sums to the parties, which can legally spend the money for a host of activities that benefit their favored candidates.[2]

After years of public agitation, progressives have convinced the public to view soft money as if it posed *the* acid test for campaign reform. But success in plugging this loophole will only catalyze a new cycle of shattered expectations. The new reform legislation must define soft money contributions in legal language of greater or lesser clarity. As soon as the ink is dry on the statute books, big donors and ambitious politicians will make every effort to continue their ongoing relationships—paying lawyers handsomely to create new modes of transaction that skirt the law and create new loopholes. Because lawyers tend to be good at this sort of thing, a decade hence there will be a need for another Senator McCain—and perhaps this time, he or she may actually win the White House by rousing populist appeals against the continuing evasions of "special interests."

Loophole plugging isn't entirely pointless. Statutes can be more or less successful in raising the costs of deal-making, and higher transaction costs generally lead to marginal reductions in the regulated activity. But until we change the incentives of big donors and ambitious politicians, we will not get to the heart of the problem. This is the point of the secret donation booth—by disrupting the informational conditions under which donors and politicians can deal with one another, the new structure deprives the two sides of the incentive to hire lawyers to design new forms of evasive transaction.

Until we take this step, the reform-evasion cycle promises to continue with only one certain consequence—the political environment will become increasingly penetrated by a proliferating set of laws and regulations specifying the do's and don'ts of particular campaign transactions. Proliferation will generate pathologies of its own. Politicians and donors will be increasingly obliged to master a complex rulebook, and their knowledge of the rules will be tested under very difficult conditions. Political campaigns are high-stress affairs. Time is of the essence, the stakes are high, and campaign coffers are filling up with checks from a broad array of contributors. Campaign staffers will almost inevitably accept some gifts that violate one or another loophole-closing provision—sometimes innocently, sometimes less so.

The predictable—if unintended—result is the criminalization of politics. After the election, criminal prosecutors will engage in the leisurely inspection of the massive record generated during the feverish days of the campaign—especially the records of the losing side. They are virtually certain to uncover irregularities, readily dramatized by the media. Suppose, for example, that Senator McCain and others succeed in plugging the soft money loophole by proscribing certain kinds of gifts to political parties, and suppose that donors respond by giving "softer money" to other groups that cooperate with political parties in ways that occasionally break the rules. Imagine the outrage that follows when a triumphant prosecutor discovers this fact.

The offending donors and politicians will profess ignorance—underlings blundered, it was an honest mistake. But skeptics will abound—and they may well be right in impugning the motives of the top dogs. Whatever the truth, it will take a year or two for prosecutors, judges, and juries to find out (as best they can).

During all this time, the reputations of political leaders will be dragged through the mud—with indelible effects regardless of the truth. Even if a case ends in formal acquittal, the mere act of criminal prosecution will suffice to cast a shadow. While the wheels of justice grind remorselessly after each campaign, the shadow darkens on the entire democratic process as leading politicians and lobbyists take their turn in the dock to protest their innocence and proclaim the political motivations of their prosecutors.

The result will be a parody of the reformers' noble intentions. Even if their controls actually succeed in cleaning up politics to a significant degree, it will not seem that way to the general public—who will be much more aware of the sensationalist charges and countercharges traded in the press. Nor will the "successful" prosecution and conviction of errant politicians and lobbyists encourage the next generation to view politics as an honorable profession. Mudslinging and criminality will repel many otherwise honorable men and women from a political career that is risky enough without adding the prospect of a jail sentence.

We have already seen the rise of this pathology during the past decade. Although none of the high-profile scandals has yet sent a leading politician or lobbyist to prison, the tendency toward criminalization is clear. Unless we change course, it is only a matter of time before a leading statesman will be sent away in handcuffs. As the television cameras whirl and paparazzi pop, how will the general public understand the scene—as an expression of the majesty of the law or as final confirmation that all politicians are crooks?

Granted, there *are* times when politicians deserve to go to jail. But we should beware lest the criminal law become a normal weapon of ordinary politics. When politicians can throw one another in jail on a regular basis, the risks of losing elections become too great, the loss of civility too profound, the cynicism of citizens too corrosive.

Reformers should rethink their traditional emphasis on ever-tighter control of suspect transactions. Rather than proliferating the web of transactional regulation, command and control should be a matter of last resort. To put the point in operational terms, our two structural initiatives—Patriot dollars and the secret donation booth—have already greatly reduced the power of powerful interests to make special deals with politicians. If these reforms were ever enacted, why not end all efforts at further command-and-control regulation?

Let anybody give any amount to any candidate, party or political organization—provided, of course, that all campaign gifts go through the secret donation booth. Let's lift the free-floating legal anxieties that currently afflict all donors and politicians as they go about giving and getting campaign resources. Let's send the lawyers packing, and tell everybody that nobody is going to jail for giving too much to politics, or giving to the wrong people at the wrong time. Let's rely instead on Patriot dollars and the secret donation booth to restrict the role of special interests and guarantee that ordinary citizens remain at the center of campaign finance. Let's achieve effective citizen sovereignty and increase political liberty at the same time.

We emphatically endorse these sentiments, but not to the point of embracing complete deregulation. A few good reasons remain for capping the amount any individual can give during any campaign cycle. But this cap should be set far above the current $1,000 limit—at a stratospheric height that will be practically insignificant to all but the very richest Americans.

Defeating the Donation Booth?

Consider how the secret donation booth undermines the traditional rationale for low contribution limits. As long as politicians know how much their donors are giving, big givers can buy special influence. Within this information-rich environment, low contribution limits make sense: How else to curb corruption?

But once politicians cannot verify big gifts, they can no longer reward the givers, and there is no longer any need to impose low limits to repress influence peddling. The traditional rationale for transactional regulation is relevant only if contributors can defeat the anonymity of the donation booth by making extremely large contributions.

To define the parameters of the residual problem, take a glimpse at the brave new world inaugurated by the secret donation booth. To receive legal contributions, politicians and political organizations must open a blind trust at a bank regulated by the new Federal Election Commission. A donor makes out her check in the name of the FEC and attaches a form naming the beneficiary. After she sends in the check and the form, she has five days to ask for a refund (once the trust has cashed her check). When she receives her canceled check for $10,000 from her bank, the donor will be free to show it to her favored candidate—but she will not be able to establish that the check was accompanied by the appropriate beneficiary form, or that it wasn't rescinded during the subsequent five-day period. Even if a donor can flaunt a check, she will have a hard time convincing a skeptical politician that she has made good on her promise of a big gift.

Leaving further details to Part II, let us focus on the obvious objection to our basic design: Can't the donor and recipient defeat the blind trust by coordinating their behavior? Suppose Donor D tells Candidate C that she will be giving him $10,000 on June 1, and that he should expect to see his blind trust account increase by that amount at the end of the recission period on June 6. If C's account does in fact jump by $10,000 on the 6th, won't that be proof that the deal went through?

Not if lots of donors are giving at the same time, and even more people are promising phony gifts they have no intention of making. If twenty people say they have given $10,000 apiece to C on June 1, what is he to think when he sees his balance jump by $27,000 on June 6?

But if we leave the matter at this level, really big givers will find it possible to defeat the donation booth. Suppose D tells C that she will be depositing $100,000 on June 1; and suppose that D's campaign chest has been growing at about $10,000 a day for the past few weeks. Then the 6th comes around, and A's account suddenly jumps by $110,000. Surely this eye-catching jump will vastly enhance the credibility of D's earlier promise—and a grateful C will not forget D's largesse if he wins on election day!

We propose to make C's guessing game much more difficult. Rather than automatically crediting his account with all funds received after the five day recission period, the FEC will instruct the blind trust to use a secrecy algorithm designed to make it especially difficult for candidates and donors to establish credible connections between particular deposits and particular increases in trust balances. Under the algorithm, C won't receive D's entire $100,000 contribution on June 6 but will see his account increase by that sum over the next couple of weeks, under a formula calculated to make its ready identification difficult. For example, it will sometimes happen that D's big gift on the 1st will trigger a modest *decline* in the $10,000 amount C ordinarily receives on a daily basis—with this decrement compensated by (randomized) increments over the next few days until the entire $100,000 becomes available. During all this period, of course, C will be receiving more gifts, further complicating his task of determining whether D gave him the $100,000, or whether his mushrooming campaign balance comes from other donors (who will have a tendency to exaggerate their generosity). In short, our secrecy algorithm creates such a "noisy signal" that it will defeat almost all efforts at accurate identification.

But not all. If Bill Gates gives C a billion dollars on June 1, our happy candidate will quickly begin to notice that something truly wonderful is happening to his trust balance—if not on the 6th, then soon enough to make him think that Gates wasn't fooling when he made his promise.

So there remains a case for stratospheric limitation on the traditional special-dealing rationale. How high this limit should be depends on the level (and volatility) of background contributions from other givers. While a concentrated gift of $100,000 might be enough to defeat the algorithm at an early stage in the race for a seat in the House of Representatives, a serious candidate for the presidency wouldn't be able to identify gifts of this size, because so many others will be giving as well.

We discuss the technical and policy issues arising in the construction of the algorithm in Chapter 7 and in a special appendix. But we have said enough to make our main point: The traditional anticorruption rationale for low contribution limits no longer operates in the world of the new paradigm. Our new structural remedy, the donation booth, displaces the old paradigm's transactional remedy, contribution limits, and transforms it into a regulation of last resort.

Equality

But there is a second rationale for low contribution limits. They constrain the inegalitarian bias of a system dominated by private giving. To be sure, any system of private finance gives the upper hand to the upper classes—but at least the $1,000 limit makes it impossible for a tiny number of oligarchs to dominate.

Recent trends seem to reinforce this point. Over the past twenty years, big donors and their lawyers have been extremely creative in evading the $1,000 limit by designing new transactional forms that violate the spirit, if not the letter, of the law: Enormous gifts of soft money now flow to political parties, and other—perhaps more pernicious—legal evasions are proliferating at great speed. As a consequence, the American system is indeed veering dangerously toward oligarchy. Within this setting, we sympathize with traditional reformers, like Senators McCain and Feingold, who seek to plug existing loopholes in a desperate effort at avoiding the worst oligarchic excesses. If this were the only way to shore up the dike against the tides of big money that threaten to overwhelm American democracy, we would be lending a hand—despite the doubts that we will soon be expressing about their proposed statutory solutions.

But we believe that our structural approach renders the transactional focus of McCain-Feingold obsolete. With citizens voting 5 billion Patriot dollars, fears of impending oligarchy become melodramatic—especially when the overall amount of private giving will decline substantially once the donation booth makes it impossible for donors to purchase influence.

In Part II, we shall take operational steps to assure the overall dominance of public funding: If private contributors give more than a third of all money during any campaign cycle, our model statute triggers an increase in each citizen's Patriot allowance to assure that public funding makes up at least two-thirds during the next electoral period. Although this macro-guarantee is fundamental, we do not think that it obviates the need for all regulations of last resort on particular donations to particular campaigns.

To define the residual problem, consider that—despite the macro-guarantee of two-thirds public funding throughout the nation—a few plutocrats could still overwhelm patriotic finance in particular races. Suppose a multibillionaire—call him Bill—was especially interested in determining the outcome of the Senate race in the State of Washington and was prepared to outspend his fellow citizens single-handedly. This should be forbidden even if the local exercise in plutocratic domination was masked by reassuring national figures indicating overall compliance with the macro-guarantee.

This anxiety about localized plutocracy is analytically distinct from our previous concern with special influence. Suppose, for example, that Bill never gave an enormous gift on any single day but simply contributed a steady stream of funds, making it impossible for his favored candidate ever to verify that Bill was financially responsible for his victory. Even if Bill's role were entirely unknown, one single man should not be allowed to dominate politics behind the scenes.

Given this antiplutocracy principle, the next task is to define an appropriate regulation of last resort. The State of Washington has about 3 million registered voters, and under our proposal they will be in a position to vote 15 Patriot dollars on each Senate race, yielding a potential sum of $45 million. Because many Washingtonians won't use their accounts, overall patriotic contributions will be a lot less than $45 million, but consider that nonplutocrats will also add their private gifts to the pool. With total public and private contributions in the $20–30 million range, what should be the upper limit of Bill's donation?

A lot more than $1,000. We leave a precise number for later, but it is immediately obvious that the current limit is much too low to survive under the new paradigm.

Crime and Punishment

Consider the clean lines of criminal responsibility emerging from our approach. There is one basic rule, easily understood by everybody: Never give or accept gifts that haven't passed through the secret donation booth. Any direct transfer of cash is a felony comparable to vote-buying, and punishable accordingly.

The remaining regulations concern a few big givers. But they can readily afford hiring lawyers and accountants to keep clear of the stratospheric limits imposed on their activities. The rest of us can give and get without fearing a host of complex and obscure rules threatening severe punishments.

Once this threat has been removed, a policy of strict law enforcement becomes a serious option for the first time. Prosecutors have generally proved lethargic—in part because winning politicians don't want their own campaigns scrutinized, but also because everybody is vaguely aware that everybody's campaign can be caught in the proliferating net of legalisms. Most prosecutors are decent people who are reluctant to use the blunt tools of their trade to scapegoat a few campaign workers for "crimes" many others have also "committed." Why waste precious time on such fringe matters when so many accused rapists and embezzlers urgently demand attention?

Once in a while, a front-page scandal may generate an uproar that propels prosecutors into a paroxysm of hyperactivity. But these interventions may only show the difficulties involved in rebutting professions of innocence when rules and transactions are complex and ambiguous. In contrast, there is nothing very ambiguous about a direct transfer of cash to a politician. It will be tough to convince a jury that a check for $10,000 was really a birthday present!

Redefining campaign crime is only the first step toward a credible enforcement strategy. There is also the obvious risk of political vendetta. Losing candidates cannot be singled out to bear the brunt of prosecution. Without genuinely impartial administration, the threat of criminal sanctions can generate perverse incentives—encouraging both sides to cheat on the donation booth, gain electoral victory, and send their opponents to prison.

This is a very serious problem, and we take it up in a later chapter as part of a sweeping reform of the Federal Election Commission. In calling for a redefinition of the role of the criminal law, we have taken only a first step toward its credible use. But it is an essential one. Without a narrow focus on commonsense notions of criminal behavior, our initiative will be eroded by increasingly cynical violations of the basic rules protecting the secret donation booth.

McCain-Feingold

A good way to summarize our critique is by considering the alternative— the effort by Senators McCain and Feingold to breathe new life into the old paradigm. In examining their initiative, we do not mean to criticize the senators themselves. The old paradigm has been the only intellectual game in town, and it was perfectly natural for them to use it as a legislative framework. After all, lots of universities and think tanks can generate new ideas, but there are only a hundred senators who can serve as leaders in a campaign for reform. They were perfectly right to take the best reform thinking of their time and try to make it into a political reality. Thanks to Senators McCain and Feingold, the nation is much more conscious of the importance of campaign reform than it would have been otherwise. Nevertheless, a study of their concrete proposals only serves to confirm the need for fresh thinking.

On the plus side, we completely endorse their effort to sweep soft-money contributions to political parties into the regulatory framework. Our model statute does the same thing, and we shall explain in Chapter 8 why this expansion of the regulatory net is constitutional under the existing doctrine of the Supreme Court.

But the bill has two important weaknesses.[3] First, it continues to rely on low contribution limits as the primary way to prevent quid pro quo corruption. Although McCain-Feingold increases these limits (lifting from $1,000 to $2,000 the amount that any individual can give a candidate's campaign), they will still operate as a binding constraint on hundred of thousands of Americans.[4] If these limits are rigorously enforced, we risk making too many lobbyists and politicians into criminals.

This is the first campaign finance statute that includes sentencing guidelines.[5] Others may take this as a strength, but for us, it is an ominous sign indeed. The only thing worse than lax enforcement would be rigorous enforcement: Do we really want hundreds or thousands prosecuted for campaign finance crime after each election?

Second, McCain-Feingold restrains free speech by expanding the definition of express advocacy. It defines as "electioneering communication" any broadcast communication which (1) "refers to a clearly identified candidate for Federal office" and (2) is made within sixty days of a general election or thirty days of a primary election.[6] The bill then prohibits corporations and unions from spending money on electioneering communications and requires other organizations to disclose the sources of their funds.[7] We reject this effort to expand the regulatory net. Rather than restricting the right of interest groups to endorse candidates, the new paradigm solves the problem of special influence by diluting it with Patriot dollars and constraining it through the secret donation booth. Once this framework is put into place, such draconian restrictions on electioneering will seem unnecessary.

This is the place to say good-bye to some of our readers: If you haven't been convinced by now to reassess the old paradigm, you should put down this book and find better things to do with your time. But for those attracted by our proposal, there is a lot of hard work ahead: How to transform the new approach into operational reality?

II

The Paradigm in Practice

5 | Mixing Paradigms

In Part I we set the stage by contrasting old and new pathways to reform. Now that we are getting down to practical proposals, we must move beyond this simple dichotomy. Paradigms are tools for problem solving. The new paradigm provides a host of promising options, but it does not guarantee good answers to all questions. Campaign finance is not a single Big Problem but a series of interrelated middle-sized issues—some of which may be solved better with the tools provided by the old paradigm. We are not purists but pragmatists, and see no need for a one-size-fits-all approach. The challenge is to use tools from both old and new paradigms to construct a whole that is more than the sum of its parts.

The traditional approach is especially useful when it comes to a threshold issue. As the next election emerges on the distant horizon, potential candidates start testing the waters. First-time challengers launch trial balloons. Incumbents consider whether to run for reelection or try for higher office. All this exploratory activity costs money. How should it be raised?

The Limits of the New Paradigm

This is an especially sensitive stage. By hypothesis, politicians don't want to declare their candidacies, and it would be wrong to force them to come into the open prematurely. At the same time, they need chunks of money up front—to do some polling, assemble a small staff, travel around potential or existing constituencies, and the like. And they need it quickly, in a hassle-free way—without the elaborate fund-raising apparatus which nowadays serves as a signal of serious candidacy.

These are things that the new paradigm won't readily provide. At this early stage, hardly anybody is focusing on the next election—except for potential candidates and their most fervent backers. Appeals for Patriot dollars are likely to go unanswered—and the appeal itself costs money and staff which, by hypothesis, the noncandidate doesn't have. There is no harm in authorizing a politician's "exploratory committee" to appeal for Patriot dollars, but we shouldn't suppose that this will ordinarily suffice to generate the needed political grubstake.

The secret donation booth is also problematic. Without much help from fund-raising staff, potential candidates will spend lots of time soliciting promises of financial support, only to find that donors aren't following through, and that a lot less money is arriving through the blind trust than had been promised. Instead of sounding out potential constituents, would-be candidates will be condemned to a lot of wasted motion.

Politicians do have some real friends—people who believe in them for their own sake, and not for their instrumental value. Friends can be trusted to mean what they say and deliver their checks, but the secret donation booth seems a pretty pointless ritual here as well. Every politician will believe it when his college roommate or childhood pal says that the check is in the mail.

The donation booth also works less efficiently at the exploratory stage. When candidates are already receiving $10,000 on an average day, it will be impossible for a politician to know whether any particular donor has made good on his promise of $5,000. But a contribution of this size will stand out if the average take is only $1,000 a day, and only a very few donors have even promised to deliver such a large amount. Our secrecy algorithm will kick in to create an especially noisy signal when the candidate receives a relatively large gift—rather than reporting the $5,000 on the fifth day after it is deposited, the formula adds money into the account over the next few weeks.[1]

But during this early phase, the delay required to create the noise may be costly. While the candidate is waiting for the algorithm to cough up enough funds for him to complete his preliminary canvass, some rival may preempt him, and he may lose a precious opportunity to enter the race.

Surely it is in society's interest to encourage a thousand flowers to bloom at this stage. Although Patriot dollars may well suffice to support the exploratory efforts of some politicians with mobilized followings, the donation booth won't reliably deliver for many other serious contenders. To solve our problem, we must rely on tools drawn from the old paradigm.

Back to the Old?

Not every tool will do. The promise of centralized bureaucratic subsidies seems limited. As we have seen, such schemes always confront a problem designing threshold criteria that applicants must satisfy before they can qualify for subsidy. These problems reach their maximum in the present case—if a centralized scheme offered hefty subsidies for "exploratory campaigns," needy politicians would line up from here to eternity; if subsidies were skimpy, the lines would be shorter, but the sums would be inadequate to provide an adequate grubstake.

There is a standard technique for ameliorating—if not eliminating—this problem. Often, applicants are required to gather a significant number of signatures on petitions of support to qualify for the subsidy. But this solution is obviously a nonstarter during the exploratory phase—when, by hypothesis, the politician hasn't decided whether to place himself before the voters and declare his candidacy officially in the first place. Insofar as public subsidy is a plausible response to the problem, it makes more sense to allow the exploratory committee to register for the receipt of Patriot dollars and hope that some citizens will be alert enough to notice.

We are left with the classic response of the old paradigm: Let readily identifiable donors give private money to politicians, constrained only by full information and contribution limits. This solution is heavily biased in favor of the rich and well organized, but that bias is tolerable—as long as the old paradigm is restricted to the exploratory phase.

Almost anybody with any chance at a House or Senate seat has at least a few friends with money. The problem of bias becomes more acute over the longer haul, when candidates servicing the rich get lots more money than those appealing to other interests. The residual bias of private money is also partially offset by the availability of patriotic finance.

So let us reject the donation booth, and accept private giving of the traditional sort, as the more appropriate response to the problem of exploratory finance. This leads to a series of design questions. Under the old paradigm, private giving is acceptable only if we stringently limit the amount of any particular contribution and require its full disclosure to the public. Are these responses plausible in the exploratory context?

We must also set an overall limit to the size of the exploratory fund. We are accepting the old paradigm only for the earliest phase of the campaign. There comes a point at which politicians should put up or shut up, retire from the field or declare their candidacies and confront the rigors of a serious race for office. During the bulk of the campaign, we propose to channel private giving through the secret donation booth. Operationally, this requires us to organize a smooth transition from the old to the new paradigm for private giving.

But first things first: There is a straightforward case for full public disclosure for all gifts into the exploratory fund. Although it is easy to overstate the benefits generated by this traditional solution, it is certainly better to publicize all the facts than to allow secret deals.

Setting contribution limits is a more complicated business, and is best addressed after we consider the overall size of the exploratory fund. We shall be proposing different caps for different offices: $50,000 for the House, $250,000 for the average Senate seat, and $1 million for the presidency. In each case, this is a small fraction of the total amount spent by winning candidates—ranging from 5 percent for the average House member in 2000 to 0.6 percent in the case of President George W. Bush.[2] In short, we are really talking about an *exploratory* fund—not a convenient label to disguise the continuation of the old regime. If a politician cannot convince large numbers of Americans to vote with their dollars—either through the donation booth or with their patriotic currency—his candidacy will soon run out of steam.

Keep this point in mind as we proceed to the next basic question: How large a limit should we set for any individual donor's contribution to the exploratory fund?

A sensible answer requires a balance between two competing values. On the one hand, we want to make the exploratory process relatively hassle free—rather than spending all her time on fund-raising, the "explorer" should be out testing public sentiment in her potential constituency. But on the other hand, a concern with efficiency has unacceptable implications when taken to its extreme. Some politicians can make a phone call to a single rich friend and get the $50,000 or million she is allowed. This might be efficient, but it invites egregious influence peddling.

No politician should feel herself so heavily indebted that she will pay back bigtime in legislative favors after the election. A big gift to the exploratory fund carries a heightened risk of special dealing within an overall regime dominated by the donation booth. It provides the *only* occasion during the entire campaign when big givers can be identified, and therefore rewarded, by the grateful politician. How to resolve the trade-off between efficiency and special dealing?

Try to define the minimum number of donors that will effectively reduce the problem of special dealing. Taking a House race as an example, suppose we required a minimum of twenty-five donors to the exploratory fund—with each donor contributing no more than $2,000 to the $50,000 pot. Given the million-dollar price tag of modern House campaigns, a $2,000 donation can't buy very much influence. Nor can the giver suppose that his $2,000 is an irreplaceable part of the exploratory fund. Any serious candidate could have found somebody else to chip in this relatively small sum. Politicians will be grateful to their initial backers. But their appreciation will be tempered by the recognition that no single giver was really crucial to the initial pump-priming effort.

Although a minimum requirement of twenty-five donors will reduce the risk of influence peddling, it won't be much of a time waster. Politicians will reach their $50,000 limit without spending too many hours on the phone trolling for dollars.

Moving from the House to the Senate and the presidency, the "twenty-five-donor" rule seems less satisfactory: Is it really acceptable for twenty-five donors to contribute $40,000 apiece to the million-dollar fund authorized for presidential candidates? We don't think so, and we insist on at least fifty donors contributing no more than $20,000 apiece. Obviously, there is nothing sacrosanct about these numbers. Feel free to fill in different ones in section 12 of our model statute.

Before penciling in your bottom line, consider how a distinctive doctrine of constitutional law inevitably complicates the analysis. The Supreme Court has repeatedly upheld contribution limits more rigorous than the ones we are proposing, but it has created a curious exemption so far as a politician's personal pocketbook is concerned. Under the Court's famous decision in

Buckley v. Valeo, rich politicians have a constitutional right to spend their own money on their own campaigns without any limit whatsoever. This leads to a fairness question: If a rich politico can finance his explorations out of his own pocket, shouldn't his poorer rival be allowed to ask a rich friend to do the same, and thereby save the hassle of a broader-based fundraising effort?

We defer a sustained confrontation with the Court to Chapter 10—the deeper constitutional questions are best addressed after we have developed the operational issues more fully. In the meantime, we shall be adopting a dual stance on doctrinal issues. On the one hand, we have designed our operational program and model statute to conform fully with all existing constitutional requirements. We thereby refute the pessimistic view of the current Supreme Court as an immovable obstacle to serious reform. To the contrary, our model statute demonstrates that sweeping and effective reform is perfectly possible within the limits of existing law. On the other hand, we think that Americans should make up their own mind on fundamental issues of constitutional principle, not rely on the Court as a crutch. As a consequence, we won't hesitate to point out where existing doctrine strikes us as wrong-headed.

That is the case here. Quite simply, we reject the notion that rich people should have special privileges when they compete for public office in democratic politics. If we were on the Court, we would not allow the Forbeses and Corzines of the world to buy political prominence that they could not otherwise earn by the force of their political personalities, public service, or programmatic ideas. But facts are facts—we don't expect to be on the Court anytime soon, and the current majority of the justices do believe that the Constitution requires an exemption for free-spending plutocrats with political ambitions. So our model statute respects this "plutocrat exemption" but refuses to expand it beyond the limits set out by the *Buckley* Court, or to allow the exemption's existence to undermine the egalitarian principles inspiring the rest of our program.

To put the point concretely: We agree that the Court's plutocrat exemption adds a measure of unfairness to our proposed contribution limits—because it grants billionaires an unlimited right to bankroll their own campaigns while forbidding other politicians to ask wealthy friends to do the same. Nevertheless, it is better to live with this imbalance than to give every politician the right to serve as the political plaything of an obliging plutocrat. Don't you agree?

Problems of Transition

Some politicians won't try to fill up their exploratory fund to the brim before moving into the donation booth system. To see why, consider that there will be pluses as well as minuses involved in the transition from the old to the new paradigm.

Fund-raising minus: The politician no longer knows the names of her big donors, so she can expect the flow of very big gifts to diminish. Plus: Her donors can now give a lot more than they could previously—they can now hand over an additional $25,000, and not only $2,000, to House candidates; $150,000, not $20,000, for presidential hopefuls. This means that a candidate's old donors can give a lot more if their ardor is not cooled by the prospect of the secret donation booth.

Some candidates will find that the pluses are bigger than the minuses—and they should be allowed to shift into the new paradigm at their earliest convenience. But of course many others will make a different cost-benefit analysis and fill up their exploratory coffers before braving the hazards of the donation booth. Our statute gives them a right to do so even if they publicly declare their candidacies before reaching their exploratory maximum.

Our permissiveness on this matter may seem paradoxical. When we first introduced the exploratory fund, we emphasized the special predicament of politicians who had not yet officially declared their candidacies. Why, then, shouldn't exploratory funding come to an end as soon as the candidate formally tosses her hat into the ring?

Consider the problems of gamesmanship this would entail. If a candidate thinks that she will profit financially by filling up her exploratory fund, she will be tempted to deny (with a wink) that she has made up her mind to run, and yet act as if she were a candidate in all other respects. This allows her to have her cake and eat it too.[3]

Far better, then, to design the transition in a way that discourages this kind of cynical manipulation. By eliminating all funding consequences from the formal declaration of candidacy, we avoid evasive behavior that erodes respect for reform measures. At the same time, the relatively small size of the exploratory fund will require serious candidates to shift quickly into the donation booth system.

Different transitional issues arise on the public side of the equation. One problem arises out of the Court's special exemption for free-spending plutocrats. *Buckley v. Valeo* does not deprive the public of all tools to constrain the exercise of plutocratic power. It expressly allows Congress to use a carrot, if not a stick, to induce billionaires to renounce their free-spending ways. Although Congress can't restrict self-financing directly, it may deny public subsidies to any plutocrat who refuses to waive this right. We propose to take full advantage of this doctrine in designing our Patriot program. No politician has an unconditional right to fish in the huge pool of Patriot dollars unless she voluntarily agrees to restrict her access to her own bank balance.

The limits we propose are those that apply to all other givers who use the donation booth during the campaign—ranging up to $100,000 for presidential races. This means that wealthy candidates still have a small advantage when competing with poorer rivals. But this residual advantage seems minor in the overall balance of public and private finance established by the new paradigm, and we are trying, wherever possible, to avoid proliferation of special regulations. What is more, even our generous limits on individual contributions will operate to deter the worst abuses perpetrated by candidates Steve Forbes, Ross Perot, Michael Huffington, and John Corzine. These four men have together spent a quarter of a billion dollars out of their own pockets in recent races![4] Under the new paradigm, plutocrats will be put to a hard choice—will they allow their opponents to fish in the patriotic pool without competition, and while they spend huge sums from their personal bank accounts, or will they restrict their free-spending ways and compete with the hoi polloi for billions of Patriot dollars?

To eliminate unnecessary hassle, we shall mark the plutocrat's moment of truth with a bright line. During the exploratory phase of the campaign, the Forbeses and Corzines of this world are free to finance themselves without any complex regulations. But when they reach the limit set for the exploratory fund, they must make a final decision on their waiver option: Will they register with Patriot Co. and live with the contribution limits imposed on all other participants, or will they forgo patriotic funding?

We have gotten our candidates to the starting line. They have all raised their exploratory funds, and they are ready to make their case to the American people.

No longer will their further success be a function of their ability to raise huge sums from special interests. Their campaigns will be fueled instead by the individual decisions of tens of millions of Americans voting with their public and private dollars.

This is, at least, the promise of the new paradigm. But can this promise be redeemed in the hard coin of operational success?

6 | Designing Patriot

Who should get Patriot dollars? How many? Who may compete to obtain them? Under what terms?

There is no single answer. But the effort to provide solutions concentrates the mind—forcing a complex sorting of relevant principles and practicalities into a concrete judgment. This will sometimes require difficult balancing acts—weighing incommensurable principles against intractable realities to reach operational solutions. And yet serious statesmen must learn to live off-balance—it is never possible to achieve principled reform without awkward accommodation; the challenge is to avoid mindless compromise that loses all sight of animating ideals.

We would be surprised if any future statute tracked all our concrete conclusions. But our effort to sum up competing factors into practical judgments should help others clarify their own sense of the hard choices required to transform the new paradigm into operational reality.

Who?

In an ideal world, all Americans of voting age should qualify for Patriot accounts. Even if they haven't registered to vote, why prevent them from voting with Patriot dollars during the campaign? Nonregistrants remain citizens, and their views on funding are entitled to respect. And if they actually exercise their patriotic option during the campaign, this may encourage them to register for the general election. Voting with dollars will encourage voting with ballots. So why not throw the net of eligibility broadly?

Because practicalities require more restrictions. Every time a person tries to obtain an account, Patriot Co. will need a quick and easy way to determine whether she is an American citizen who could, in principle, register to vote. Long lines and complex procedures will deter tens of millions of Americans from opening a Patriot account. Instead of creating an independent system, we piggy-back on the existing voter registration process. Before any American can open a Patriot account, she must register to vote.

Voter registration will only serve as the first of many opportunities to sign up. Whenever a citizen comes to the polls, she will get another chance to open a Patriot account.[1] For most Americans, enrolling will be an easy matter. After establishing her voting qualifications, the applicant will write the number of one of her existing ATM or credit cards on a registration form. She will then be notified in her next bank or credit card statement that her Patriot account has become active.

Registered voters will also be able to transform their Visa or ATM cards into Patriot accounts via the Internet, telephone, or even traditional mail. The applicant would begin this process by sending her ATM or credit card number to Patriot Co., which would then see whether the applicant was a registered voter who had not previously opened an account. If so, Patriot would send a letter to the applicant's home address with an individualized activation code. She could then activate her account (attached to her pre-existing ATM or credit card) by dialing an 800 number and punching in the code. This strategy is already used successfully by credit card companies to assure the integrity of their systems. If the voter later canceled the credit card tied to Patriot, she could tell the company to roll her campaign finance account over to one of her other electronic cards.

Voters also have the right to request and receive a distinct Patriot card, but these free-floating cards carry a special corruption risk. Shady politicians will be tempted to buy them for greenbacks—offering $10 in ordinary money for a $50 Patriot card. Our model statute makes it a crime to engage in these transactions, but prosecutors would be overwhelmed if millions of cards were bought and sold on a vibrant black market. Although they could (and should) use selective prosecution as a weapon against big-time card-buying efforts, our aim is to prevent the rise of a black market in the first place.

Holders of free-floating cards will be required to prove their identity to an impartial official before entering a secret donation booth to vote their Patriot dollars electronically. A government bureaucrat need not be involved. The policymakers at Patriot Co. may, for example, negotiate with banks to allow their tellers to serve as identity checkers. This task could also be entrusted to existing governmental personnel—postal clerks, Social Security officials, and voting registrars. Nevertheless, the costs of providing a control system will be substantial. If most Americans chose the free-floating card, the escalating costs might force an anxious reappraisal of the entire effort to democratize campaign finance.

But nothing like that will occur. One hundred twenty-eight million Americans are registered to vote, but more than 150 million have ATM or credit cards.[2] The Federal Reserve estimates that "in 1998, 90.5 percent of families had some type of transactions account" that is generally associated with an electronic card.[3] Most of the rest won't go cardless, thanks to recent federal regulations requiring states to deliver welfare benefits and food stamps through an electronic card—with a machine-readable strip enabling linkage to Patriot Co.[4] Because 17 million Americans received food stamps in 1998, state-provided cards would integrate many poor and near-poor voters into the system.[5] Some eligible voters undoubtedly will fall through the cracks, but the number is already quite small, and getting smaller.

Nor will many voters resist the opportunity to link their Patriot account to an electronic card already in their possession. After all, they can use their linked cards in a hassle-free fashion—going to the ATM whenever they like and punching in their patriotic choices. In contrast, the free-floating card will require them to go to an office during business hours and wait on line. Why go through the extra trouble?

Perhaps in the hope that a shady politician might buy the free-floating card, and then corrupt a neighborhood bank or postal official to enable him to vote the dollars under an assumed name. But it seems unlikely that many politicians would find such a complex and risky enterprise attractive. Each Patriot card is worth only $50, so card-buying would make financial sense only if attempted on a large scale. Yet it will be virtually impossible to keep massive card-buying secret; once word leaks out, the public outcry would almost guarantee criminal prosecution.

This game isn't worth the candle. There isn't enough incentive for many Americans to sabotage the system by de-linking their Patriot accounts from electronic cards. The only voters who will request free-floating cards are people without any electronic alternatives—and these, as we have seen, are not numerous.

Nevertheless, "free-floaters" will be at a relative disadvantage. They will be obliged to go through the hassle of identity checks before voting their dollars—and as a result, their participation in the system will be reduced. Many at the very bottom will be saved this indignity thanks to the electronic cards provided by the government. But the few Americans who remain card-less will undoubtedly be disproportionately poor. The resulting class bias is real, but seems almost trivial compared to the overwhelming inequalities of the existing finance system.

So much for the bad news. The good news is the surprising ease with which we have designed a system that is both hassle- and corruption-free for the overwhelming majority of Americans. It is also surprisingly inexpensive. We estimate the costs of the system to be about $300 million a year (see Appendix D).

In our brave new world, Americans simply go to their neighborhood ATM and vote their Patriot dollars under three ground rules.[6] The first gives each voter five days to change her mind. This not only encourages sober second thought but makes a black market tough to organize. To see why, suppose that a fraudster offers Citizen X $20 in private money if she allows him to accompany her to the ATM and watch her transfer 50 Patriots to his favorite candidate. X accepts the offer, executes the transaction, takes the $20—and then returns the next day to countermand the order!

Not a good deal for the fraudster, especially if we add two rules. Patriotic contributions should be anonymous—making it impossible for the fraudster to contact his favored beneficiary to see whether the transaction sticks.[7] And the ATM will accept only Patriot accounts linked to standard electronic cards. This prevents the fraudster from demanding possession of X's ATM card for the five-day cooling off period, thereby making it impossible for her to change her mind. While X might give away a free-floating Patriot card, she will refuse to surrender a standard credit card to somebody who is not, by definition, very trustworthy. If she ever gets her American Express card back, she may find not only that her Patriot account is empty but that the fraudster has used it to finance his trip to Las Vegas![8]

As a final anticorruption safeguard, all Patriot accounts will expire after six years. Renewal will be easy—a citizen must simply vote once during the period, and swipe his card once again through the electronic reader available at his polling place. Regular renewal prunes the files of dead and incapacitated cardholders—cutting out another source of fraud. To be sure, it also eliminates people who fail to vote once in six years. But this seems entirely acceptable: Nonvoters can regain their patriotic status simply by reregistering.

When all is said and done, the two-card system of Patriot accounts represents a compromise with principle—justified by the excessive costs involved in designing a fraud-proof system that allows all adult Americans, regardless of their voter registration status, to sign up for an account. Perhaps we will soon be in a position to dispense with these awkward compromises when everybody has an Internet connection—which may make it far cheaper to administer a workable system of universal eligibility.[9] But even today, our rough and ready compromise represents a massive breakthrough for democracy at a cost that doesn't seem excessive.

For Whom?

Our basic principle is citizen sovereignty. No longer should campaign finance be a rich man's sport. Ordinary Americans should be free to use their Patriot dollars any way they think best. If a citizen wants to give directly to candidates, that's fine; if she wants to give to a political party or interest group, which then gives money to candidates, that's fine too. If she doesn't want to give at all, and leaves her Patriot account untouched, that's okay as well.

Citizen sovereignty is the bedrock principle of American democracy, and we do not propose to explore its historical or philosophical underpinnings.[10] Nevertheless, the principle is open to different interpretations, with different implications for program design. How to choose among them?

Begin with a basic, relatively uncontroversial issue. We do not require citizens to vote with their Patriot dollars; we simply give them the chance to do so. In places like Australia, where voting is mandatory, this might seem too permissive. If Australians can be required to vote on election day, why not require them also to vote with their dollars during the campaign? But such a suggestion is a nonstarter in America, where all voting is voluntary.

We take a different kind of challenge much more seriously. Under our proposal, citizens are free not only to send their patriotic currency to the candidate of their choice. They may also send it to political parties and other political organizations. Is this expansion of citizen sovereignty really appropriate?

When election day comes around, we don't let a citizen delegate his vote to a friendly representative of the Democratic Party or National Rifle Association: "Hey Charlie, do me a favor, and go into the voting booth for me!" Why, then, allow citizens to send their Patriot dollars to such organizations? Why not restrict voting with dollars in the same way we limit voting with ballots—and insist that all Patriots be sent directly to candidates, and nobody else?

Because of a basic difference in the informational environment. When a voter casts her final ballot, she may not be very well informed—but she is as informed as she is going to get. The time has come for a final civic judgment, and she should not be allowed to escape a sense of personal responsibility for the fateful decision the polity confronts.[11]

Voting with dollars occurs at an earlier stage—when no voter supposes that he is relatively well-informed. The whole point is to structure the process of collective learning and debate in ways that are worthy of democratic citizens. We confront a circularity problem that has no analogue on election day: How are relatively uninformed citizens to identify the best ways of funding the process of deliberation?

When faced with this question, it is perfectly sensible for a responsible citizen to respond: "At the present time, I'm not informed enough to say which candidate I will finally support. But I am informed enough to say which organization I trust. Moreover, I may not make up my mind until the last minute, and it may then be too late for my Patriot dollars to make a useful contribution to the collective debate. So I maximize my citizen sovereignty by contributing to the Sierra Club or Republican Party now, without waiting to get more information about the candidates and their views."

Many Americans won't have too much trouble finding the candidates who best express their views. But there is no reason to deny others a different, but no less responsible, path to citizenship engagement. By expanding the range of choice to include political organizations, our proposal enables citizens to escape a choice between two unattractive options: Plunk prematurely for individual candidates or remain paralyzed by indecision.

This conclusion leads us to refine, if not entirely repudiate, an important aspect of the reform tradition. In developing our new paradigm, our main aim has been to develop a systematic alternative to the three affirmative planks of the traditional agenda—bureaucratic subsidy, full information, and comprehensive regulation. But there is a darker side to the progressive

tradition—a set of diabolical images which the movement cultivates to ener-
gize its partisans. Within this familiar demonology, the position of Public
Enemy Number One is reserved for the political action committees (or PACS)
that serve as the conduits for the obscene sums flowing from special interests
to cynical politicians. The overriding aim of reform is to stanch this flow
through ever-tightening regulation—with every failed effort generating a call
for more comprehensive controls.

The rise of Patriot prompts a more discriminating assessment. As long
as PACS depend on the supply of green money, reformers are right to emphasize how they contribute to special-interest dealing. But once we place them
within a patriotic framework, the PAC is no longer a public enemy. Allowing
citizens to give Patriot dollars to PACS can represent a massive increase in
freedom of association.

Let the NRA and Sierra Club, and countless other groups, compete for
patriotic funds. There is absolutely nothing wrong when citizens use them
as vehicles for their political ideals. To the contrary, patriotic PACS will allow
millions of Americans to exercise their citizen sovereignty in a responsible
fashion. If they proliferate under the new paradigm, this simply emphasizes
the need to revise traditional reform demonology. Ever since Tocqueville,
Americans have been celebrated for the dynamism of their civic organizations, and the complex ways they contribute to a healthy democratic life.
We embrace this pluralist ideal and see patriotic finance as a way to sustain
the Tocquevillean tradition into the twenty-first century.

Our model statute creates a fundamental distinction between patriotic
PACS and those based on private finance. As we explain in the next chapter,
green-money PACS can only ask their members to make campaign contributions through the secret donation booth. In contrast, patriotic PACS can operate in a richer informational environment—but one carefully designed to
accommodate competing concerns.

Consider that patriotic giving can be a two-stage process. During the first
stage, citizens go to their ATMS and send Patriots to PACS and political parties.
During the second, these intermediaries send Patriots to the candidates of
their choice. We propose different informational regimes for these distinct
stages of the financial journey.

We have already explained why Patriot holders must remain anonymous
when sending contributions to patriotic PACS and political parties. Otherwise, it would be too easy to bribe cardholders with private dollars and ob-

tain Patriot dollars at bargain prices.[12] Just as the secret ballot prevents candidates and political organizations from buying citizens' votes, anonymity should prevent them from buying Patriot dollars.

But this simple point doesn't cover the second stage of the financial journey—when political organizations send patriotic funds to the candidates of their choice. Should the Sierra Club or Republican Party be allowed to publicize how much they are contributing to their favorite candidates? Or should these transactions also be cloaked in anonymity?

We see no reason for secrecy at this stage. Return to the circularity problem that provides a major motivation for the entire reform exercise. The more big money shapes the direction of American politics, the less democratic politics can serve as a primary legitimator for economic inequality. If economic inequality is to remain (relatively) legitimate in our society, democratic politics must retain its integrity as a sphere of (relative) equality.

This basic point serves as the foundation for our effort, via the secret donation booth, to purge private-money donations of their worst characteristics. When we make it hard for candidates to identify contributions with certainty, we make it hard for them to respond readily to the influence of the underlying inequality of private resources. By disrupting potential quid pro quos, we enhance the credibility of the claim that political deliberation and decision is something more than, and different from, the reflexive servicing of economic privilege.

But this rationale does not apply where Patriot dollars are concerned, for these resources are distributed equally, reflecting our status as equal citizens. Suppose, for example, that a group of autoworkers formed "Automobile Lovers of America" and managed to raise 100,000 Patriots to support car-friendly legislators.[13] The democratic status of this PAC is quite different from that of a PAC established by the auto companies with private money—precisely because the dollars funding the patriotic PAC have been collected on an egalitarian basis, and do not exacerbate the circularity problem.[14] To put the point more affirmatively, the formation of patriotic PACs is best viewed as an integral part of a temporally extended process—citizens intervene during the campaign by using their equal shares of Patriot dollars to shape the discursive agenda, and they intervene at the end of the campaign by casting equal votes to help resolve the issues raised in part through the agitation of patriotic PACs.

Within this context, it is a serious mistake to allow a justified concern with the use of big money to taint an entirely legitimate part of the democratic enterprise. Rather than using an anonymity rule, as in the case of private-money PACS, our model statute allows patriotic PACS to make public the precise amounts of patriotic cash they are giving to each of their favored candidates.

Under this full-publicity regime, politicians will undoubtedly compete for the favor of patriotic PACS—just as they do today in the case of private-money PACS. But this competition for financial support should no longer generate anxiety about the PACS' "undue influence." Because the underlying distribution of Patriot dollars is equal, the flow of patriotic PAC money reflects the views of equal citizens. When politicians compete for the support of patriotic PACS, they are doing something that makes the process more democratic, not less so.

We do not generally condemn a politician when he shapes his public views to gain the support of a majority of his fellow citizens on election day. By the same token, we should not condemn him for heeding the views of citizens when they are expressed through their contributions to patriotic PACS. To the contrary, the active and public involvement of patriotic PACS is a sign of the vitality of the democratic process.

Going further, we would expect the public and the press to sit up and take notice whenever the Federal Election Commission reports the flow of patriotic contributions to each candidate. Under our model statute, these reports will announce the total number of Patriots each candidate has received directly from citizens—but for anticorruption reasons, the commission will not announce the individual names of these donors. In contrast, the report will detail precisely how many Patriots have come from each patriotic PAC and each political party. (It will also announce the total amount of private money received through the secret donation booth, as will be explained in greater detail in the next chapter.)

These reports will provide insights into public opinion that will rival those offered by public opinion polls. Although Gallup and the rest may report what Americans say about the candidates and issues, patterns of patriotic expenditure will reflect what Americans do when distributing scarce patriotic funds to many deserving causes. Each commission report not only will suggest that citizen sovereignty is a real force in our democracy. It will serve as a feedback loop that shapes and reshapes public opinion over the course of the campaign—precipitating a flood of public commentary, as pundits speculate about the meaning of the ebbs and flows in the candidates' fiscal fortunes, and as PACs and parties launch renewed appeals for additional support. Reformers should celebrate, rather than demonize, the role of voluntary associations in the process of public debate.

Our emphatic defense of patriotic PACs leaves us with a final design issue. Although our model statute allows these groups to play an important part on the political stage, it carefully circumscribes their role. They can serve as political brokers—collecting Patriot dollars from citizens and passing them on to candidates. But they cannot serve as political spokesmen in their own right—they cannot refuse to hand over their Patriots to candidates and use them instead to finance their own "independent" campaigns on behalf of issues and politicians. If the Sierra Club or the NRA wishes to take this further step, it must raise private funds for this express purpose.

Does this limitation make sense? Given our pluralist celebration of the role of patriotic PACs, why not give them greater freedom of action? Why not leave it up to them to decide whether to hand the money over to candidates or whether to spend it on their own issue-oriented campaigns?

Good questions. If our reform ever takes off, and experience proves positive, perhaps the next generation of reformers might well wish to expand the new paradigm by giving each American a second patriotic account for more general communicative purposes. Call it a First Amendment account, which might be used for a host of purposes, including the support of political organizations to serve as spokesmen as well as brokers.[15]

But it is a bit premature to consider the extension of our initiative before anybody has tried it. For the next decade or two, let's see whether we can summon the political will to use patriotic finance to check America's visible decline into oligarchy. If the technique works here, there will be time enough to consider whether it will work elsewhere.[16]

What?

You are now standing in front of an ATM with your Patriot-linked card in hand. You insert the card into the electronic reader—and, presto, we come to our next big policy decision: What options should be displayed on the screen?

Our basic commitment to citizen sovereignty permits a drastic simplification of the inquiry. Absent compelling reasons, each American should be free to use Patriot dollars in the way that makes the most sense to her. Supposing there are 50 Patriots in her account, why not allow her to give all fifty to a single candidate or party or patriotic PAC?

We do not treat citizen sovereignty as only one aspect of a multifactored cost-benefit analysis. This would make it far too easy to whittle away the principle by an appeal to some amorphous notion of "efficiency." We place a strong burden of persuasion on all efforts to narrow the range of citizen choice. Within this framework, only three countervailing principles seem worthy of serious consideration.

The first is the constitutional separation of powers. To fix ideas, assume that all three federal offices—House, Senate, and presidency—are up for grabs in the election. Should you be allowed to spend all $50 on one of these races, leaving nothing for the others? Or should the screen allocate a fixed amount—say $10, $15, and $25, respectively—to each race?

Citizen sovereignty points to free choice, but the separation of powers suggests the creation of distinct subaccounts. Each elected institution has its own constitutional dignity; each performs interdependent functions. If one remains starved of public funds, this will affect the entire system. Yet if one race is particularly exciting, this basic constitutional point may be ignored by most voters. By creating office-specific accounts, our system will require citizens to consider that presidents can't even make Cabinet appointments unless the Senate cooperates, and that lawmaking is a matter for all branches. By making three distinct patriotic decisions, each citizen will be reenacting and reaffirming the fundamental character of the separation of powers in our constitutional system.

Subaccounts will also avoid a recurring problem in assuring the fair distribution of patriotic funds. During each electoral cycle, only two-thirds of the states hold senatorial elections; and the presidency opens up every other election. This not only means that we will be distributing different amounts of patriotic money during different cycles, but that voters in some states should get more because they will be financing more elections.

This leads immediately to our distributional problem. Suppose, for example, that voters in New York get $50 in their accounts because all three offices are up, while voters in California only get $35 because no Senate race is being contested. Suppose all New Yorkers and Californians choose to spend all their Patriots on the presidential race. This will give New Yorkers a lot more power, per capita, simply because their patriotic coffers are swelled by a senatorial contest. Office specificity avoids this absurd result.

We have reached our first important conclusion: When you open your Patriot account, you won't be given a single lump sum to spend on any race that suits your fancy. You will be confronting a screen revealing three subaccounts, each containing an appropriate amount for the open races in your constituency.

So far, so good—but our talk of "office specificity" conceals an important ambiguity. To see the problem, suppose you are trapped in a House district where your opinions are permanently in the minority, and any donation to a candidate from your party will be money wasted. Rather than spending your $10 on any of the candidates running in your district, you want to give it to the Sierra Club or National Rifle Association, and let them decide where the money is best spent. Should this be permitted?

Competing analogies point in opposite directions. On the one hand, holders of private dollars are free to give to any House race in the country, either directly or indirectly, regardless of where they live. Why shouldn't holders of Patriot dollars have equal freedom? On the other hand, you must vote in the district where you live. You can't transfer your ballot to a district where you can make more of a difference. Why should Patriot dollars be more transferable than your vote?

We find it easier to deflect the analogy with the vote. After all, the wisdom of the Anglo-American tradition of voting in geographic districts is open to question. Most democracies outside the English-speaking world have long since opted for systems of proportional representation—which do allow local minorities to aggregate their votes with voters elsewhere to elect representatives. We do not suggest that this feature of proportional representation makes it decisively superior. Defenders of the Anglo-American system may point to advantages that offset its failure to afford local minorities direct representation. Most notably, voting in geographic districts encourages the development of two broad-based parties and avoids the shifting coalition governments common on the Continent. While this is an advantage, nobody denies that it comes at a price—the potential alienation of local minorities who never see "their" candidate emerge victorious in a House election.

Our position on Patriot promises to ameliorate this cost while retaining the advantages of the traditional system. By allowing local minorities to transfer their Patriots to other House races, we give them some sense of political efficacy: Even if they will never elect a friendly representative from their own geographic district, they may influence races elsewhere.

We take the same position on the transferability of senatorial Patriots, but it is a closer call. First, there is a variation on the distribution problem that haunted full free choice. If I live in Connecticut, my capacity to influence elections in New York or California will depend on whether there is a Senate race occurring in my home state. There is undoubtedly a certain arbitrariness here.

The Senate is also distinctive in representing the states qua states, and so there is a constitutional quality to a concern about undue influence of patriotic dollars from out-of-staters. But this concern has never proved decisive in the regulation of private money.[17] Nor should it trump the decisions made with patriotic currency. As the Fourteenth Amendment makes clear, we are citizens of the nation first, and citizens of the states only derivatively. And in fact, our national life has become so interdependent that many citizens may plausibly consider their own state's race less important than a contest somewhere else.

We certainly agree that the problem posed by the Senate is not as easy to solve as the one posed by the House. But in cases of good-faith doubt, we follow the principle of citizen sovereignty. We leave it up to each American to decide which Senate race is most deserving of his patriotic concern.

Our reflections on the separation of powers have led us to fundamental, but limited, incursions on the principle of citizen sovereignty. We reach the same conclusion after confronting a second principle: fairness between the candidates in the general election.

Fundamental fairness may be compromised if one candidate conducts an expensive primary battle while the other doesn't. The problem is at its maximum when a sitting president is running for reelection. The man (or woman!) in the White House comes to the table with such great advantages that he may avoid a significant challenge in the primary. This will allow him to stockpile the pool of Patriots from members of his own party while challengers raise and spend large sums for the privilege of running against him in November. By the time the out-party selects its candidate, the successful nominee may confront a serious problem raising patriotic donations from the party faithful. Many will have spent their wad during the primaries, leaving the challenger to face an incumbent sitting on a large patriotic stockpile. It is tough enough ousting a sitting president without giving him this further advantage.

The problem is of constitutional dimension. After Franklin Roosevelt's four-term presidency, the American people said "never again," and enacted a constitutional amendment checking the power of incumbent presidents by limiting them to two terms in office. Our approach to Patriot is guided by this decision. In the case of incumbents running for reelection, we divide the 25 Patriot dollars allocated to each presidential account into two subaccounts—allocating $10, say, to the primaries and $15 to the general election.[18] This will permit the out-party to wage a fierce struggle over the nomination without compromising its capacity to run an effective race in the fall.

We refuse to impose subaccounts in other races—though the balance of argument is rather close in some cases. Begin with races for the presidency which don't involve an incumbent.[19] With nobody running from the White House, a serious contest is almost certain on both sides, so structural unfairness isn't an issue.[20] When viewed from the vantage of individual Patriot holders, the subaccount system represents a serious restriction on citizen sovereignty. Some may well think the primary is a lot more important than the general election. If their party makes the wrong choice, they may believe that the general election won't be worth fighting anyway. So why shouldn't they be given the right to spend all $25 on the primaries?

Our reluctance to constrain this choice is reinforced by a final factor. Generally speaking, presidential nominees have been determined on the basis of early primaries, leaving many states farther down the line engaging in an empty ritual. Although a few citizens in these states will be engaged enough in national politics to vote their Patriot dollars in early primaries, most will fail to participate effectively at any point in the primary process. If we impose a subaccount system, a disproportionate number of citizens in late-voting states will never use the dollars allocated to the primary. Having the right to vote the full $25 in the general election compensates them a bit. Although voters in early primary states will spend more of their Patriots determining the nominees, other voters have more financial power in the final fall contest.

The decisiveness of early primaries also makes it more hazardous to engage in the fine-tuning required for the subaccount system to work: Should we allocate only a small amount to the primaries, on the ground that they will be over in three or four weeks, or should we allocate more to them because they may go on for months?

Putting the problem of presidential incumbency to one side, we are happy to leave these questions to the good sense of the American people, who can calibrate their patriotic donations to their shifting sense of the dynamics of particular presidential contests.

This means that the party that selects its nominee more quickly may gain a marginal financial advantage in the final election. But there are also benefits attached to more controversial primary contests—which may sometimes result in a mobilized party and a better-tested candidate. Given the large pool of patriotic funds available for presidential candidates, we do not think that this residual unfairness outweighs the serious constraints that a subaccount system imposes on citizen sovereignty.

Turning to congressional races, we reject subaccounts for primaries entirely. When a citizen dials into his Patriot account, the screen will reveal that he has, say, $10 to spend for House races and $15 for the Senate, but he will be entirely free to decide whether to spend the money on primary contests or general elections.

Our argument against further subaccounting begins, once again, with the distinction between open seats and those in which an incumbent is running for reelection. But the distinction plays out differently in the congressional context. Because there are roughly 470 races for Congress in any election cycle, both "open" and "incumbency" contests are going on simultaneously. We believe that this basic point makes it unnecessary to create a special subaccount for primaries in an effort to protect challengers to incumbent senators and house members.

This may seem paradoxical at first glance, because congressional incumbents are notoriously successful in gaining reelection. During the 1990s success rates in the House and Senate ran consistently above 88 percent.[21] These numbers exaggerate incumbency advantage, because they don't include the sitting congressman who "voluntarily" retires when polls tell him that he faces a tough race.[22] Nonetheless, the data point to a very real phenomenon. Why, then, shouldn't we give challengers special subaccount protection, just as we have in the case of a sitting president?

Our answer is that we are worried only about a special kind of unfairness—one generated when a primary contest in the out-party so depletes
the patriotic resources of party loyalists as to make it hard for them to fund
the primary victor in the general elections. We don't think that this kind of
"structural unfairness" will be common.

Most incumbents are so good at currying favor in their districts and states
that they regularly win by large margins, and would do so under any realistic
system of campaign finance. If this is a problem, the remedy is term limits
for members of Congress, not campaign finance reform. Undoubtedly, the
large infusion of patriotic currency will make it easier to fund aggressive
challenges in some districts, but we should not expect miracles. Many House
districts, and some states, simply contain many more members from one
party than another, and an incumbent wins because the majority wants it
that way.[23]

This basic point not only limits the number of districts where structural
unfairness is a serious problem. It also provides us with an "invisible hand"
solution to the problem that remains. Quite simply, many residents in "safe
districts" will ship their House and Senate Patriots elsewhere in search of
contests where their funds will be more productive. And we can count on
a host of organizations to encourage the export trade: "Don't waste your
House and Senate Patriots by sending them to a sure loser (or winner). Send
them to us and we will find the districts where the money will make a big
difference!"

Many Americans are interested only in their own House and Senate races.
These homebodies will refuse to ship their Patriots off to unknown candidates in distant places. But some money will make it out of the district.
Moreover, many incumbents will find that their own patriotic PACs are overflowing, and they will also send excess Patriots to needy candidates running
elsewhere.[24]

Even if a credible challenger spends lots of money in the primary, then,
she will not be starved for funds in the fall campaign. A host of patriotic
PACs will be on the lookout for challengers who stand a chance of ousting
incumbents. After all, if PACs place their bets wisely, and some of their challengers actually win, they can brag about their successes the next time
around.

We propose, in short, to rely on the exercise of citizen sovereignty, mediated by patriotic PACS, to get sufficient funds to those challengers with a serious chance of winning. In contrast to the case of presidential incumbency, there is no need to create subaccounts to counter structural unfairness. Patriotic citizens will solve the problem on their own.

PACS will also play a constructive role in "open" districts—generally 10 to 15 percent of the total—where no incumbent is running for reelection.[25] The departure of an incumbent generally prompts hot primary contests in both parties and a spirited campaign in the fall—requiring lots of money. These large sums are well spent, for the winner will enjoy the advantages of incumbency and may represent the constituency for many years. But once again, there is no need to fine-tune the system to accommodate this point. Open seats will operate as magnets for patriotic PACS throughout the nation, which will be quick to appreciate their strategic importance.

Our reflections on two basic values have led us to limit, but not eradicate, our fundamental commitment to citizen sovereignty. The constitutional separation of powers provides the more important constraint—rather than allowing each citizen to spend her 50 Patriots on any race she likes, the model statute creates three distinct subaccounts for the presidency, the Senate, and the House. We have responded more cautiously to the problem of potential unfairness between incumbents and challengers at the final election. Except in the case of a sitting president running for reelection, citizen sovereignty will take care of the problem.

Our third, and final, exercise in fine-tuning requires some thought about the limits of citizen sovereignty itself. Most Americans don't pay a lot of attention to the earliest stages of campaigns—just at the time when lots of politicians are exploring their options, hiring personnel, and seeking grassroots support. These crucial explorations and plans may be starved of resources if citizen inattention is sufficiently pervasive. Patriotic donations may be most needed when they are least forthcoming. Shouldn't something be done about this?

We have struggled with this question before. Selective citizen attention was one big reason for opposing the abolition of private giving. Many private donors are more politically aware than ordinary citizens, and their contributions reduce the danger of a financial drought early in the campaign. We have also made it particularly easy for candidates to collect an exploratory fund of private money.

But this reliance on the private sector comes at an obvious price in terms of fairness and equality. We have argued that this cost is bearable, but we confess to residual anxiety on this score and propose a modification which will increase the early flow of public dollars. Our model statute provides a bonus for early patriotic giving up to the point where 5 percent of all available Patriot dollars have reached the candidates. During this early period, donors can double their contribution—if their account gives them $10 for House races, their gift will generate $20 in their favorite candidate's coffers, and so forth.

We have been trying to resist efforts to micromanage the donation process over the course of the campaign. For one thing, too many bells and whistles will make the entire patriotic initiative seem too gimmicky to the general public. For another, any change in the formula during the campaign places pressure on the impartiality of the Federal Election Commission. To put our bonus system into operation, the FEC will be obliged to determine, in a fair and impartial way, when the 5 percent threshold has been reached and to declare the bonus period at an end. Commissioners might abuse this power in favor of a candidate whose campaign is just coming into prominence at the crucial moment.

But the quantitative determination required here seems sufficiently ministerial, and the risk of partisan abuse sufficiently unlikely, that the enhanced fairness purchased by the bonus system seems worth the modest dangers involved.

So let us add the bonus for early giving to the other modifications of citizen sovereignty on our list—subaccounts for House, Senate, and Presidency, and another subaccount for presidential primaries when incumbents are running for reelection—and move on to the final big design question.

How Much?

To fix ideas, we have been imagining that Patriot had been introduced in time for the 2000 elections, and that the 100 million Americans who cast ballots had also voted with their Patriots during the campaign. This implies a yield of approximately 5 billion Patriots.

Contrast this with reality: Candidates for federal office received only $235 million in public funds, but more than $3 billion in private money.[26] This flood from the private sector would diminish under the new paradigm—both because of the secret donation booth and because private money is simply less productive in a world of Patriot dollars. If only one billion private dollars came into the pool, total funding would still double—from $3 billion to $6 billion—but patriotic finance would dominate private by 5 to 1.

But we can hardly guarantee this scenario. Predictions will be especially hazardous during the first few electoral cycles after the transition from the old paradigm to the new: How quickly will ordinary Americans learn to take their Patriot dollars seriously? How quickly will political organizations perfect fund-raising techniques that reach out to their new and massive patriotic audience? So far as private giving is concerned, how energetically will big donors try to defeat the anonymity of the donation booth? How much will ideology and generalized self-interest motivate big donors to continue giving?

Even after the transitional period, the total financial pool will expand or shrink unpredictably as Americans' interest in the candidates and the issues ebbs and flows. Managing these fluctuations will require a certain budgetary sophistication. But these technocratic complexities should not divert attention from the main point—the unpredictability of financial support is one of the greatest merits of the new paradigm, not a shortcoming. It reflects the basic point that concerned citizens, and not special interests or entrenched politicians, have taken control of campaign finance—and that the system is responding to *their* changing sense of political opportunities, rather than the organized imperatives of big donors or incumbent politicians to stabilize a steady exchange of money for political support.

Nevertheless, this shift to citizen sovereignty does present a crucial design problem. At the beginning of each campaign cycle, the new Federal Election Commission must determine the amount of patriotic currency going into each citizen's account. How should the model statute structure this decision? We restrict ourselves to basic principles, deferring a more fine-grained analysis to Appendix A, which yields our proposed stabilization algorithm.

Begin with some worst-case scenarios. Suppose that Congress responds to a massive groundswell by enacting our model statute in time for the 2004 elections—only to find that our rosy predictions are belied by facts on the ground. As the campaign proceeds, relatively few Americans take the time to march to their ATMs and vote their 50 Patriot dollars—while 100 million make it to the polls on election day, only twenty million bother to exercise their patriotic privileges, yielding a mere billion dollars for candidates.

At the same time, the secret donation booth has a devastating impact on private giving, revealing that most of the money given in 2000 was motivated by special dealing. Now that these hopes have been eliminated, private contributions sink to one billion or so. As a consequence, total funding goes down by a third—from $3 billion to $2 billion (half Patriot, half private).

Call this a financial drought, and we would consider it a disaster. Like most serious students, we reject the frequent claim that Americans are already spending "too much" on political campaigns.[27] A few numbers put such banalities into context: Contrast the $3 billion contributed during the 2000 campaign cycle with the $13 billion spent in 1999 for advertising by the auto industry alone, and the $66 billion spent on broadcast spots by all advertisers during the same year.[28] We hardly wish to downplay the importance of choosing the right car, nor do we disdain the informational nuggets swept along by the steady stream of commercials. But is the annual expenditure on auto advertising worth four times the quadrennial expenditure involved in picking a proper president and Congress?

It's easy to criticize how candidates spend the $3 billion flowing into their coffers. If they were more inspired by Madison than by Madison Avenue, they could communicate twenty times as much at half the price. But it hardly follows that Americans would be more informed and engaged if candidates had even less to spend. To the contrary, the best empirical studies suggest otherwise.[29]

Large spending reductions would also redound to the advantage of incumbents, who need to invest less in getting their name and positions before the public than do challengers. "Campaign reform" that ends up entrenching incumbents involves an exchange of masters—replacing the power of big money for the power of established politicians.

But there is even more at stake. Political conversation is the lifeblood of democracy—and any substantial reduction in its flow, regardless of its short-term consequences on incumbents and citizens, is enough to motivate grave concern. We have set the initial patriotic allocation at the relatively high sum of $50 to reduce the risk of financial drought. But we propose two extra safeguards in the unlikely event that a shortfall should occur. Both involve the construction of "feedback" loops that enable the FEC to respond by injecting more patriotic funds into the system.

The first feedback authorizes the commission to rectify a fiscal shortfall by increasing the patriotic allocation the next time around. Suppose that the election of 2004 generates $1 billion Patriots and $1 billion through the donation booth, leading to a $1 billion shortfall from 2000 levels. The model statute instructs the commission to double the patriotic allocation from 50 to 100 Patriots for the next presidential cycle. The Commission's overriding statutory goal, in short, is to assure that overall funds flowing into the reformed system are no less substantial than those flowing under the old regime.

Despite this feedback loop, the actual results in 2008 might still fall short. Perhaps private funding drops once again—from $1 billion in 2004 to $500 million in 2008. Or perhaps even fewer Americans take the trouble to vote the $100 Patriots now in their accounts, and the anticipated $2 billion does not materialize. If this happens, the statute instructs the commission to make another compensating adjustment for the next presidential election.[30] And so forth.

This dismal scenario suggests the possibility of something even worse. Funding levels might get so low as to warrant immediate action from the commission—rather than waiting for four years, perhaps it should inject more funds immediately into the ongoing campaign?

To fix ideas, let us say that "severe drought" conditions exist when public and private giving fail to generate $1.5 billion during a presidential election cycle (or half of what prevailed under the old regime). Under the proactive approach, the model statute instructs the commission to monitor total collections over the course of the campaign: Every month or so, it must announce the total amount of public and private money collected by all candidates. If the entire pool is less than 50 percent of the average generated at comparable stages of past campaigns, the FEC will instruct its computers to grant a compensating bonus to every candidate in proportion to the number of Patriot dollars that he or she has collected.[31] If a candidate has collected 10 percent of Patriots redeemed, he will receive 10 percent of the bonus, and so forth—with the overall bonus calculated to eliminate the severe drought. In principle, a proactive approach holds promise as a tool for responding to the worst of the worst-case scenarios.

But in practice we have very serious doubts, and not only because devising a good algorithm is a tricky business. For example, it will be hard to prevent a scenario in which one or another candidate will find it in her interest to discourage giving for the next accounting period in an effort to gain a bonus, and only then encourage her supporters to give generously. Gamesmanship of this kind can easily undermine the system's integrity in the eyes of the public (see Appendix A).

Putting strategic problems to one side, proactivity comes at a heavy political price. As every monthly decision date came around, the commission would return to the spotlight—will it declare the existence of a drought? How big will the bonus be? Which candidates will be helped or hurt?

The result would be a distortion of the political conversation—away from the candidates and their issues, and toward the commission and its policies. Worse yet, there will inevitably be a certain amount of discretion required in rapidly calculating the relevant sums—and candidates will be quick to claim that the agency is abusing its discretion in favor of their rivals. Even if it acts with the best of intentions, the commission will sometimes make technocratic mistakes. When these are later discovered, they will be used as further evidence of agency partisanship. Such charges will predictably cloud the closing weeks of the campaign and further divert public attention away from the merits of the candidates and their competing programs for America.

And of course, it is always possible that the commission will succumb to the heat of the campaign and make a last-minute intervention for partisan ends. One such episode could destroy the legitimacy of the entire patriotic initiative. Isn't it wiser to respond to a severe drought by telling the candidates that they have nobody to blame but themselves for failing to inspire their followers to march up to their ATMs and vote with their dollars?

At the very most, we are prepared to consider proactivity as a transitional device. It may take some time for ordinary Americans to start voting with dollars in great numbers—and it would be wrong to starve the political process in the meantime. Whether this risk is serious enough to warrant transitional measures is hard to say. We really don't have any disciplined way to estimate likely response rates. The best we can do is scan the horizon for existing programs that bear some resemblance to our initiative. Unfortunately, this exercise can't provide a solid basis for serious predictions—there isn't anything in the real world that is close enough to Patriot dollars to permit meaningful extrapolation.

But it won't hurt to do some tea-leaf reading. The most significant place to look is federal tax law. Since the Watergate scandal, taxpayers have been invited to check off a box that allows them to send a small portion of their tax dollars—initially $1, now $3 ($6 for a joint return)—to the special fund financing presidential campaigns. The early response was heartening, with twenty-one million taxpayers—or 25 percent of all filers—checking off the box. But participation has declined over the years, as presidential candidates became experts in finding loopholes that allowed them to take public subsidies and continue the hunt for large private contributions. By 1996 only fifteen million taxpayers—one filer in eight—chose to divert three of their tax dollars into the fund.[32]

Which part of this story is more relevant to Patriot—the early hopes or the later public disillusionment? In any event, our initiative breaks enough new ground to make the relevance of this experience problematic. Most obviously, Patriot holders give directly to their favorite candidate or political organization, but tax payers merely check off their dollars to a nonpartisan fund. They are merely cogs in a bureaucratic machine of distribution, without any sense that their choices are making a concrete difference to one candidate or another. This not only makes a big psychological difference, but it also creates different incentives for candidates. At present, nobody acts as if he cares whether you check off a box on the dark night in April when you finally fill out your tax return. But under the new paradigm, there will be many candidates and organizations reaching out for your Patriots— and they won't be doing it on tax day but throughout the entire campaign season! This should make a big difference.[33]

Such tea-leaf reading exercises only emphasize the difficulty of predicting early response rates. We cannot be sure whether allocating $50 to each Patriot account will generate $5 billion or $1 billion during the first election cycle. Given the range of indeterminacy, it seems irresponsible to ignore the risk of a severe financial drought, and our model statute gives the FEC power to intervene proactively to prevent the worst case.

We endorse this only as a provisional measure for the first eight years under the new paradigm. By this point, the commission should have enough experience to set the Patriot allocation for the next electoral cycle without nasty surprises. In spite of the FEC's best efforts, it may fail to generate adequate aggregate funding. Even if it continually hiked patriotic allocations, droughts may continue if citizen participation plummets continuously—with fewer and fewer Americans taking the trouble to vote with their dollars.

But if this happened, we would respond by rethinking our fundamental premises. Patriot simply cannot function in the long run without tens of millions of Americans using it as an occasion for active citizenship. If our initiative fails to generate broad engagement, our country is in worse trouble than we thought, and much more than Patriot is in danger.

But enough of worst-case analysis. Although it would be irresponsible to ignore the dark side, we don't really think there is a serious danger of severe financial drought. Americans love novelty. The prospect of voting with Patriot dollars is more likely to generate a burst of civic enthusiasm than a slough of indifference—as well as noisy efforts by candidates and political organizations to reach out and win the financial support of a newly empowered citizenry. We would be very surprised if the first election cycle under the new paradigm did not generate more funds than the last cycle held under the current system. (But we have been surprised before.)

A second problem strikes us as more serious. Under this variation on our transition scenario, there is no financial drought during the year 2004—to fix ideas, we suppose that a total of $4 billion flows into the system (or an increase of one billion over 2000). A closer inspection of the books, however, reveals that only $2 billion comes from patriotic contributions and that the other half is generated by private gifts flowing through the donation booth.

This finding should be a cause for serious concern. We have opposed purists who seek to prohibit all private giving and have argued for its supplementary role to patriotic finance. But our arguments do not imply that America's 4 million private givers should be equal participants with 130 million American Patriot holders in determining the flow of campaign money.[34] Whenever the share of private contributions exceeds one-third of the whole, we consider this a dangerous sign of incipient oligarchy. To prevent swamping of the system by private money, our model statute instructs the FEC to increase patriotic allocations for the next comparable election—with the aim of restoring a 2-to-1 funding ratio. Call this "swamping control," and as in the case of drought prevention, this forward-looking technique can never guarantee success. Suppose, for example, that the commission doubles the patriotic allocation from $50 to $100 for 2008 in the hope of doubling the patriotic contribution from $2 billion to $4 billion, thereby establishing the

2 to 1 ratio. This aim may be defeated in two ways: Either patriotic giving might fall short, or private giving might increase beyond the $2 billion level.

Even if our feedback loop operates perfectly, it will hardly console losing politicians who were swamped by private money in the 2004 election. Rather than waiting until next time, they will want a statute that provides proactive relief.

As in the case of droughts, it is technically possible to satisfy this request. The commission could continuously monitor the ongoing mix of public and private funding. If private money was swamping patriotic contributions, the FEC could instruct its computers to grant a compensating bonus to every candidate in proportion to the number of Patriot dollars that he or she has collected.[35]

It is a mistake to go down this path. We don't deny that swamping can be a real problem in particular races. But the cure is worse than the disease. God help the commission when it occasionally blunders in calculating the bonus required to offset the swamping effect! Protecting the commission's integrity will be hard enough without making it the target of repeated political vendettas.

We rely instead on the power of citizens to shift their patriotic gifts to hot elections where swamping by private dollars is most likely to be a concern. After all, it is not as if politicians confronting the prospect of swamping will be entirely powerless. They will predictably use their predicament in their own fund-raising appeals: "My fellow Americans, don't let my opponent crush my campaign under an avalanche of private dollars. Send me your Patriots ASAP!"

Sometimes this appeal will work; sometimes it won't. But as long as the FEC responds to swamping by increasing Patriots at the next election, the remaining problem doesn't seem serious enough to warrant aggressive intervention that might undermine support for the entire program.

We are now in a position to glimpse a happier future. Our initiative does not create a dismal landscape of financial droughts and swamps. Instead, it generates a wave of enthusiastic citizen engagement—even more Americans vote with their patriotic dollars than go to the polls in November. After all, there will be many more opportunities to go to an ATM than to show up at the voting station. The result, say, is that 125 million citizens give between

$6 billion and $7 billion in Patriots, overwhelming the billion or two in private money flowing through the donation booth.

Success breeds problems of its own—notably cost containment: Surely there comes a point at which we are pouring too much public money into political campaigns. How to decide when enough is enough?

Begin by putting the costs of Patriot into perspective. Because federal elections don't occur every year, we should annualize their budgetary cost. Even if Patriot boomed, no more than $3 billion a year, on average, would be disbursed—$7 billion during presidential years, $3–4 billion during off-years when only Congress is at stake. Estimating costs of administration is hazardous, but we suspect that they will run in the annualized range of $200–250 million (see Appendix D).

Three billion a year isn't peanuts, but it isn't Star Wars either. And it provides a misleading indicator of true budgetary cost. The program will also save taxpayers money. Our present system generates costly special-interest legislation motivated by the recurring political need to raise large campaign gifts from the private sector. There is no way to provide hard estimates of the savings that will result once this incentive is eliminated or dramatically reduced, but there is every reason to believe that the sums are substantial. Even when measured narrowly in dollars and cents, Patriot may easily pay for itself.

Nevertheless, success will undoubtedly generate agitation from cost-cutters. To pacify these critics, we envision gradual reductions over time in allocations to citizen accounts when total Patriot expenditures exceed a statutory ceiling. Our model statute also includes a budgetary protection provision which kicks in whenever patriotic contributions exceed $6 billion in presidential years (or twice the amount spent in 2000).[36] We leave the details of this capping algorithm to the statute and the associated Appendix A. It suffices to say that we have eliminated the danger of an open-ended run on the treasury.

Technocratic responses to financial droughts, swamps, and gluts should not deflect attention from the main point. We have every reason to expect the new paradigm to increase vastly the resources flowing into the political marketplace.

This basic point allows serious reformers to transform the terms of the constitutional debate surrounding campaign finance. Old paradigmers have allowed themselves to be portrayed as egalitarian zealots grimly determined to suppress free speech in their relentless pursuit of a level playing field. Once this characterization is accepted, the Supreme Court can be relied upon for a knockout punch: "The concept that government may restrict speech of some [in] order to enhance the relative voice of others is wholly foreign to the First Amendment."[37]

This famous dictum simply does not apply to the new paradigm. We are not in the business of restricting speech. We are interested only in enhancing the capacity of all Americans to join the debate. Even when private money swamps the system, we simply add extra Patriots to the mix: The more private money flows through the donation booth, the more public money flows through patriotic accounts. But there is never any effort to repress speech in the name of equality.

Our object is very different. We aim for nothing less than the construction of a marketplace of ideas more equal *and* more vibrant than anything experienced in American history.

7 | Designing the Donation Booth

The gap between theory and practice sometimes seems as wide as the Grand Canyon. The analogy to the secret ballot is attractive, but will the secret donation booth really work in practice? Won't clever politicians and powerful donors figure out some way to crack the system? And when they succeed, won't our reform become a nightmare?

Millions of dollars will flow through the secret donation booth, and the public won't have the foggiest idea who is paying whom for what. But the big givers and their favorites won't be in the dark. As they wink and nod at one another, our so-called representatives will indulge in orgies of special-interest legislation—amid increasing rumor and escalating suspicion that the donation booth has become a facade. Some great scandal will finally emerge to sink the entire structure and destroy the reformist hopes of an entire generation.

We have argued that the traditional nostrum of "government in the sunshine" isn't much of a cure for the special-interest dealing that afflicts the polity. Even if this grim diagnosis is correct, perhaps the full-information remedy generates a smaller risk of systemic collapse? The old paradigm also suffers from scandals, as secret dealings between big donors and friendly politicians are uncovered from time to time. But in such cases, prosecuting the villains may suffice to restore the public's faith in the overall integrity of the system. In contrast, scandals surrounding the donation booth may catalyze pervasive suspicions: Do the shocking discoveries merely reveal the tip of the iceberg? Because secrecy prevails, rumors will multiply, more easily demoralizing the general public with the entire reform project. Is this risk really worth it?

Similar doubts were raised when the secret ballot was introduced, but this hardly implies that critics won't be right this time.[1] We have taken pains in designing our system to minimize the risks of cheating. But we can't promise to prevent all scandals. The question is whether our design is sufficiently credible that scandals, when they occur, will not undermine public confidence in the system as a whole.

We can't know unless we try, and there is no avoiding guesswork here. In deciding whether the game is worth the candle, recall that our proposal does promise big benefits if it can be made to work. We have already emphasized how anonymous donation will disrupt special dealing, while full information only makes everybody feel good about themselves. Now is the time to add a second big point: Our initiative will check one of the most disturbing political trends of our time—the tendency of the president and members of Congress to spend increasing time raising funds at the expense of governing the country.[2] Only the secret donation booth, not the full-information remedy, promises to reverse this shift.

To see why, begin by considering a hidden ambition linking our proposal with the traditional remedy of full disclosure. The two initiatives may seem diametrically opposed, but they share a common goal: informational parity. Both systems try to guarantee that candidates know no more about their gifts than the public does. Mandated disclosure aims for parity by giving equally good information to the public and the candidate; mandated anonymity, equally poor information. Either system fails if the candidate ends up knowing more than the public.

"Full information" regimes are bound to fail. At the very most, the traditional remedy requires candidates to issue a report containing only three bits of information: name of donor, amount of donation, and date of gift. It doesn't require publication of a final piece of the puzzle: what the politician and the donor say to one another in the process of giving and getting.[3]

Nor should it. Such a sweeping invasion of conversational privacy would be a blatant violation of the First Amendment. It is also a bad idea. Public officials need space to test proposals before publicly endorsing or opposing them. It would be silly to consider extending the full-information requirement to enable the public to eavesdrop on all conversations between politicians and affected interests, and nobody has ever suggested otherwise.

This means that the "quasi-full informational" remedy proffered by the old paradigm creates perverse incentives. To get big gifts politicians not only must solicit big givers. They must do it themselves and cannot afford to delegate the job to professional fund-raisers. When speaking privately, they can make all sorts of assurances to big donors without saying anything blatantly criminal like "Give me $100,000 and I'll vote for your tax break." The very fact that Senator X is spending a whole hour in private conversation with the donor attests to the seriousness of his concerns, making such blatant illegalities unnecessary.

But Senator X will find it harder to signal genuine commitment through professional fund-raisers: *Of course,* staffers will say that the senator takes the interests of industry Y to heart—that's what they're paid to say. Perhaps they might make their protestations credible by producing a written statement, signed by Senator X, promising prompt legislative action. But no sensible politician will sign anything the least bit suggestive of a quid pro quo, lest the paper fall into the hands of prosecutors or political opponents.

As a consequence, a regime of quasi-full information will remorselessly require politicians to spend inordinate amounts of time "dialing for dollars" (preferably on bug-proof lines). Only by talking personally can they talk credibly without violating antibribery laws, and thereby gain access to the deep pockets of special interests.

The new paradigm eliminates these perverse incentives. Politicians will dispense with most private sessions with big donors when they can no longer tell whether there is a real payoff. Personal time is a politician's scarcest resource, and begging isn't the most pleasant pastime.

The new paradigm is no miracle cure. We fully expect incumbents to continue fund-raising on a year-round basis. But they will suddenly delegate much more of the job to paid professionals, and will preserve more of their own time for the mission that was supposed to motivate their journey to Washington—governing the country.

But this benefit, and all the others, will prove chimerical if the donation booth doesn't really work.

The Basics

Begin by refining the proposal. We envision the Federal Election Commission establishing a blind trust that will receive all private contributions to candidates and allied organizations. Donors must follow one central commandment: "Send your checks directly to the blind trust, and don't give them to anybody else." Just as taxpayers make checks payable to the Internal Revenue Service, donors will write theirs to the Political Contribution Blind Trust without specifying their beneficiary more precisely. The name of the favored candidate or organization will appear only on a separate form.

Candidates and allied organizations open accounts with the trust—and receive checkbooks but no deposit slips. The deposits come only from contributors, and the aggregate amount available in each account is reported on a daily basis—instantly available for public inspection on the Internet.

What isn't available is a breakdown of each account into the precise contributions provided by each donor. As long as the trust operates a perfectly secret donation booth, it keeps the candidates and the public entirely in the dark on these matters.

We have become convinced, however, that all-encompassing secrecy isn't necessary to achieve our goals, and so we have modified the regime as it applies to small donors. Consider the situation of Joe Citizen, who proudly gives $100 to the Cause and urges his friends and neighbors to make similar contributions. There is nothing wrong with allowing the trust to confirm his gift—after all, nobody supposes that $100 can buy influence, so why not allow the trust to confirm the small donor's gift, and thereby help him encourage others to mail in $100 gifts of their own?

The problem of special dealing arises only with big gifts, and we tailor our informational regime accordingly. Our model statute authorizes the trust publicly to acknowledge that a donor has given up to $200 to a particular candidate. But bigger givers can only obtain a statement that they have contributed "$200 or more." Of course, donors retain the right to remain completely anonymous if they so choose; but the only bit of information which *must* remain secret is whether they have given the sort of gift that could, if revealed, buy special access and influence.[4] Because more than 80 percent of all donors give less than $250, this refinement enhances the expressive interests of most participants at no cost to the larger aims of our initiative, and we embrace it enthusiastically.[5] (To avoid tedious technotalk, we will continue referring to the "secret donation booth" as if the term were synonymous with a regime of limited disclosure.)

More fine-tuning is in order as we turn from givers to getters. Precisely

who must register with the trust? All candidates will obviously open accounts, because they are barred from receiving direct contributions. But the
line starts to get blurry when we turn to political parties and political action
committees (PACS): Are they also obliged to register with the trust, or may
they continue to receive identifiable donations?

We shall return to this question later, but it suffices to say that existing
Supreme Court doctrine will be our guide. In other words, we have absolutely no intention of forcing the secret donation booth on any organization
that runs issue-oriented campaigns independent of a candidate's control. If
John Doe and his rich neighbors want to buy a full-page ad in the *New
York Times*, they are perfectly free to do so. But candidates cannot evade
the discipline of the donation booth simply by directing big donors to give
their money to organizations that they control or influence. Such organizations must also register with the blind trust and receive all gifts through the
donation booth.

So much for the supply and demand sides of the political marketplace.
Turn next to the process of giving and getting, and consider how the basic
commandment—"Give to the blind trust, and nobody else"—transforms
existing arrangements.[6] Candidates remain perfectly free to ask individuals
for support, but they can no longer close the deal. Fund-raising events may
continue apace, and candidates can restrict invitations to rich members of
their own political party or allied interest groups. But invitations can't be
conditioned on campaign contributions, and the dinner can't be priced
above cost.[7] When donors sit down at the table, they may find that their
plate is covered with a postage-paid envelope addressed to the blind trust,
but only they can determine what happens next. Campaign workers can't
pass the hat at the end of the meal. Donors can't give their checks to anybody
for inspection or collection, but must go to the post office themselves to
mail their envelopes. The basic commandment also puts an end to another
feature of the present system:

> The loophole, called bundling, works in the following way; a PAC, for
> example, solicits contributions from the members made out to a particu-
> lar candidate and then turns over these contributions or otherwise ar-
> ranges for them to be channeled to that candidate. Because the contribu-
> tions technically originate with the person who signs the contribution

check, the contributions involved do not count toward the $5,000 limit on the amount the PAC can contribute to a candidate. The PAC, however, gets the credit—and the influence that flows from it—for giving the total amount of bundled contributions to the candidate.[8]

Our statute effectively outlaws bundling. PACs are perfectly free to recommend candidates and urge their members to contribute to their campaigns. But PAC officials cannot serve as intermediaries, and hence cannot pressure a candidate by threatening to destroy a stack of envelopes containing checks directed to his blind-trust account.

It will be a crime to violate the basic commandment, and effective enforcement is crucial to the entire effort. As long as donors act individually, it will be a lot easier for us to design systems that defeat sophisticated efforts to undermine the secret donation booth. Before moving on to consider complex counterstrategies, we must open a second front and guard against a different kind of crude assault. What is to prevent givers and politicians from corrupting the administrators of the blind trust?

Similar problems arise under the secret ballot. Here too administrators must be prevented from (1) publicizing the votes of individual citizens and (2) crediting votes to the wrong candidate. But with donations—unlike votes—there is the added risk that the administrator will convert the dollar contribution to her own private benefit. We don't think this distinctive risk will apply in the real world. The same problem arises in the administration of the Internal Revenue Service—and while the IRS has many problems, embezzlement of tax dollars is not one of them.

The real problem is misapplication—a $10,000 check comes in for Bush, and a rogue bureaucrat credits it to Gore. Our first line of defense is rigorous internal audits. Such systems are effective throughout the world in policing complex financial transactions, and there is no reason why they won't work here.[9]

A second line of defense is provided by the ability of donors to verify their gifts. To be sure, the trust will report only that a donor has given "$200 or more" to a particular account—and so the donor cannot establish that the rest of his gift has gone to the right place. But at least he can prevent crude misappropriations, requiring rogue bureaucrats to engage in more elaborate, and easier to detect, shenanigans.

New technologies may allow us to go further. We envision a system of digital signatures permitting a donor to trace the flow of her contribution through the blind trust to the account of a particular campaign—but which blocks the campaign from determining the identity of the donor.[10] With this technology, a big giver could simply go to an office of the blind trust, sign on to a special computer terminal, and verify the entire sum. (For obvious reasons, only the original giver, unaccompanied, can be allowed to engage in this inquiry; nor can she leave with a printout of her account verification. She can only look at the screen and file a complaint, including her canceled check, if she did not like what she saw.[11])

We suspect that this technology will be perfected long before our model statute is enacted. But if we are wrong, we provide for a cruder backup: Ten years after each election, the FEC will publish a complete contributions list. This will prevent the system from enduring if it tolerates widespread misapplication by rogue bureaucrats. Donors will scream to high heaven when the published lists indicate serious mistakes. And after ten years, the data will be too stale for donors and politicians to use as a basis for future-oriented dealings.[12]

Finally, there is the danger of sheer corruption—donors and politicians bribing trust officials to leak the data they need to grease the wheels of quid pro quo. Criminal prosecution is only part of a sound strategy. The FEC should also organize the blind trust to minimize the number of officials with access to the secret information, and we propose to insulate these sensitive positions in two different ways.

The first imposes a ten-year ban on employment by any big donor or candidate. No "sensitive" official can be seduced into spilling the beans by the offer of a cushy job outside the blind trust. If this effort to close the revolving door is successful, it will increase employment costs—because officials will rightly demand high pay to compensate them for the loss of a vast array of employment opportunities. Although these high salaries may serve as cannon fodder for sensationalist newspapers, the aggregate amounts will be relatively modest—and in any event, they are an essential price of a serious operation.

Premium salaries, in turn, will serve as an additional spur for official integrity. Once trust officers have accepted sensitive positions, they will have powerful reasons to avoid discharge for suspicious activities; even if they are not criminally prosecuted, they will both lose their premium salaries and find it hard to obtain comparable work in the private sector. This grim prospect will encourage them to avoid even the appearance of corrupt dealings.[13]

A second set of regulations will reinforce this message. Officials holding sensitive positions should be barred from associating with candidates or their representatives outside the office. Antifraternization regulations are a standard technique for cordoning off sensitive functions from casual corruption.[14] They are especially important here, where the most innocent dinner table conversation between a trust official and a candidate will generate waves of rumors.

Controls on revolving-door employment and fraternization cannot do the whole job. In the final analysis, it will be up to the leaders of the Federal Election Commission to foster a spirit of genuine independence for their watchdog agency—a spirit that will inspire officials to take pride in a job well done. We reserve these critical matters to Chapter 9.

For the present, it suffices to note the many public agencies that have sustained such a spirit over the decades—from the United States Marines to the National Institutes of Health to the Social Security Administration. If properly structured, the Federal Election Commission might also become an object of pride for a cadre of long-term, highly paid civil servants—or so we hope to persuade you.

Safeguarding the System

Suppose that our blind trust is manned by an honest crew of officials determined to maintain the integrity of the secret donation booth. Suppose further that both donors and politicians have internalized the basic commandment and largely refrain from bundling contributions or passing large wads of cash under the table—leaving the remaining sociopaths to the tender mercies of criminal prosecution. Suppose all this, and we have only taken the first step toward a credible and effective operation.

First, and most obviously, won't an unscrupulous donor undercut the secret donation booth by showing the candidate his canceled check for $10,000, and telling her that she was the beneficiary? Even though the check is made out to the Federal Election Commission's Blind Trust, won't the candidate find the donor's check persuasive?

Second, can't a donor enhance his credibility by bombing the trust with a series of large donations after telling the candidate to watch out for corresponding jumps in the available balance in her blind trust account?

Third, we have already noted that donors remain free to maintain campaign initiatives that operate independently of the candidates' control or coordination. Even if we can solve the preceding problems, won't big givers simply respond by diverting their funds to "independent" issue advocacy campaigns? If these campaigns help candidates get elected, won't grateful officials pass special-interest legislation in compensation? Won't these independent end runs around the donation booth ultimately destroy its effectiveness?

Big questions. We take up the first two now and defer the third to the next chapter.

THE MIMICRY PRINCIPLE

We refuse all coercive responses to the canceled check problem: Let the $10,000 donor say anything he likes to his favorite candidate. We simply allow others who have *not* given $10,000 to mimic his statements, and thereby require candidates to negotiate in a "noisy" environment, full of potentially misleading signals.

To be concrete: Our model statute gives each donor a five-day cooling off period during which he can retract his initial gift. If the donor exercises this option, the trust cashes his initial check but sends him a reimbursement check—a process similar to the Internal Revenue Service's issuance of refund checks to citizens who have overpaid their taxes. At the end of the day, the retracting donor will have two documents: a canceled check for $10,000 made out to the trust and a fresh check for $10,000 made out by the trust.[15]

This puts politicians in a pickle. When a big giver comes up waving his canceled check for $10,000, how is the candidate to know whether the trust has returned the money? Because the reimbursement check can be cashed or posted to a different account, the donor will not get very far by showing the candidate a few bank statements. Even experienced auditors will have a hard time determining the truth. Individuals are under no legal obligation

to keep all of their cash in publicly verifiable accounts: Has the reimbursement check been sent to a Swiss bank, or is it sitting in a drawer waiting
to be cashed after election day?[16]

To be sure, politicians won't be fooled by some faux donors. If Rush
Limbaugh tries to convince Ralph Nader that he contributed $10,000 to the
Green Party, Nader won't be impressed by Limbaugh's canceled check for
$10,000 to the Federal Election Commission's Blind Trust. But such primi-
tive sifting devices are insufficient to provide politicians with the information
they need to make less obvious credibility assessments. There are a lot of
conservatives and liberals out there, and even more opportunists, who will
give to anybody who has a good chance to win and reward them with governmental largesse. But only a small fraction will ever give to any particular
candidate. How, then, is a candidate to know whose canceled checks are to
be taken seriously?

Imagine that we lived in a world where all purchases of BMWs were nego-
tiated through a blind trust operating under the revocation rules we have
established. Joe Shmoe walks into the showroom flashing a canceled check
for $75,000 to the Luxury Car Purchase Fund and demands his new BMW
725. The car dealer would smell something fishy if Shmoe's bank statements
revealed that he was making $4,000 a month and spending all of it on the
mortgage, groceries, and the like. But suppose Shmoe was making $400,000
a year and could "afford" the car. How is the dealer to determine whether
Shmoe indicated a preference for BMW rather than Cadillac on his luxury
car preference form? And how to separate the good-faith purchasers from
the sly revokers? The dealer's guesswork will predictably bankrupt BMW
within months.

Candidates will face analogous problems. They might, we suppose, frame
a two-part response. The first might involve assigning a campaign worker
to watch the donor as he writes his check, attaches a form naming the candidate as beneficiary, and marches to the mailbox to send the whole thing off
to the blind trust. During this mailing ritual, the campaign worker is careful
to avoid violating the basic commandment: It is the donor, not the worker,
who is the active agent at all times.

The second part is trickier: A rich donor will not happily allow the campaign worker to become his intimate associate for the next five days, merely
to verify that he hasn't cheated on the deal. Nor will he be much amused

if the candidate instructs her staff to spy on the donor without his knowledge or consent. If the donor ever learns of such a scheme, the candidate's future looks grim indeed!

A more plausible response is the creation of a "ritual of honor": The donor puts his hand on the Bible, or gives his solemn word as his bond, and swears that he will not exercise his revocation option. The credibility of such an oath depends on the circumstances. It will be least credible in "hold-up" situations—when the candidate is bullying donors into gifts by threatening to punish interests that withhold support. Given such quasi-extortionate demands, many donors will think it appropriate to revoke regardless of their oaths to the contrary.

But let us put such extreme provocations—which are not at all uncommon—to one side.[17] Revocation will also be a real option in a much broader class of cases. These involve opportunistic donors who look upon large gifts as business propositions and often give to both sides to assure a favorable reception regardless of the outcome. Opportunists will be sorely tempted to adopt a cynical stance to any oath-taking ritual—especially if they suspect that other opportunists are covertly revoking their promises: Why should I keep my promise of $10,000 when Unscrupulous is going to wave his $10,000 check despite his revocation, and the Candidate doesn't really appreciate that I'm not Unscrupulous?

Even ideologically motivated givers will be tempted to cheat. By hypothesis, they aren't giving in the hope of some material benefit. But they can still further their ideological interests through a strategy of revocation. To see how, suppose Ideologue has allocated $10,000 for the campaign and wants to use it to push as many candidates as possible in his favored direction. He will be tempted to wave a check for $10,000 dated January 1 in front of Candidate A early in the campaign, then show Candidate B another canceled check for $10,000 dated February 1, and so forth. But this strategy requires ideologues to engage in serial revocation.

Given the manifold strategic possibilities, most politicians won't put much stock in rituals of honor. Givers who repeatedly swear their fidelity may even find themselves under suspicion for "protesting too much." Nevertheless, even the skeptical enactment of such rituals creates a moral environment that suggests it is acceptable for big givers to weasel their way around the system. As a consequence, we propose the construction of a counterritual that emphasizes the social importance of supporting the secret donation booth.

We require that the very biggest donors actually enter a physical donation booth if they wish to make a gift of more than $10,000. The cubicle will resemble a traditional voting booth and will be open during business hours in offices designated by the blind trust.[18] The donor will be required to close the curtain behind her before making her gift. Once inside the booth, she is under no obligation to write a check for $10,000 or more—indeed, she is perfectly free to walk out of the booth without giving any gift whatever. But if she wishes to make a large contribution, she can do it only within a physical setting that emphasizes the social importance of anonymous giving.

Our point is to disrupt the symbolic force of competing rituals of honor.[19] Even as they swear an oath about their big transaction, both giver and getter know that when the donor pulls the curtain, nobody can tell whether she has actually made any gift at all, and if she has, who she has named as beneficiary. These basic facts will frame the social meaning of any competing ritual of honor—undermining its credibility and enhancing the donation booth system at a vulnerable moment.

Requiring a visit to a donation booth will impose a minor inconvenience on big givers.[20] But this modest burden is not unreasonable, given the grave risk of corruption from large gifts. Because the number of big givers is minuscule, the overall burden on the citizenry is small.

THE SECRECY ALGORITHM

Imagine yourself a candidate operating within the new informational environment. You regularly encounter rich men and women who show you canceled checks with big numbers on them and say supportive things. You smile and shake their hands enthusiastically, but you know that they know that you don't know whether they have given anything at all.

But one day, a rich guy—call him Mr. G—tries to penetrate the haze: "I will be giving you $50,000 today. So look closely at your trust account next week, and you will see your balance take a really big jump after the five-day revocation period expires." Even though our blind trust reports a combination of both Patriot and private contribution receipts, a sufficiently large private contribution would tend to stand out. Let's call this check-bombing, and it obviously threatens to destroy our anonymity shield if it carries sufficient megatonnage.

Some counterintelligence is required. One simple response: We have been supposing that the blind trust updates each account on a daily basis. But why not lengthen the updating interval to a week or two? This accounting maneuver dilutes Mr. G's big gift by mixing it with a larger number of others, making the $50,000 bomb harder to identify. Suppose Candidate X has been receiving about $50,000 a day. If we extend the updating period to a week, there will never be a moment when X sees his daily take double from $50 to $100 thousand; he will merely observe a weekly rise from $250 to $300 thousand. Since many others besides Mr. G have promised big gifts to X during the preceding week, it won't be so clear that Mr. G came through and that the others were merely puffing. (And keep in mind that the number of promises—and false promises—will multiply under the new regime!)

This simple solution is too crude. Many candidates won't be the beneficiary of bombing raids, and yet they will experience unnecessary delays in gaining access to their money. This is a serious problem, because candidates can't engage in serious campaign planning without an accurate sense of their financial resources.

We propose a more sophisticated solution. Candidates will normally get their money on a daily basis, except when there is reason to believe that a bombing campaign is actually under way. We will apply special measures only when there is a truly remarkable increase in receipts arriving on a particular day, and only when the uptick is attributable to a small number of big gifts. To implement this policy, we provide the trust with a "secrecy algorithm." In response to the sudden surge, the algorithm sequesters some of the money, and the candidate does not see it until later—when it is distributed in a random pattern over the next accounting window (two weeks during an election year, and four weeks at other times).

We have tailored the algorithm further to allow mass surges of support to register without randomization. After his victory in the Republican primary in New Hampshire, John McCain raised more than $1 million in small contributions within forty-eight hours.[21] Because our algorithm is triggered only by a small number of large gifts, it would not prevent these contributions from flowing immediately into McCain's coffers after the five-day recission period.[22] We defer further details to Appendix B, restricting ourselves only to a few basic points.

Most obviously, big contributors may devise sophisticated bombing strategies in an effort to overwhelm our algorithmic defenses. Given our particular formula, donors might try giving moderately large amounts on successive days. If the average daily amount received by a candidate is $50,000 and the standard deviation is $30,000, then an individual donor wishing to make a $200,000 contribution might give $25,000 on eight successive days. Breaking up the total gift into smallish amounts reduces the chance that the algorithm will be triggered on any particular day—so that the candidate might more confidently infer the presence of the gift by calculating whether her donations went up by a daily average of $25,000 compared with the periods before and after the bombing raid.

To respond to this threat, our algorithm aggregates an individual's past contributions to determine whether the randomization mechanism should be triggered. Continuing our previous example, this means that on the seventh day of the bombing raid, our hypothetical donor will be treated as giving $175,000, not $25,000, in determining whether the biggest donors on that day had accounted for an extraordinary surge of contributions.

Our secrecy algorithm also deters gamesmanship by making randomization a function of dollar amounts that are not precisely knowable by either the candidates or contributors. It is triggered by calculating the mean and standard deviation of actual contributions—not the amounts reported in the trust account (which are, of course, subject to randomization). As a consequence, contributors will have trouble designing their bombing campaign to fly just below the radar.

The secrecy algorithm poses distinct problems at the beginning and at the end of campaigns. In the beginning, large contributions are more likely to stand out because candidates normally receive fewer background gifts—so we would expect the algorithm to kick in more often.[23] This is undoubtedly an inconvenience. But recall that our exploratory committee device, which doesn't employ anonymity as a tool, allows candidates to raise substantial amounts of funds early without delay. And it will usually take only a week or so for most of the funds to be available. So the problem, while real, doesn't seem particularly serious.

Perhaps we are underestimating the vulnerability of the algorithm during the early campaign. Given the low level of contributions, candidates may attempt to assist bombing campaigns by actively dissuading general contributions on particular days. If nobody else gives on Monday, Mr. G may be able to make a big gift without triggering randomization. To continue our previous example, suppose that contributions are flowing in at $50,000 a day, with a standard deviation of $30,000. If a candidate can persuade all other donors to abstain from giving on a particular Monday, Mr. G could contribute $75,000 without triggering randomization, and thereby credibly claim credit for his gift.

We could respond by refining the secrecy algorithm further, but we are content to let experience determine whether this is necessary.[24] There are a limited number of days in a campaign, and even if the strategy is successful, an individual donor can give only so much before triggering randomization. (In the preceding example, the maximum gift was $80,000.) Our model statute leaves such refinements to the sound discretion of the commission.

A different problem arises at the end of the campaign—when time is of the essence as the competing candidates make their strategic media buys. If the secrecy algorithm is hiding a lot of money, this is a serious problem. But happily, the risk seems remote. With large sums flowing into candidates' coffers in the late stages, strategic bombing must be massive indeed if it is to stand out in a credible way. To explore the matter further, we have analyzed the impact of our algorithm on daily contribution data from actual elections. Using Monte Carlo simulations, we find that current patterns of giving rarely trigger our algorithm; once the algorithm is triggered, the excess donation normally is fully reported within a week; and in general, there is an exceedingly small deviation between actual and reported amounts of giving (on average, 96 percent of the total amount contributed to date had been reported five days later). Donation patterns will differ substantially under the new regime, but the results of these simulations are reassuring (see Appendix B).

There can be no hope of devising the perfect strategic defense against saturation bombing. If Bill Gates tells his favorite candidate for the Senate to expect $100 million to arrive in his trust account, and this eye-popping sum does show up over the next accounting period, Gates's credibility will be as good as gold—and there is nothing our algorithm can do to change this fact.

Our response will be some regulations of last resort. The risk of truly massive strategic bombing provides a rationale for retaining some legal limits on the amount that any individual can contribute to a campaign. These limits will be much higher than those prevailing today. But it would be irresponsible to dispense with them entirely and allow billionaires to bomb their way out of the anonymity that the donation booth imposes upon the rest of us. We elaborate this point in the next chapter.

The Patriotic Contribution Ratio

We can now sum up the distinctive informational regime created by our model statute. The Federal Election Commission will publish a daily contributions report for each candidate and political organization that includes:

1. A list of all private money contributors and the amount they have given up to $200. Bigger contributions will remain secret, and individual givers are free to remain completely anonymous.
2. The total amount of private and patriotic money that is available (after passing through the secrecy algorithm) for spending.
3. The total amount of private and patriotic money that remains unspent.
4. No information concerning individual patriotic contributors—neither their names nor the amounts they have given—either to candidates or political organizations.
5. The names of political organizations which have given Patriot dollars to candidates, and the dates and amounts of their contributions.
6. The Patriot-to-private ratio of received funds.[25]

We have explored the rationale for each aspect of the new paradigm. But the whole is greater than the sum of its parts. Consider the commission's running report of the crucial ratio that compares patriotic and private contributions flowing to each candidate. We envision the mass media using it to provide ordinary Americans with a single number that tells them how much each candidate is depending on the patriotic support of equal citizens. We hope these "patriotic contribution ratios" will take their place in the public mind with other leading indicators of public welfare: the unemployment rate, the crime rate, and the like. It is up to the electorate, of course, to determine the range of tolerable ratios, and the point at which private contributions become so dominant as to suggest that a candidacy has become the tool of special interests. But one of the new paradigm's great virtues is its ability to keep this question at the forefront of public concern.

An Idea Whose Time Has Come?

Is it time to take the secret donation booth seriously?

The basic idea isn't new.[26] Sixteen states of the Union have already tried to prohibit judicial candidates from learning who donates to their (re)election campaigns.[27] The rationale, of course, is that judges shouldn't know the identity of their donors lest they reward them later on in the courtroom. When measured against the model statute, these existing judicial schemes are very primitive.[28]

More elaborate initiatives are taking place overseas. Korea amended its Political Fund Act in 1992 to give donors the option of contributing anonymously.[29] The criminalization of politics provided a major impetus for the change—as "donors to opposition parties were under a high risk of being tax audited by the authorities once their donation was made public."[30] Chile is seriously considering a statute that makes anonymity a requirement, not merely an option. Although developed independently, the Chilean initiative shares several features with our model statute—including a government-run blind trust with a ten-day cancellation period.[31] The British Conservative Party has also proposed for discussion "the establishment of an independently administered blind trust—a 'Political Donations Institute.' "[32] As in the case of the secret ballot, perhaps a success in some faraway place will encourage Americans to take the new paradigm seriously.

There is no need to wait. America has the rule of law tradition, and the technocratic skills required for a serious experiment. Given the bankruptcy of the existing reform paradigm, it is time to take a new approach. The secret donation booth is within our operational horizon. In conjunction with patriotic finance, it promises a genuine democratic breakthrough.

Not a magic cure-all. Even if our model statute becomes a reality, the commission will be playing an endless cat-and-mouse game with the latest check-bombing program. Indeed, the agency will predictably fail unless it can also back up the secrecy algorithm by restricting the freedom of the biggest givers to make unlimited donations.

How should these backstop regulations be designed?

8 | Plugging the Gaps

Exploratory fund + patriotic finance + secret donation booth—this is not a formula for eliminating private money from politics. It is an effort to channel its flow into a larger framework that puts citizen sovereignty at the center of American democracy. As long as the patriotic decisions of ordinary citizens dominate campaign finance, there is nothing to fear from private giving. To the contrary, a mixed system can serve a host of valuable functions—provided that private dollars move in ways that restrict opportunities for undue influence.

The question is whether big money will mock our efforts to put it in its proper place. The previous chapter already introduced one obvious problem: What is to stop the biggest givers from overwhelming the donation booth with enormous checks that make their claims instantly credible?

Even if we can solve this problem, a larger one remains. This is a free country, and big donors will undoubtedly devise new ways to gain special influence. If we make it impossible for them to bomb their way out of the donation booth, won't they respond by making an end run around it?

Under this alternative, big givers simply undertake their own independent media campaigns on behalf of their favorite causes. After all, the First Amendment guarantees them a constitutional right to make their personal opinions known to the world—including grateful candidates who will appreciate the extent to which these "independent" media blitzes redound to their electoral advantage. Rather than breaking the informational link between givers and getters, will the donation booth merely induce the protagonists to create new patterns of special dealing behind the protective shield of the Constitution?

Recent writers have found this question particularly demoralizing. They have come to view the problem like the effort to dam the Mississippi. You may stop the river from flooding a town at one point, but this only leads to terrible destruction elsewhere. Like water seeking its own level, private money will push its way through the doctrinal exemptions, and around the reformist barriers, to swamp the democratic process. Bewitched by this hydraulic metaphor, some generally progressive writers have recently pronounced serious structural reform an exercise in futility.[1]

We do not agree. We do not expect to eliminate all bombing raids and hydraulic pressures. But we can keep them under control by a focused set of regulatory measures. These strategies will sustain the overriding ambition of our initiative—to establish citizen sovereignty as the central reality of campaign finance.

We owe our cautious optimism to a distinctive way of setting up our problem. Under the old paradigm, comprehensive regulation was the strategy of first resort—and it is easy to see why despair followed. Under existing law, for example, the Federal Election Commission is charged with assuring that nobody ever gives a candidate more than $1,000. This is a hopeless task: There are simply too many givers, and too few regulators, to expect ongoing and evenhanded enforcement. If a bureaucratic miracle happened, givers and getters would respond with evasive measures requiring endless cycles of heroic effort from outstripped officials.

Our problem is different. Command-and-control regulation is our last resort. Our principal tools are patriotic finance and the donation booth. We use classical regulatory techniques only to plug holes that might otherwise destroy our market-channeling strategies. This focused ambition makes it possible to be a realistic optimist. By bringing bureaucratic energy to bear on a few trouble spots, we can hope for the ongoing engagement and occasional creativity needed to keep the remaining problems under control.

We begin with bombing, and our principal defense against it: the secrecy algorithm. As we have explained, only the biggest bombing raids pose a serious threat to our algorithmic defense of the secret donation booth. Because a few thousand dollars will no longer buy special influence or access, there is no longer a need for very low contribution limits. Under existing law, a donor can give no more than $1,000 to any candidate's campaign, but our model statute allows gifts of $5,000 to individual House candidates; about $15,000 to candidates for the Senate (depending on a state's population);

and $100,000 to aspirants to the White House.[2] We also impose an annual cap of $100,000 on the total amount a private donor can give to all candidates running for federal office.

This big change promises a vast increase in both individual freedom and bureaucratic effectiveness. During the 2000 campaign, more than six hundred thousand Americans gave $1,000 to a candidate—pushing them up against the existing limit and inviting bureaucrats to determine whether they had gone over the line. But few people would come close to the stratospheric limits we are proposing. This not only frees the vast majority from any concern with the sanctions of the criminal law. It also—and for the first time—promises rigorous enforcement against the small number of donors who might threaten the integrity of the new paradigm.

This focused bureaucratic reaction will, in turn, generate a cautious response by big givers. Given the risks of discovery, and the resulting threat of criminal prosecution, illegal bombing raids will be few and far between. Our first set of regulations, then, promises to plug one obvious hole in our market-channeling strategy.

Which returns us to the hydraulic critique. If big donors no longer can get credit for their direct donations to candidates, will they respond by funneling more cash into independent issue advocacy campaigns?

Yes, but not nearly enough to threaten the centrality of patriotic finance. Before expecting you to agree, we must describe the regulatory regime required to plug this last large hole in the dike.

The Limits of Algorithmic Secrecy

Imagine Candidate C soliciting funds under the new regime. Day after day, she and her staff approach big givers, who tell them that they will mail their checks immediately. A week later, C looks at her account balance, and tries to determine whether the big givers have come through. This will require two inferences.

First, maybe none of the big givers delivered. This won't be so easy to determine, because small givers will also be sending money and patriotic donations will be flowing into the candidate's blind trust account. During most of the campaign, this flow will be substantial and it will vary considerably on a daily basis. In statistics, this volatility is measured in terms of standard deviations. If the standard deviation of total daily patriotic and private contributions is large, it will be difficult to tell whether a jump in the trust balance was caused by big givers or by normal fluctuations. When the standard deviation is small, it will be easier for big gifts to stand out.

Second, even if a sudden surge suggests that a bombing raid is under way, C will encounter a distinct problem of attribution: how to determine which big givers gave and which were only talking? This problem dissolves if the balance jumps so decisively that it is clear that all givers are following through on their promises. But in the absence of such a decisive signal, the second stage will be tricky indeed. C may know that somebody is giving in a big way, but often there will be lots of big talkers claiming credit.

Our algorithm makes the first inference difficult and the second virtually impossible. Whenever the daily increment in C's account fluctuates by more than one standard deviation, the algorithm distributes the amount in a random pattern over the next accounting period (two weeks during the campaign year, four weeks during the precampaign).[3] Once a particular fluctuation triggers the algorithm, C may not even see her daily balance increase on the day when the big deposit is ordinarily scheduled to appear in her account. One third of the time, our algorithm instructs the computer to register an abnormally low amount in C's account on that day—compensating for this initial decrease by adding extra amounts in C's account, at random, over the accounting period.

When faced with such a noisy signal, C would be silly to consult one-day changes in her trust account to test the credibility of her big givers' claims. Instead, she will direct her attention to the aggregate changes reported over the accounting period. If the aggregate contribution over the last period shows a big divergence from previous periods, there may be reason to infer that a burst of bombing has occurred. But even when this is true, C must take a second step and attribute the increment to particular givers. And once we have extended the period from one day to two or four weeks, this is no easy matter: Ordinary politicians will meet lots of folks who make lots of promises.

There is only one practical way for the politician to solve this problem. We imagine C pinpointing one major donor in every accounting period as a special target, whom we shall call Donor T. C tells T that he has a special opportunity to prove that he has put his money where his mouth is: "I will be looking at my balance for this accounting period, and if I see a big jump, I will be crediting the entire surplus to you and only you. Now bomb away!"

With this incentive, T will try hard to induce others to step up their giving during the accounting period. But except for close family members, he won't be in a good position to determine whether they are following through. Indeed, T runs the risk that rivals for C's affection may reduce their giving so as to make his contribution appear nonexistent or negligible in the eyes of the candidate. Nevertheless, C's invitation does give T and his intimate associates a special chance to penetrate the information barrier.

This selective targeting strategy frames our first set of regulations of last resort. The Federal Election Commission's goal is clear: It should forbid any giver from making a contribution during any accounting period that is so large that it can penetrate the algorithm's noisy signal. But how large should this amount be?

As she looks at her running account balance over the accounting period, C's problem is similar to one confronted by financial economists on Wall Street seeking to determine the market impact of a particular piece of news—say a merger or new invention. Financial economists regularly examine abnormal changes in stock prices to assess whether one or another bit of information has enabled market participants to obtain "abnormal" returns on their stock holdings.[4] When they suspect that it will take a while for market participants to assimilate the news, they typically define an "event window"—say ten days—to determine whether the cumulative abnormal change in stock price is large relative to the multiple-day standard deviation. Candidates will revert to a similar analysis in seeking to detect evidence of a large bombing raid.

Appendix C provides details for readers eager to improve the performance of their stock portfolios. But for us the critical policy question is how hard we want to make the candidate's guessing game. As the candidate's statistical analyst scrutinizes the data for the previous accounting period, he will not be able to come to a hard-and-fast judgment as to whether T has kept his promise. Instead, he will give the candidate a report of probabilities: "I can tell you, with a __ degree of certainty, that T has given X dollars."

The key regulatory question involves the blank. Suppose we want to reduce C's certainty to the 20 percent level; then the two-week ceiling on T's gift should be one-quarter of the standard deviation in the variability of C's daily account balance over the accounting period. Suppose that a 38 percent certainty level is acceptable; then the ceiling should be half the standard deviation; suppose 50 percent, then T's gift can be as large as two-thirds the standard deviation; and so forth.

To make this point concrete, imagine that C is running for a House seat and checks her bank account at the Federal Election Commission on a daily basis. Once the algorithm has done its work, suppose that her daily increment bounces around over the accounting period with a standard deviation of $10,000. (This figure approximates the historical ten-day standard deviation of contributions to House races.) If we wish to permit our candidate a maximum confidence of 20 percent in T's veracity, our regulations should impose a $2,500 ceiling on any gift during a two-week accounting period. If an individual wishes to give more than this at one time, he is free to write a larger check—but the algorithm will distribute the rest of his money at random over the next accounting period.[5]

During any particular period, individuals will be able to contribute as much as $2,500, $7,500 (on average), and $50,000 to candidates for the House, Senate, and presidency. Appendix C explains why these stratospheric limits should prevent candidates from confidently attributing bombing raids to particular donors. Our model statute authorizes the FEC to modify these limits as it gains more experience in evaluating the variability of private contributions under the new paradigm.

Note the larger strategic implications of the fact that the biggest gifts will spill over into subsequent accounting periods. This will paradoxically help defend the integrity of the donation booth. Quite simply, excess contributions of previous givers will clog up the candidate's contribution dance card. There are only thirty-nine accounting periods between house elections. If five donors claim to have given a candidate the maximum amount during an accounting period, the candidate will be hard pressed to know whom to credit when her aggregate balance falls short of the total claims. Shortfalls are inevitable because the incentive for individual claimants to chisel on the promises increases with the number of claimants. By forcing the largest donations into multiple accounting periods, our two- or four-week contribution limits greatly exacerbate a candidate's attribution problem.

We also propose an overall limit on the total amount that any giver can donate to any particular candidate over the course of the campaign. These limits are double the numbers for donations during a single accounting period—$5,000 for a House candidate, $15,000 for a Senate candidate (on average), and $100,000 for a presidential contender. The campaign limits serve as a last line of defense against the possibility of bombing over multiple accounting periods.[6]

But are even these stratospheric limits too low when it comes to donations to minor-party candidates? Because these hopefuls have virtually no chance of winning the election, special interests won't be beating a path to their door. With the risk of corruption low, why not allow them to solicit larger sums from any rich supporters they can interest in their cause?

Minor-party candidacies have greatly enriched political debate over time—ventilating issues which later move to the center of American politics. Given their historical importance, we are inclined to allow private donors to triple the amount they can give—increasing the sum from $5,000 to $15,000 for House seats, and so on. We refuse to provide third-party hopefuls any further exemptions: They must use the donation booth and run the gauntlet of the algorithm like all other candidates. Even if they have no plausible chance of winning, they may wield power as spoilers and can negotiate for substantive agenda priorities before throwing their support behind a major-party candidate.[7] As a consequence, special interests might well be tempted to bankroll a minor-party hopeful if he can credibly promise to bargain with the major players on their behalf.

Our limited exemption may give the Pat Buchanans and Ralph Naders a slightly easier time raising funds without generating very much of a risk of corruption. At the end of the day, such candidacies will take off only if their protagonists can engage the hopes of millions of citizens who respond by forwarding their Patriot dollars. But together with the exploratory fund, the special exemption will help keep their cause alive long enough to make a serious appeal.

So much for our regime as it applies to particular candidacies. We also propose (1) an overall limit of $100,000 on the amount that any donor can give to all campaigns and political committees during a calendar year; and (2) a $25,000 limit on the amount during a calendar year that any donor can give to political committees to fund express advocacy.[8] The overall annual limit of $100,000 cuts off more complex bombing strategies under which a group of House candidates, say, target the same T for the same accounting period—and thereby give him the chance to gain credibility by bombing a host of candidate accounts simultaneously (see Appendix C). The $25,000 annual limitation helps assure that individuals do not use contributions to PACs to attempt an end run around the anonymity requirement and signal to candidates the source for particular express advocacy campaigns. This restriction also limits the ability of plutocrats to set up a series of essentially private PACs (think of the Forbes family PACs) to fund independent express advocacy that directly signals their support for particular candidates.[9]

All these stratospheric limits will apply only to a handful of the richest Americans. But that is just their point. The rest of us can give freely, and only the few who continue to aim for special influence should confront regulations of last resort. If they insist on playing "target" with their favorite candidates, they should be prepared to hire a lawyer as part of the cost of doing business.

The Hydraulic Critique

We don't want to promise too much. Candidates and donors will occasionally outsmart the secrecy algorithm—requiring the commission to fine-tune its regulatory responses in an endless game of cat-and-mouse. It is foolish to aim for a foolproof scheme. The realistic goal is to sustain public confidence in the integrity of the donation booth. This won't be destroyed by the occasional breach—as long as the FEC is actively policing and refining its regulations of last resort. Of course, it is a fair question whether any agency will have the independence required to enforce the rules rigorously against the most powerful politicians and donors in the land. We take up this question in the next chapter.

For now, consider a different objection—which supposes that we succeed in coming up with a workable design, but condemns this "success" as an exercise in futility. Even if we manage to channel the direct flow of private money through the donation booth, won't big givers simply redirect their cash into other channels? Because they can no longer gain special influence by direct gifts to candidates, won't they run their own independent issue advocacy campaigns on behalf of their favorites? If these costly efforts deliver votes, won't grateful candidates respond by delivering favors? If so, haven't we merely displaced—not solved—the basic problem of big money in politics?

This is the hydraulic critique. We have been shadowboxing with it throughout the book, but now is the time to confront it squarely. A proper assessment begins with the Supreme Court's decision in *Buckley v. Valeo*, which established two legitimate bases for regulating contributions. The first focuses on the content of speech, the second on the nature of the speaker. Although reformers have traditionally concentrated on the first ground, the new paradigm focuses on the second.

Begin with the more traditional route to regulation: The justices have squarely upheld the power of Congress to limit independent expenditures that expressly endorse a candidate. But in addition to this content-based rationale, *Buckley* also authorizes Congress to regulate the funding of speakers whose activities are a part of the candidates' campaigns. The Court expressly upheld two sorts of speaker regulation. Call the first noncoordination: Advocates must design the timing and content of their public communications independently of candidates. The second authorizes regulation of funding if a speaker's "major purpose" is "the nomination or election of a candidate."[10] To put these points in a single line: Congress can restrict funding for express advocacy; but citizens are free to finance unlimited amounts of issue advocacy, as long as they are really independent of entities (candidates and "major purpose" organizations) that are trying to get candidates elected.[11]

Reformers have traditionally attempted to broaden the regulatory net by expanding the definition of express advocacy.[12] McCain-Feingold is illustrative: It defines any advertisement as an exercise in express advocacy if it pictures or names a candidate within thirty days of a primary election or sixty days of a general election.[13] We doubt that the present Court would uphold such a definition, and even if it did, we doubt that the restriction would have a large effect. Given the operation of free markets and private property, there will always be lots of market winners who—with perfect legitimacy—have made lots of private money from their economic activities. And these people will predictably get as close as possible to the Court's "free speech" line and use their wealth to express their opinions on matters of political importance. If the Court upheld McCain-Feingold, advertisers would quickly figure out ways of alluding to candidates without mentioning them; and if this were somehow rendered illegal, rich people would respond by publishing more newspapers and editorializing more aggressively; and if this option were somehow cut off, they would find compelling political uses for their Web sites; and so on. Short of the abolition of free markets and private property, there is simply no way to eliminate the influence of private money on democratic politics—and to paraphrase Madison, surely this cure is far worse than the disease.

We do not deny that a modest statutory redefinition of express advocacy might have a modest effect on the flow of money to independent campaigns. But we look elsewhere for a decisive response to the hydraulic critique. To join issue, we shall assume that the Supreme Court refuses to permit any further legislative expansion of express advocacy.

Our regulations of last resort are based on the second rationale for regulation marked out by the *Buckley* Court. As we have seen, the justices have already endorsed the power of Congress to regulate issue advocacy by organizations that "coordinate" with candidates or whose "major purpose" is the election of candidates. These regulatory rationales do not require government agencies to police the content of speech. They focus on the kinds of organizations doing the speaking—insisting that they must be truly independent of the candidates' campaigns. We hope to show that "organizationally targeted" regulations provide a decisive response to the hydraulic critique.

DILUTION

Begin by considering how much patriotic finance will dilute the hydraulic shift of private dollars toward issue advocacy. As we have suggested, 5 billion Patriot dollars may well be the normal flow during presidential elections; even if the donation booth cuts the flow of private money by a third or a half, this will still yield a pool of $6–7 billion.

This compares with $100 million spent on independent issue advocacy during the 2000 year cycle.[14] The hydraulic effect must reach hurricane proportions before it can overwhelm the new financial landscape. Even if expenditures on issue advocacy doubled or tripled, there is no cause for concern. The $6–7 billion flowing to candidates will assuredly determine the major thrust of the political conversation. As long as independents don't seize control of the agenda, it is good—not bad—to give them a chance to emphasize issues that the candidates have pushed to the periphery.

But of course, we may be wrong in our predictions; and in any event, increasing flows into truly independent advocacy may threaten the balance between public and private funding of the campaign as a whole. As a consequence, our model statute authorizes the commission to take countervailing steps to offset serious hydraulic effects. To assure that at least two-thirds of total funds come from patriotic sources, we have already designed a stabilization algorithm to guide the commission. Whenever patriotic finance falls below two-thirds of total funding, our algorithm kicks in to increase each citizen's patriotic balance for the next election cycle, thereby reestablishing the 2-to-1 ratio over time.

We propose to extend this approach to the hydraulic threat raised by independent issue advocacy. On a finding that independent finance is increasing its relative share of total revenue flows, the commission should include these funds in determining whether the overall 2-to-1 funding ratio is endangered. If the balance tips toward the private side once the independents are included, our stabilization algorithm instructs the commission to enhance each citizen's patriotic allotment the next time around. As always, our response to an increase of private money is to increase public money.[15]

REGULATION BASED ON THE IDENTITY OF THE SPEAKER

We add this dilution refinement only as a precautionary measure, because we don't think there is much risk here. To see why, consider how the new paradigm changes the decision-making calculus of potential contributors to issue-advocacy campaigns. One aspect of the new calculus will rightly feed the hydraulicists' anxieties. Organizing an "independent" campaign allows givers to inform candidates of the magnitude of their contributions. Suppose, for example, that you and your friends contribute a million dollars to Citizens for Energy Independence, a new organization that happens to support the very same positions that Candidate C hopes to use to defeat his rival. The First Amendment guarantees you the right to affirm publicly your financial support of the new citizens' group, and word of your large contribution will undoubtedly get back to a grateful C. This means that big givers have a new decision to make: Should they get together to give, say, $1 million to Energy Independence, or should they give the money to C's blind trust account?

If they choose Energy Independence, C may sharply discount the value of their efforts.[16] By hypothesis, Energy Independence is not coordinating its campaign with the candidate. Although they converge on the general issue, the two campaigns may often run at cross purposes—with Energy Independence spouting the wrong things at the wrong time in the wrong places. The organization's media invasions may sometimes be entirely counterproductive—requiring C to spend precious time and money offsetting the damage done by its ill-advised advertising cannonades. But more typically, independent campaigns will be valuable to C, but much less valuable than a direct contribution of $1 million to his blind trust.

This sharp discount won't necessarily deter big givers from deflecting donations away from the donation booth. After all, if they take the independent route, they can take advantage of the First Amendment to publicize the precise amount of their financial contribution and thereby get direct credit from the candidate. Even if C applies an 80 percent discount to a million-dollar campaign, it is still worth $200,000 to him. And because he will have no trouble identifying the contributors to Energy Independence, they can expect him to be grateful for the $200,000 contribution once he gains office.

At the same time, the discount does make the independent contribution less attractive: If donors give the million dollars directly to the blind trust, C will have a better chance of winning the election—because he will be in a position to devote the entire million to its highest and best use, and not sit idly by while big givers waste $800,000 in their effort to penetrate the anonymity barrier. To be sure, if the big givers deposit their million into the donation booth, a triumphant C won't be able to pay them back by providing special access and influence. Nevertheless, they will gain generalized benefits—because C's positions on energy independence are more favorable than his Green opponent's.

The overall hydraulic effect will depend on how individual givers weigh these options. We do not doubt that in the aggregate, overall investment in independent campaigning will rise, but not nearly enough to destroy the integrity of the new paradigm. Recall that funds for independent advocacy now hover around the $100 million mark; doubling or quintupling this amount won't make much of a splash in a $6 billion pool.

Our confidence is strengthened by the ways candidates will predictably use the extra billions made available under the new paradigm. Speaking broadly, they will be spending their patriotic money for more media time, and this means that they will typically place a lower value on the marginal value of independent expenditures. If Candidate C thought an issue-advocacy campaign by Energy Independence generated $200,000 of value under the old regime, she might consider the same campaign worth only $100,000 now that she has so much more to spend. This likely decline in marginal value will lead rational actors to reduce, not increase, their investments in independent contributions—though it is anybody's guess whether this depressive factor will outweigh the expansionary factors canvassed previously.[17]

Defining Coordinated Speech

We have been talking about "independent" issue advocacy as if it were possible to create an effective barrier against coordination with the candidate and his campaign staff. This premise is central. If candidates can create organizations that masquerade as independents but function as integral parts of their campaign, they will no longer encourage givers to use the blind trust. Pseudoindependents will serve as conduits enabling givers and getters to maximize their self-interest at the expense of the donation booth. Givers to pseudoindependents get name recognition for their big gifts; candidates get full value for the money without the heavy discount imposed by truly independent expenditures. Unless this loophole is plugged, the hydraulic effect will indeed overwhelm the donation booth (though the patriotic component of the new paradigm will remain intact).

We have a two-pronged response. The first defines the sorts of transaction that deprive a group of its independent standing. Any group that submits any of its advertisements to the candidate for review, for example, should be stripped of independent status. Similarly, independents cannot hire any consultants who are also working for candidates—because they will predictably discharge the forbidden coordination function. The FEC has recently been taking the independence requirement more seriously—promulgating new and detailed regulations usefully expanding and clarifying what constitutes coordination.[18] Our model statute builds on these rules, but they will not be enough to plug the dike. Givers and getters will come up with clever new ways to coordinate, and the commission should be empowered to strike down evolving evasions as they arise. There is an inevitably Sisyphean aspect to such labors. But as long as the commission's rules are relatively responsive to evolving practice, candidates will continue to place a heavy discount on contributions to independent advocacy campaigns, and the hydraulic effect will remain under reasonable control.[19]

Specific rules are especially important because they constrain a fundamental aspect of American political life. American politicians will continue to speechify endlessly at interest-group dinners and find many other ways to reassure issue-oriented organizations of their undying concern. We have absolutely no intention of abolishing such practices, which are the very life-blood of American politics. But it is one thing to talk until dawn, quite another to plan a concrete campaign strategy—with dollars, dates, and messages for advertising spots. The commission's regulations will target these kinds of concrete activities, and it is in everybody's interest to know in advance the sorts of transactions which cross the line from talk to action.

Defining "Major Purpose"

We have thus far been confronting a classic problem raised by American pluralism: given the multitude of ever-changing interest groups appearing on the political scene, how to identify pseudoindependents that merely serve as fronts for the candidates themselves? Our second strategy confronts a more tractable problem—the status of political parties. When Al Gore talks to his friends at the Democratic National Committee, and the DNC subsequently spends $1 million on ads for "independent issue advocacy," it is impossible to believe that these media buys are not part of the Gore campaign. Certainly donors to the DNC would be grievously disappointed to learn that their gifts were not part of a coordinated effort to beat Republicans in November!

In recognition of these deeply rooted attitudes, our statute treats all political parties as their candidates' alter egos, and requires all their campaign expenditures to come through the secret donation booth. We could, of course, reach the same result through the transactional perspective—for it would be odd if the party and its candidates did not share consultants or engage in other obvious forms of transactional coordination. But we see no reason to insist on a pointless ritual when the link between candidates and political parties is plain to anybody with common sense.

This point is already recognized by existing law. All contributors of more than $200 per year to a political party must currently disclose those gifts—even if parties spend the money on issue advocacy without explicitly endorsing candidates. Such requirements would be unconstitutional if applied to organizations that were truly independent of candidates. But nobody has ever raised a constitutional challenge—since the linkage is so obvious. Our new rules should also pass constitutional muster for the same reason. No sensible court will allow candidates to defeat the donation booth by pretending that their political party is an independent strategic player.[20]

A harder question is how far courts will allow Congress to regulate non-party organizations on the ground that they too have as their "major purpose . . . the nomination or election of a candidate."[21] There are obvious dangers involved in granting the FEC a roving commission to determine the "major purpose" of organizations on a case-by-case basis. The very effort to target some groups will predictably generate cries of political partisanship. And the determination of "major purpose" can too easily degenerate into an ad hoc, and potentially arbitrary, process.

Rules help channel discretion, and the FEC has recently sought comments on a proposed rule designed to clarify what types of organizations trigger "major purpose regulation."[22] But our model statute relies principally on a very different approach. Rather than placing the burden on the FEC, we give incentives to interest groups to identify themselves when their major purpose is the election of candidates. Recall that voluntary associations may qualify for Patriot dollars by registering patriotic PACs and soliciting for funds. These PACs, however, cannot spend their Patriots themselves, but can only pass them along to the candidates of their choice. They are, in short, organizations whose "major purpose . . . is the nomination or election of a candidate." As a consequence, we give all organizations a choice—if they do not wish to solicit Patriot dollars, they are free to raise private funds outside the donation booth; but if they wish to organize a patriotic PAC to obtain public dollars, then this PAC can obtain private funds only through the donation booth, because it is, by definition, a PAC that falls within *Buckley*'s regulatory rationale.[23]

Of course, some voluntary organizations will respond by organizing two PACs—one that receives patriotic money, and another that solicits private money for independent advocacy. If this second PAC is truly independent of the first, it remains perfectly free to solicit unlimited funds from named donors, without recourse to the secret donation booth.

But the second PAC must be truly independent. The Sierra Club's "issue advocacy fund" cannot coordinate with any candidate or any other organization that has opted to receive Patriot dollars—including the Sierra Club's Patriot fund. There are already prophylactic rules to stop individual entities from nominally propagating many PACs to end run current contribution limits.[24] And a combination of these rules and our expanded anticoordination rules should suffice to deter such shenanigans.

We have no doubt that some voluntary organizations will establish truly independent PACs for issue advocacy. Although these groups may well play important roles in particular races, their overall impact will be rather small—as long as they comply with restrictions based on their "major purpose," their ongoing "coordination" with candidates, and their "express advocacy" of particular candidacies.

Plugging the Dike?

We do not minimize the ongoing regulatory work required to protect the integrity of the system. Do newly sophisticated bombing strategies make a change in the stratospheric contribution limits imperative? How should stopgap regulations be modified in the light of the most recent scheme to coordinate pseudoindependent expenditures?

These questions will not only tax the regulatory intelligence of our new Federal Election Commission. They will also test the FEC's political fortitude—for major politicians and big givers will be seeking to undermine it at every step. We confront this problem in the next chapter, and propose new ways to assure the FEC's independence.

Assume, for the moment, that we are successful, and that the FEC proves to be an energetic dike-mender. If this turns out to be right, there is nothing troubling about the never-ending prospect of sophisticated check-bombing and tragicomical shenanigans surrounding pseudoindependent advocacy. To the contrary, we are almost inclined to celebrate these ongoing evasions as reflecting a larger truth about life in a liberal democracy. As long as we are committed to both market freedom and democratic legitimacy, there can be no hope of liberating ourselves from the tensions generated by our conflicting ideals. Yet it is better to live with the tension than to abolish either of our basic commitments.

During much of the twentieth century, progressives tended to overestimate the capacities of democratic government to control the market for the public good. But as a new century dawns, we confront a different danger—a skepticism that challenges the very possibility of democratic progress (that precious word).

This is the reason why we have taken the hydraulic critique so seriously. But we hope you are convinced by our response. The rich and powerful will undoubtedly adapt to the new paradigm, and salvage some of their existing influence. But they will not unleash forces that entirely overwhelm our market-channeling reforms.

Our regulations of last resort will not perfectly plug the dike. And the resulting leakages will disappoint the utopian aspirations secretly shared by most hardened skeptics. But the new paradigm can redeem a more modest hope—that the American people may rejuvenate the spirit of liberal democracy for a new generation.

9 | Safeguarding the Guardians

A serious reform effort will invariably encounter powerful resistance. However pretty the new paradigm looks on paper, political forces will try to undermine its real-world operation. Unless we block these predictable counterthrusts, we will be writing yet another chapter in the sorry history of reform—good intentions once again defeated by the organized power of political and economic self-interest. Can sound institutional design promise relief from the remorseless cycle of hope and despair?

Agency Takeover?

The key pressure point will be the new Federal Election Commission. If candidates think that they can cheat on finances, and then use their extra money to win elections, and then pressure the FEC to suppress awkward investigations into their conduct, many politicians will walk this winding path—and those who resist may reconsider when they are defeated by cynical opponents who come out ahead. Our response is to insulate the commission from these predictable pressures as much as our constitutional tradition permits.

But how much is that? On the level of first principles, the basic ideas motivating the separation of powers support our effort; and we have designed our model statute to avoid any doctrinal barriers that obstruct our path.

Begin with first principles. From the *Federalist Papers* onward, American constitutional thought has taken a complicated view of man as a political animal. On the one hand, ambitious men and women *will* exploit opportunities for self-aggrandizement provided by the institutional structure, and if we give them enough rope, they will hang us. But on the other hand, we should not view the political class as if it were largely composed of predatory monsters. Many leaders are genuinely concerned with the public good, and if we do not tempt them too severely, they will act according to their better angels, at least most of the time. The aim, famously, is to design structures that set ambition against ambition so as to bring the temptations of political power within tolerable limits—to economize on virtue, and thereby encourage all of us to make the most of the little we possess.[1]

We begin with the crucial question of personnel: How to identify a group of men and women whose interests and ambitions will lead them to resist the temptation to turn a blind eye to illegalities perpetrated by powerful donors and candidates?

The best group of potential watchdogs, we think, are retired judges. Our model statute requires that all five members of the new FEC will previously have served as federal judges long enough to qualify for a full judicial pension. When nominated by the president, and confirmed by the Senate, commissioners must resign from the judiciary and devote themselves exclusively to the FEC. (They will, of course, continue to receive their judicial pensions in addition to their salaries.)

These seasoned professionals have reached an age when they no longer lust after high political office, but we do not suppose them to be selfless creatures.[2] Assured of comfortable salaries and pensions, they will still lust after fame—and seek to ensure that their names receive honorable mention in the annals of the republic.

The use of fame as a motivator was well known to the Founders.[3] Like every other human passion, its pursuit has a dark side—it can, for example, tempt a president to dangerous overseas adventures in a vainglorious effort to redeem his reputation before the high court of History. But in the present context, an appeal to fame is just what Dr. Madison ordered. Retired federal judges, after all, *are* aware of our great constitutional legacy, and *are* alive to the honor that goes with making a genuine contribution to its sustenance. They have also been socialized into the cast of mind necessary for the successful operation of the FEC—cultivating habits of impartiality in the name of the rule of law. If they cannot transcend the temptations of party and seek to apply the new campaign contributions law impartially, who can be trusted to do so?

We are dealing with human beings, not syllogisms, and there can be no guarantee of success. In spite of their training, and the risk of demonization in the history books, commissioners may succumb to temptation and abandon serious efforts at impartial and energetic law enforcement—using their power to engage in the time-honored exercise of punishing political foes and rewarding old friends.

But this doesn't seem very likely—especially because we are confiding responsibility not to a single person but to a board of five members, each serving a single nonrenewable term of ten years. As long as the founding commissioners are selected wisely and set the FEC on a strong initial course, it will be tough for succeeding presidents and Senates to undermine the agency by searching the senior judiciary for its most partisan members and pushing them onto the commission despite protests from the larger public.[4] To make it even tougher, our statute creates a staggered appointment schedule, under which one seat on the commission opens up every two years. This means that the same political coalition would need to control both the presidency and the Senate for six years before it could pack the commission with a strongly partisan majority.

If all goes well, our new agency chiefs will display two important characteristics. They will be nonpartisan—concerned with the impartial implementation of the law. And they will be decisive—engaging in the ongoing oversight necessary to assure the integrity of the system.

Members of the existing FEC are selected for very different traits. Current law creates an agency with six commissioners and requires that three members come from each major party.[5] Each commissioner is thereby invited to think of himself as part of a bloc whose main mission is to protect party interests. This effect is enhanced by the even number of commissioners— at least one member of each party bloc must join a 4–2 majority before any action can be undertaken.

This is a recipe not for impartiality but for something very different— call it bipartisanship. The structure encourages initiatives that entrench the leadership of both parties from challenge by insurgents or third parties.[6] Any proposal that damages the interests of leading politicians of either party will be greeted skeptically, and embraced only if it promises to do more damage to the rival party—in which case it is likely to be vetoed by the other three-member bloc. The existing structure also generates indecisiveness, virtually guaranteeing administrative failure on a broad front.[7] "With no constituency, little money and few friends . . . [it is] an agency whose administrative decisions are vilified by politicians, ridiculed by lawyers and overturned by courts."[8]

But there is no reason to suppose that our new commission will continue this dismal performance. To be sure, the Supreme Court's shocking decision in *Bush v. Gore* has shaken the public's confidence in the impartiality of judges on high-stakes electoral matters. But the situation of our commissioners will be very different. We are not inviting them to rush into the fray after the election has occurred. They will never be placed in the tempting position of directly naming the president. Nor will their judgment be clouded by a desire to retire from the Supreme Court under an ideologically compatible administration. They will have retired already, and their concern will be focused on the integrity of the process before the votes are counted. No single decision of theirs will determine the winner; and every decision will be scrutinized by all sides for potential unfairness. Within this environment, most retired judges will have their eyes on the history books, and will seek to discharge their duties with impartiality and decisiveness.

These virtues will be especially important, for our reliance on the policy tool of donor anonymity places a heavy burden upon the agency. Donors to blind trusts must have confidence that the trustees are not putting the money into their own pockets, or diverting it to rival candidates. And the same is true for patriotic contributors—because, for anticorruption reasons, they too will be unable to trace their contributions.

We do not expect a bunch of elderly judges to take primary responsibility for the hands-on operation of complex operational tasks. But we do expect them to provide a crucial buffer against political pressures when it comes to selecting the chief officers of the agency's operational divisions. Although the president and the Senate will be fully involved in the appointment of the five retired judges, they will not have a direct say in the selection of the agency's key bureau chiefs. Instead, the five judges will have the sole authority to make these appointments, without any vetting by Congress or the president.

In spite of our statutory effort to insulate these key appointments from direct political control, the FEC will undoubtedly be buffeted by intense informal pressures. The bureaucrats operating the Patriot program and the system of secret donation booths will have real power over the electoral fates of every politico in Washington, D.C., and beyond—and it is only natural that the politicos will try their hardest to get their buddies into the key posts. Will the members of the FEC have enough backbone to resist?

Compared with this question, all others are unimportant. There can be no serious doubt about the constitutionality of insulating these key FEC appointments from presidential and senatorial review. The Constitution explicitly says that "the appointment of . . . inferior officers"—in our case, the principal bureaucrats serving the five commissioners—need not be vested in the president and the Senate but may instead be placed exclusively in the "Heads of Departments" whenever Congress thinks this is "proper." And there is ample precedent establishing that Congress may use this constitutional provision to vest appointive authority in an independent agency like the FEC.[9] The issue is not constitutional power but whether the five retired judges on the commission will make good use of it.

The commission's main hiring responsibility will be to fill three top posts. One will be charged with the task of managing Patriot, one with operating the donation booth, one with law enforcement. Neither Patriot nor the donation division is expected to fulfill its mission with its own personnel. Each will be encouraged to contract with existing governmental and private institutions. But when all is said and done, the task of the chief operating officers will not be easy. And the statute provides that they, and their top associates, should be compensated accordingly—at the same level as the salary received by the chairman of the Federal Reserve Board.[10] With the political stakes so high, the commission should be in a position to bid for the most honest and competent executives in public or private life. To further secure their authority, all division heads are guaranteed six-year terms in office, subject to termination for cause as determined by a majority of the FEC.[11]

The statute also creates an enforcement division consisting of trained examiners who will make frequent and unannounced inspection visits to the operating divisions, and their private and governmental affiliates. We envision this branch following the traditional practice of the comptroller of the currency—running spot checks, without notice, on the banks under its jurisdiction.[12]

By separating enforcement from the operating divisions, we aim to create a functional system of checks and balances. Enforcement has no incentive to cover up operational blunders; to the contrary, the quicker errors are detected and cured, the better the bureau looks. The more vigorous the bureau, the greater the pressure on the Patriot and donation divisions to avoid the sanctions generated by incompetence or breaches of trust.

The head of the enforcement division will be the agency's general counsel. Our model statute grants him power to act effectively without kowtowing to the attorney general. After all, the attorney general is the president's appointee, and the president has the most to gain from suppressing any investigation into the financial underpinnings of his recent electoral victory. If there is any area ripe for special statutory protection of prosecutorial independence, this is it.[13]

As Kenneth Starr has recently brought to everybody's attention, the Supreme Court has upheld the constitutionality of a statute creating a prosecutorial arm that is virtually independent of supervision by the executive branch.[14] But we do not choose to push the Supreme Court's case law to its utmost limit. Our model statute grants the general counsel full independence to investigate any matter within the FEC's jurisdiction, but it does not authorize criminal indictments without giving the attorney general an opportunity to review (and veto) the general counsel's prosecutorial decisions. If the attorney general wishes to overrule the counsel's request to indict a violator, he must do so promptly and in a public document explaining his grounds for intervening. This publicity requirement will force any attorney general to think long and hard before exercising his prerogative. The public reaction to high-visibility suppression of an FEC prosecution is likely to be furious: "Why is the administration attempting this desperate cover up?"[15] No attorney general will provoke a hailstorm of criticism unless the commission has discredited itself by its own blatantly partisan behavior. It will make sense for the attorney general to block a prosecution only if he is intervening to prevent a deplorable political vendetta.

Budgetary Counterattack?

Assume that we have accomplished our first mission. The commission has earned a reputation for impartial and effective execution of the new campaign laws. Politicians and donors have learned that crime doesn't pay, and the few who haven't gotten the message find out the hard way.

We are not out of the woods. The commission's success may only drive established political and economic interests to more devious methods. Why not starve the agency of funds? Congress has often used its fiscal powers as a club to batter agencies into line when they offend powerful interests.[16] A senator or representative can be expected to swing this club in the commission's direction whenever its general counsel begins a truly independent investigation into the dark side of the legislator's own campaign finances.

The fiscal threat is magnified by the terrible procedures used by Congress when it makes its annual appropriations. During good years Congress passes most of its thirteen major appropriations bills in a mindless rush to meet the fiscal deadline of October 1. During bad years, most of these bills are wrapped up into a gigantic "omnibus" law and passed under conditions that allow for almost no meaningful oversight of last-minute changes.[17]

This is a recipe for disaster. No senator or representative will gladly take the heat for starving the FEC to death, but many will happily overlook a last-minute killer amendment that strangles the agency in retribution for some threatening act of political independence. Assaults on the agency will not be lost forever in the fog of fiscal detail surrounding the passage of an omnibus bill, which sometimes runs to four thousand pages.[18] But when the sneak attack comes to light, investigative reporters may find it hard to determine who did what during the midnight session when the commission was skewered by the quiet introduction of section 7422(G)(11)(a)(iv) into the omnibus. As the finger-pointing and evasion proceed, the fiscal fact of the matter remains—starved of funds, the FEC becomes a paper tiger, and Congress dallies until the commission makes it clear that it is calling off sensitive investigations.

This scenario need not actually occur before it has a chilling effect. A commission composed of worldly-wise retired judges will anticipate the problem, pull its punches, and see its reputation as a watchdog slowly disintegrate.

There is only one way out: Insulate the agency's budget from annual congressional review. There are many precedents. Social Security provides a useful example. Congress does not dole out money for this "entitlement program" on a year-to-year basis. It passes a framework statute that endures beyond a single congressional session and serves as a token of its lasting commitment to the program. Rather than reopening the fiscal foundations of pensions annually, the framework statute instructs the treasury to pay whatever it takes to redeem the pensions promised all qualifying workers.[19]

We propose the same for Patriot. Every time a citizen goes to an ATM and votes her Patriot dollars, her decision will operate as a command to the treasury to pay the amount to her favorite candidate or political organization. Each citizen's right to Patriot dollars, no less than her right to a pension, should be put beyond the vagaries of normal politics—and for many of the same reasons. Just as ordinary Americans should be encouraged to plan for the future in the secure knowledge that Congress won't be playing around with Social Security, they should have the same degree of confidence in the stability of campaign finance. After all, if politicians suspect that Congress can pull the financial plug on Patriot in the near future, they will continue to curry favor with big economic interests—whose deep pockets will provide them with political insurance if patriotic finance proves ephemeral. Only if politicians expect Patriot to continue indefinitely will they shift decisively into a new politics that is respectful of the financial power of the sovereign citizenry.

An enduring appropriations statute is likely to breed a "virtuous cycle" that makes underfunding less likely over time. When politicians are convinced that patriotic finance is here to stay, they will master the new fundraising techniques required, and once they learn to win under the new rules, they will be reluctant to consider another round of sweeping revisions— why change the patriotic game, when they have managed to win?

Politicians will become even more reluctant as ordinary citizens come to appreciate their new power over campaign finance. Once Americans are in the habit of voting with dollars, only a brave representative or senator will try to take this privilege away from them. And this act of bravery will increasingly look foolhardy to legislators who have mastered the new system. In short, an initial decision by Congress to insulate Patriot from annual appropriations will increasingly insulate the initiative from political pressure over time.

Legally speaking, Congress remains free to reshape Patriot or change the statutory formula governing appropriations to individual accounts. But at least these revisions will come not during a midnight session on an omnibus appropriations measure but after a high-visibility debate—with a majority taking full responsibility for their votes before their constituents.

In dealing with appropriations, we have been focusing on Patriot for one simple reason—it is our big-ticket item. But the same logic leads us to insulate the rest of the commission's budget. The cost of administering the secret donation booth, for example, may look small compared with the multibillion appropriation required for patriotic finance, but it is also subject to midnight raids during the annual appropriation ritual. Some incumbents may find it to their advantage to starve agency oversight over the blind trusts—enabling their friends to bribe administrators to pass on precious information detailing how much particular donors are giving. Once they have corrupted the trustees, donors will jack up their contributions—for they have now restored the prospect of a quid pro quo. Only a well-funded enforcement effort will deter wide-scale bribery and make it possible to detect and prosecute the occasional rotten trustee with speed and dispatch. Because the basic arguments should be clear by now, we leave the statutory details to Part III.[20]

Crime and Punishment

We have been searching for middle ground. We have distanced ourselves considerably from the standard administrative agency—controlled by ordinary political appointees and disciplined by the whiplash of annual congressional appropriations. But we have not tried to scale the Olympian heights of total political independence. Our panel of retired federal judges gain their ten-year terms as commissioners only after presidential nomination and senatorial confirmation. And Congress and the president retain the power to rein in the agency if they are willing to take the heat required to change the FEC's framework statute, including its continuing appropriations provisions, in a high-visibility way. But if things go well, the practical political independence of our FEC will be considerable—similar to that enjoyed by the Federal Reserve Board within its own distinctive domain.

Independence of this magnitude would be intolerable if the agency were operating under the old paradigm. As we have seen, traditional reformers are committed to a style of command and control that tends to proliferate detailed regulations into every nook and cranny of the fund-raising process. If our FEC were charged with such a task, Ken Starr lookalikes would play an ongoing role at the center of American politics. Given the inevitably amateurish character of political campaigns, each election day would serve as the prelude for yet another series of prosecutorial investigations. As the general counsel's office examines the books of winners and losers, most leading politicians would find themselves in the dock: "Would Senator So-and-so please explain how he could possibly have allowed some callow twenty-seven-year-old in his office to accept three $1,000 checks from the same person, thereby implicating himself in an influence-peddling scandal involving gifts that were three times the legal limit?" And on and on—for years after the election results are a dim memory.

Little wonder, then, that the existing FEC is such a paper tiger. If it ever got serious, it would chew up the reputations of most politicians—even if most investigations did not culminate in indictments, the steady stream of notables into the prosecutor's office would be enough to generate ceaseless leaks and innuendos.

Our reconstruction of the FEC makes sense only in terms of the larger reorientation envisioned by the new paradigm. With Patriot and the donation booth serving as the main instruments of reform, we can afford to eliminate almost all command and control and reserve our criminal sanctions to a few simple requirements: Don't bribe Patriot holders. Don't accept any cash or checks from anybody—tell them to send it to you via the secret donation booth. Apart from these easy-to-understand rules, only a few of the very richest contributors will require the help of a lawyer to comply with the stratospheric contribution limits that remain in place.[21]

The most sensitive remaining area will concern groups devoted to independent issue advocacy. As we have seen, politicians may sabotage the donation booth by telling donors to contribute funds to organizations that claim independence but are covertly controlled by the candidate's campaign. As a consequence, the commission must be on constant lookout for creative efforts to create sham independence, and other forms of covert coordination by candidates and donors intent on evading the anonymity barrier. This will sometimes require contentious prosecutorial scrutiny into politically sensitive relationships.

To check the potential for abuse, our model statute provides for a carefully modulated response: The general counsel can demand penal sanctions only if sham organizations proliferate to the point at which they threaten the integrity of the donation booth; if evasions are rare, penalties will be restricted to (large) monetary fines.

To decide whether to ratchet up penalties, the commission is instructed to consult data it is already collecting as part of the ongoing regulatory effort. The agency will be constantly monitoring aggregate levels of expenditure on independent advocacy to assure that private money does not swamp patriotic contributions. After each election, it will use this information to help determine whether the ratio of public to private finance has fallen below 2 to 1, and if this happens, the FEC will increase the number of Patriot dollars going to each citizen for the next election. We are now in a position to see the need for the construction of an additional ratio. This one splits the flow of private money into two components and compares the amount flowing into independent issue advocacy with the flow through the donation booth. If this ratio reveals a sudden shift away from the donation booth, there is reason to fear that candidates and contributors are conspiring to undermine the entire system by proliferating modes of sham independence. This is the time to announce a crackdown and threaten jail terms for the most egregious violators.[22]

As long as the data demonstrate the existence of a serious problem, the commission should be able to gain the public support required for an aggressive enforcement campaign. And this should be enough of a deterrent to induce many big givers and getters to retreat from the cynical use of pseudo-independent advocacy as an evasive technique—clearing the way for prosecuting hardcore violators.

This cautious use of the criminal sanction contrasts sharply with the current regime. Although the most honorable politician now has a hard time keeping up with the proliferating web of commands and controls, she can confidently stay clear of our regulations of last resort. She simply must refuse to set up phony advocacy groups and just say no to shady consultants who offer to serve as covert intermediaries to "independent" advocacy groups. By dramatically restricting the use of criminal sanctions, the new paradigm makes it realistic to create a commission with sufficient prestige and autonomy to bring prosecutions where they remain necessary.

Less is more.

We have been circling our subject. Part I provided a general overview, and we have now completed a more elaborate inspection tour: exploratory funds, patriotic finance, donation booth, regulations of last resort, the new election commission. We shall soon be cycling through the model statute to gain a different sense of the whole—and whether it is more or less than the sum of its parts.

But this is a good time to stand back and consider some larger themes: Does the new paradigm break through the constitutional conundrums that have blocked decisive reform in the past? Will it really facilitate a more democratic politics in the future?

10 Who's Afraid of the Supreme Court?

We have been walking a winding path. In the beginning, it was enough to challenge the old paradigm and glimpse the possibility of a new approach. We then set to work designing a realistic scheme that might actually restore real political sovereignty to ordinary Americans. As we blazed the trail from theory to practice, the Supreme Court sometimes crossed our path—forcing us to an accommodation with one or another legal doctrine. But at no point did the Court appear as an insuperable road-block to reform.

The Court's marginal role contrasts sharply to its traditional position under the old paradigm. Traditional reformers see the justices not as minor nuisances but as major antagonists. They regularly denounce the Court's leading decision, *Buckley v. Valeo*, as "wrong headed (not to say bone-headed)" or, worse yet, a "20th-century stepchild to Dred Scott."[1]

Demonization may be cathartic, but it serves as a prelude for a despairing diagnosis of real-world prospects. Although old paradigmers fervently pray for deliverance from *Buckley*, the Supreme Court shows no sign of converting to the reform faith. To be sure, some of the fiercest resistance comes from hard-right justices of the Reagan and Bush eras.[2] Lest reformers suppose that better times are coming, they need only glance at relative new-comers like Stephen Breyer. This centrist Clinton appointee quickly wrote an important opinion affirming and extending key aspects of *Buckley*.[3] If real reform must await a radical change in Supreme Court membership, we may be waiting for quite some time.

And during this extended interregnum, partisans of the old paradigm offer a pretty dismal prospect. The best we can hope for is a long slog through the trenches as we try to persuade the Court to uphold one or another form of command and control despite *Buckley*-ite anxieties. Suppose, for example, McCain-Feingold's effort to eliminate soft money to political parties survives attack in the courts. Surely nobody believes that this will revolutionize the current system—contributions to political parties may decline, but big donors will still find many ways to channel large sums to candidates.[4]

This means that reformers will return to Congress and begin agitating for a new round of more exigent regulations—hoping against hope that the Court will not make it impossible to turn the screw a bit tighter. And on and on, one small step at a time, as generation after generation marches into the sunset awaiting the great day when the Supreme Court finally repudiates *Buckley,* and "real reform" can begin at last.

We reject this grim scenario. We refuse to displace our hopes for real reform onto a remote future. It is within our own power to make a major advance. To make this clear, our model statute conforms in all respects to prevailing judicial doctrine. Our initiative might be improved further if the Court allowed us to nibble around the edges of existing doctrine—and we mark these points in our statutory commentary. But such second-order matters should not obscure the main point: If Americans take the path marked out by the new paradigm, the Supreme Court will not stand in the way of a major breakthrough for democracy. There is absolutely nothing to stop citizens from reclaiming their sovereignty—other than a lack of political will and imagination.

Demonizing the Court not only leads to despair. It also makes it impossible to confront *Buckley's* concerns in an open-minded way. It is easy to object to many of the Court's particular line-drawing exercises. But it is not easy to dismiss some of its underlying anxieties. Rather than likening *Buckley* to *Dred Scott,* reformers should face up to some serious weaknesses in their traditional approach and reconsider their long day's journey into the juridical night.

Buckley's Unanswered Question

Old paradigmers hate *Buckley* because it raises constitutional barriers to their favorite remedy—ever-more-stringent limits on the amount of private money that contributors can give and candidates can spend. Before considering the merits of their complaints, we want to emphasize a less-noted aspect of reigning doctrine. Although the Court is skeptical about restrictions on private money, it is remarkably accommodating where governmental subsidies are concerned. When it comes to adding public money, rather than subtracting private cash, *Buckley* gives Congress a remarkably free hand.

This is good news for Patriot—which is simply an innovative way of channeling government subsidies in the service of citizen sovereignty. But quite apart from our own proposal, this neglected aspect of *Buckley* raises a larger question: Is the Court right in suggesting that serious campaign reform should not happen without a significant injection of public funds?

During the past few years, practical reformers on Capitol Hill have ignored this message, preferring to demonize the messenger. Their refusal to emphasize the need for federal subsidy is explained by their reading of the present political situation. Since the Republicans took control of Congress in 1994, they have made their opposition to "handouts" for politicians unmistakably clear.[5] Rather than challenge the reigning prejudice against subsidies, activists have fashioned a command-and-control agenda that panders to prevailing tastes. But this short-term strategy is short-sighted. If a heavy reliance on command and control is misconceived, it would be better for real reformers to refuse to play the shell game on Capitol Hill, and to engage in an energetic campaign of political education.

We urge progressives to take a page out of the conservative playbook and consider the story of their successful agitation for a "voucher" solution to the problem of public education. Only a decade ago the idea of replacing public schooling with a system of parental vouchers would have been casually dismissed as a notion from the radical fringe, out of sync with "political realities." But no longer. The voucher idea can be compelling if it is placed at the service of a cogent political vision.[6] Rather than spending so much time and energy trying to overrule *Buckley*, wouldn't it be more profitable to take the path marked out by *Buckley* and seek to persuade the public that the now-familiar voucher idea—in the form of Patriot dollars—serves as the best path to genuine reform?

CONTROLLING CREEPING PLUTOCRACY

Buckley does more than secure the constitutional foundations for the Patriot program. It explicitly authorizes the use of public subsidies as a powerful tool for shaping the conditions of political access to private money. The *Buckley* Court considered the question in connection with the existing public subsidy for presidential campaigns. Under this familiar system, presidential hopefuls do not have an unconditional right to obtain federal funds to support their electoral efforts. After establishing that they have substantial popular support, they are put to a choice: They can either apply for the subsidy or try to raise unlimited sums of private money, but not both.[7] If they take federal funds in the primary, they must limit the amount of private money they can raise and spend.[8] Accepting the subsidy for the general election requires them to waive all rights to raise private money—the federal subsidy becomes their fund-raising ceiling.[9]

The Court upheld this waiver arrangement, and the statutory mechanism has been broadly effective. Only four Presidential candidates—John Connally, Ross Perot, Steve Forbes, and last but not least, George W. Bush—have found it worthwhile to spurn federal funds and depend exclusively on private resources (though Bush did so only during the primary phase of the campaign).[10] To be sure, all candidates have been remarkably assiduous in devising legal loopholes that permit their political parties and other interests to raise additional private funds on their behalf. But as a matter of constitutional doctrine, the waiver technique remains a powerful method of shaping access to private funds.

Our model statute reinvigorates *Buckley*'s waiver doctrine by placing it within the new reform framework. Our target is the increasing number of superrich candidates who take advantage of existing law to spend their own money without limit as a means of compensating for their lack of political experience or insight. We have not yet seen a political amateur like Forbes or Perot buy himself the White House. But the drift toward plutocracy is unmistakable, and we join critics of *Buckley*'s grant to billionaires of a constitutional right to crush their competition under an avalanche of cash.

And yet new paradigmers have better things to do than wait for the Court to change its mind. Paradoxically, we need look no farther than *Buckley* itself to find a practical cure for the decision's self-inflicted wound. The opinion expressly authorizes Congress to offer plutocrats a deal: The government will give them subsidies provided that they waive their right to spend freely from their bottomless bank accounts. The Court's message is clear: If you want to curb plutocracy, use carrots, not sticks.

Patriot offers a far more tempting carrot than the small potatoes offered up to candidates today. Under the existing regime, presidential hopefuls make their waiver decisions at two stages—first at the primaries and then at the general election. If they refuse federal money at one stage, they are free to accept it at the other.[11] This means that during the crucial primary season, our hypothetical plutocrat need only sacrifice $34 million of federal money if she wishes to raise unlimited private funds. If she waives this subsidy, she may gain a decisive competitive advantage over poorer rivals—because their private fund-raising ability continues to be restricted once they accept federal money. As a consequence, our free-spending plutocrat may find herself in the delightful position of burying her opponents under a media onslaught they cannot afford to answer.

Patriot makes it far more dangerous for an ambitious plutocrat to remain outside the subsidy program. If she insists on unlimited self-financing, it will be much harder to outspend opponents who are fishing in the multibillion dollar patriotic pool. Not only will the plutocrat's decision to spurn the pool allow her opponents to fish for Patriot dollars that would otherwise have gone to her, but it will also provide them a new and appealing message: "Fellow citizens, don't let our competitor buy this election. Send your Patriot dollars to us and send a message to her—America is not for sale!"

Our free-spending plutocrat will always be at liberty to counterattack: "Unlike my opponents, I refuse to feed at the federal trough. I am putting my money where my mouth is, and appeal for money only from supporters who are willing to contribute their own hard-earned cash through the secret donation booth. This kind of self-reliance is precisely the thing that the American people want from their representatives in Washington, D.C. So vote for the candidate whose campaign is run with real money from real people, not play money devised by Washington bureaucrats and ivory-tower eggheads."

The citizenry's response to these competing messages will serve as an ongoing referendum on Patriot. If most Americans come to value Patriot dollars as a genuine tool for citizen sovereignty, plutocratic counterspinning will prove pointless. Or even counterproductive—because the plutocratic critique can readily be interpreted as an insult to ordinary Americans, disparaging their right to participate effectively in democratic life.

Of course, it is always possible that the plutocratic counteroffensive will succeed—persuading most Americans to leave their Patriot accounts untouched and allow free-spending billionaires to dominate the political playing field. Perhaps democracy won't come to an end if plutocrats do succeed in buying their way into office from time to time. But if this happens frequently, we would certainly consider it definitive proof that our initiative has failed.

Which is okay by us. The best we can do is to provide ordinary Americans with tools that allow for the reinvigoration of their collective commitment to citizen sovereignty. It is up to them to decide whether these tools are worth using—or indeed, whether the entire democratic project has a future.

One thing is clear. Even if most free-spending billionaires are defeated by patriotic antagonists, others will keep on trying to buy their way into high office. To see why, imagine that you had a hundred million dollars to burn and that your name was completely unknown among the general public. If you want to get anywhere quickly in politics, your only hope is to spend your own money, because your appeal for Patriot dollars will go unnoticed. So you resist patriotic temptation and proudly invoke your constitutional right to spend your riches for the public good. The mere fact that previous plutocrats have failed surely doesn't mean that you will!

We welcome these occasional challenges. It is a good thing for the premises of any system to be questioned from time to time—once the new paradigm is given a decent trial, we are content to let the system survive only as long as it can maintain popular support. What is more, the entry of an occasional free-spending billionaire will greatly enhance the legal defense of our model statute. Opponents will seek to take advantage of some lower federal court rulings which have sought to limit the range of *Buckley*'s waiver rationale.[12]

These decisions respond to recent state legislation which tries to compensate for a weakness in traditional approaches. Most state subsidy programs require candidates to forgo private fund-raising in exchange for taxpayer money—thereby exposing them to advertising blitzes by free-spending candidates who reject the subsidy. To level the playing field, reformers have recently added an ingenious triggering mechanism: If any of a candidate's opponents refuses to participate in the public-financing scheme and tries to spend his way to victory, the state responds by increasing the level of subsidy for the candidate who has agreed to restrict his private expenditures.

To which his free-spending competitors have predictably cried "foul." They emphasize that the Supreme Court did grant them a constitutional right to engage in their free-spending ways, and argue that the new triggering mechanism makes these rights meaningless—especially if they allow subsidized candidates to match private superexpenditures on a dollar-for-dollar basis. If the free spenders can never gain any competitive advantage from their private fund-raising, the triggering mechanism has made it pointless to remain outside the subsidized system. But if this is true, it is no longer appropriate to speak of the rich "waiving" their rights to spend freely. The new triggering mechanism is simply coercing everybody into the subsidy system, and the *Buckley* Court never intended its talk about "waiver" to cover such coercive measures.

Whatever the constitutional merits of this line of attack, it has no application to our model statute.[13] The Patriot system does not require an elaborate triggering mechanism to enable subsidized candidates to overcome any "unfair advantage" obtained by rich candidates who spend "too much" of their own money. It leaves it up to the good sense of individual Patriot holders to decide whether to counteract a free-spending plutocrat's cash offensive by giving more Patriot dollars to candidates who have waived their free-spending privileges in exchange for the right to fish in the patriotic pool. If the citizenry responds by opening up its patriotic pursestrings, the free-spending candidate should be the last to complain. He is the one, after all, who is insisting on his fundamental right to spend as much of his own money as he wishes. Shouldn't he recognize that his fellow citizens have an equally fundamental right to spend their 50 Patriot dollars as they wish?

To put the point more legalistically, our model statute organizes the waiver transaction in precisely the same way as the presidential subsidy program upheld in *Buckley*. As in that case, we offer all candidates an identical option—either they may enter the subsidy program and voluntarily restrict their private cash expenditures, or they may spend as much of their personal fortunes as they like. The only difference is how the subsidy program structures this choice: While the existing system gives candidates a fixed amount of subsidy, the new paradigm makes the total subsidy depend on the candidate's success in appealing to Patriot holders. This is a big difference for policy purposes, but it makes no constitutional difference in the legal analysis of the waiver issue.

If anything, the constitutional question raised by the model statute is even easier to resolve. Under the traditional presidential subsidy, a rich candidate opting into the system must rely almost exclusively on her federal funds during the general election—she cannot raise any funds from other citizens and can spend only a limited amount of her own money.[14] In contrast, our statute not only allows candidates to dig quite deeply into their own pockets.[15] It also permits them to make a broad appeal for private funds as long as they use the secret donation booth. If *Buckley* upheld a waiver of all access to private funds, surely it supports this very limited waiver.

So the first plank of the new paradigm is constitutionally secure. Existing doctrine not only authorizes subsidy programs like Patriot. It affirmatively supports our efforts to make Patriot into a potent tool for combating plutocracy.

It's time to turn to the constitutional issues raised by our new approach to private giving.

FREE SPEECH?

Once again, we find ourselves on easy street. Begin with the Court's core constitutional doctrine. Much to the dismay of old paradigmers, the justices have been very tough on reform measures, repeatedly striking down one or another effort to restrict private contributions and expenditures. Progressive lawyers have responded with brave efforts to deflect the flow of negative precedents and maintain the constitutional respectability of the old paradigm. But all this bobbing and weaving can't disguise the hard fact of fierce judicial resistance.

Happily for us (and the reader), the new paradigm does not require this kind of fancy footwork. Despite judicial hostility on other fronts, the Court has been remarkably consistent in emphasizing that there *is* one rationale for public regulation with an impeccable constitutional pedigree. Like most sensible people, the justices are well aware that big givers can gain special influence over politicians, and they have regularly sustained legislation that can plausibly be viewed as efforts to reduce the risk—or even the appearance—of corruption.[16]

This tried-and-true rationale serves as our royal highway to constitutional legitimacy. Our approach to private giving is carefully tailored to eliminate only those donations that generate the possibility of influence peddling.

There is every reason to believe, then, that the Court will readily uphold the new paradigm against all constitutional attack.

Begin with the secret donation booth, and suppose you were considering whether to give $10,000 to support Candidate C. If you are giving the money solely because you admire C, or favor his political program, the new system should not deter you one bit. The only time you will have second thoughts is when you want special treatment—either explicitly or implicitly. If C can't be sure that you have put your money where your mouth is, he won't be very responsive to your pleas for special favors when you come around after the election. Special dealing of this kind has always been barred under the Court's corruption-fighting rationale.

We have fashioned our model statute precisely to hit our target. We simply make it a crime to hand any campaign check directly to a politician, requiring its transmission to him through the donation booth instead. We do not in any way trench upon the donor's freedom of speech. We guarantee every American the right to say anything he wants about the size and nature of his donations. You remain perfectly free to tell your favorite politician—or the world in general—that you have given $10,000 or any other number you care to name. You can even display your canceled check to the Federal Election Commission's Blind Trust. The only problem is that the trust has acknowledged your gift with a bland receipt reporting that you have contributed "more than $200," leaving it up to you to convince your beneficiary that you really have given lots more.

You'd have an easier time establishing the size of your gift if the trust had supplied a more explicit statement about the $10,000. But this isn't enough to establish a violation of the First Amendment. Although the "free speech" clause serves as a reliable shield from state suppression, it has never operated as a sword requiring the government to hand over all information in its possession. To fill this constitutional gap, the federal government and many states have passed freedom of information acts granting access. But these statutes have never granted citizens an absolute and unconditional right to all relevant information in the government's files. They very self-consciously balance the citizen's interest in information against the need to protect a wide array of competing state interests—ranging from national security, to privacy, to effective governmental operation.[17] For example, the federal Freedom of Information Act contains an exception safeguarding the secrecy of the census form that each American is required by law to complete every decade.[18] If politicians gained access to individual forms, they could communicate with their constituents in a more focused fashion, but the statute rightly subordinates this interest in political speech to each individual's right to privacy, and to the national interest in maximizing voluntary participation.

Similar trade-offs are appropriate here—though the counterbalancing interest is not personal privacy but political corruption. As long as our model statute does not suppress any individual's freedom of speech, but simply limits access to information, it is up to Congress and not the Court to serve as primary decisionmaker. The justices will defer to a good-faith congressional judgment that the policy of limited nondisclosure pursued by the blind trust serves as a potent corruption-fighting tool.

Perhaps our analysis has been too narrow. On this view, the constitutional problem is not incomplete information but misinformation. Once the secret donation booth is in place, small donors will suddenly have the ability to operate under false pretenses—by contributing $200, they will receive their receipt noting a gift of "$200 or more," and then claim credit for a $10,000 gift! Can't the big giver who has actually handed over his $10,000 protest when the state makes it so easy for others to indulge in systematic misrepresentation? Isn't it unconstitutional for the government to stand to one side and refuse to penalize such a stream of lies and exaggerations?

The short answer is No. Note that this complaint involves the generation of too much, not too little, speech. But the First Amendment is concerned only with the problem of government suppression and does not require the government to launch an aggressive campaign to purge politics of exaggeration. To the contrary, in its landmark decision of *New York Times v. Sullivan*, the Court imposed severe limits on any such campaign. Before *New York Times*, the common law of libel had served for centuries as a formidable weapon against misrepresentation in politics—allowing a wide range of litigants to recover large damages for a broad class of falsehoods and exaggerations. On first impression, it is hard to find fault with this—who can be in favor of lies? And yet the Court struck down traditional legal principles as a violation of the First Amendment—holding that the pervasive threat of lawsuits generated an unconstitutional chilling effect on vibrant democratic debate. Far better to tolerate some misrepresentation than to repress a broad swath of legitimate speech.[19]

Our model statute takes the same approach. It refuses to use the law of misrepresentation as a blunderbuss, but follows the caution of *New York Times* and seeks to keep political life free of lawsuits except for the most serious lies. Even if we had no further reason for creating an extra zone of "free speech" surrounding campaign contributions, no court in the country would second-guess this legislative decision. The Constitution serves as a floor but not a ceiling—requiring government to respect the rights of speakers in a broad variety of contexts, but never forbidding it from going further and protecting more speech than is constitutionally required.

But we are not only acting out of concern for law's "chilling effect" on politics. We are using free speech as a tool for controlling corruption. By allowing small donors to exaggerate, we undermine the capacity of big donors to obtain special influence. If we were forbidden to use free speech as an anticorruption tool, we would be required to employ command-and-control regulations to achieve this goal—regulations that would undoubtedly repress the domain of free speech, rather than expand its scope. Our decision to fight corruption by facilitating more speech, rather than less, serves as a less restrictive alternative to more speech-repressive techniques. It is certain to withstand the most searching constitutional scrutiny.[20]

FREEDOM OF ASSOCIATION?

The standard First Amendment case involves a judicial balancing act. On the one side, the Court considers how large a burden the state is imposing on the protected constitutional value; on the other, it assesses the public interest that the government is invoking to justify its controls. If the burden is sufficiently small, and the interest is sufficiently compelling, the Court will uphold the challenged regulation; if not, not.

Our free-speech analysis has been exceptionally trouble free because we could entirely avoid this classical exercise in balancing. The reason is simple: Our model statute refuses to impose *any* new restrictions on the things private citizens can say to one another. As a consequence, there was no occasion to begin balancing, because there was no effort to repress anybody's speech in the first place.

Life isn't quite so easy when we turn to the new paradigm's impact on freedom of association. Our new statute does indeed impose new limitations on this freedom, and so there will be a need for balancing. As we will show, there is no reason to fear that the balance will swing against the constitutionality of the new paradigm. Nevertheless, the very need for balancing complicates the argument.

To frame the problem, recall some basic points about the donation booth's operation. Whenever anybody wants to contribute to a campaign, he must personally deposit his gift in the mail or go to a donation booth (if it is a big gift). The politician can't do this job for the donor—it would be just too easy for her to take a peek on her way to the booth. By the same token, it is also illegal for interest groups to serve as intermediaries. Otherwise, they could undermine the secrecy of the process by verifying the gift before handing it over to the blind trust—say, by hiring a certified public accountant to inspect each check and issue a report publishing the precise amount. If the donation booth is to operate in a corruption-free way, each donor must personally send his own money to the blind trust.

It is this feature of the system—call it the requirement of personal delivery—that arguably amounts to a new restriction on freedom of association, and hence triggers the need for a classical balancing act. We say "arguably" because many lawyers will be tempted to obviate the need for balancing by recharacterizing the rights involved. They will deny that the requirement of personal delivery limits anything our tradition recognizes as freedom of association. After all, the law has always been suspicious of encounters with politicians that end up with a transfer of money. Rather than treating such meetings as an aspect of a precious constitutional heritage, bribery statutes make them into crimes without anyone raising any serious questions. From this vantage, the requirement of personal delivery is merely a new technique rendering anticorruption laws more effective. Because nobody has a right to "freedom of association" for purposes of corruption, the new restriction falls outside the zone of constitutional protection, and no further balancing is required.

Courts are likely to find this point dispositive so far as direct gifts to candidates are concerned. But the requirement of personal delivery sweeps more broadly—banning interest groups, as well as politicians, from playing the role of intermediaries. And this ban seems more difficult to justify through casuistical means.

Generally speaking, the Constitution provides a solid foundation for citizens to join together for political purposes whenever they find it convenient. And there can be no denying that such collaborations often make sense in the context of campaign contributions. By giving the money to an ideologically congenial political action committee, you can take advantage of their expertise in identifying the best uses of the money. Putting efficiency to one side, there is also an expressive dimension of a group gift that may be lacking from the individual one. When the NRA or the NAACP publicly gives $10,000 to a candidate, it is making a statement about the relation of the candidate to the Cause that cannot be readily duplicated by the same gift from an ordinary person. So it appears, in this case at least, that there is real loss in constitutional value resulting from the ban imposed by the model statute—and that some balancing is required before a final judgment can be rendered under the First Amendment.

Begin by inspecting the magnitude of the loss with some care—it is much smaller than may appear at first. Our statute only prohibits groups from creating political action committees that shunt money directly to candidates. Groups can collect as much money as they want in order to speak in their own name on the issues of the day. The NAACP or NRA remains entirely free to publicize its views on race relations or the right to bear arms—and it may purchase as much space in the media as its members' pocketbooks permit. Our statute does not touch these fundamental associational interests in expressing group commitments.

Nor does it unduly constrain opportunities for gift-giving campaigns. Groups remain free to endorse candidates and to advise their members as to which candidates most need their money. They can also engage in a host of activities that enhance the value of their endorsements—inviting a favored candidate to make a pitch for funds at membership meetings, or even providing members with preaddressed envelopes for use in making contributions. The only thing they can't do is take physical control of their members' money (or checks or credit cards) and walk the cash over to the donation booth. Only this effort to verify and guarantee member contributions threatens the corruption-control goals of the donation booth system, and only this effort is prohibited.

We have, in short, narrowly tailored our restriction to fit the particular problem—corruption control—which the Court has traditionally recognized as the primary ground for constitutionally legitimate campaign reform. We have not gone further than necessary to respond responsibly to the pervasive special-dealing that threatens to undermine the democratic process. The Court has repeatedly upheld far more severe restrictions on corruption-fighting grounds.[21]

But we have done more than merely minimize restrictions. We have simultaneously provided groups with a grand new arena for expressing their political commitments. Although corruption control eliminates interest groups as conduits of private money, the new paradigm expressly authorizes the very same groups to establish patriotic PACs, launch appeals for the new currency, and play the same role previously discharged by private-money PACs.

The birth of these new PACs should amply compensate interest groups for the minor restrictions imposed on their role in the private money market. Consider the expressive value that comes with "putting your money where your mouth is." The NAACP or NRA can no longer back up its endorsements by publicly providing candidates with 10,000 private dollars, but it can do so with a public gift of 10,000 patriotic dollars.

Of course, some organizations will do much better raising Patriot dollars than they do today raising private money, and vice versa. But this hardly suggests that the new paradigm is serving the value of freedom of association less well—only that some associations will do better, and some worse, once we have effectively restructured the system to eliminate the risk of corrupt deals between big givers and established politicians.

To make this point even stronger, recall that the flow of patriotic funds will probably be larger than the flow of private funds prevailing nowadays. Patriotic PACs will be fishing in a very big pool, and will probably be handing over bigger checks than they do today. Indeed, our model statute guarantees against a grave financial drought and provides for the effective exercise of freedom of association even under circumstances—like another great depression—which would cause private funding to dry up. Looking at the statute as a whole, any fair-minded Court should conclude that the carefully limited losses of associational freedom in the private sector are fully counterbalanced by the great gains in identical freedoms exercised in the new patriotic marketplace.[22] Call this an appeal to offsetting gains.[23]

But suppose we turn out to be wrong, and the justices refuse to consider the great patriotic gains as compensation for the new restrictions on private-money PACs. Even this drastic narrowing of focus is insufficient to condemn the constitutionality of our initiative. It means only that the analysis must finally proceed to the classic balancing question: Are the narrowly tailored constraints on freedom of association justified by the state's compelling interest in preventing the corruption of the political process?

The answer suggested by the cases is Yes. Time and again the justices have upheld restrictions that are carefully tailored responses to the threat of corruption. For example, the Court had no trouble upholding a flat ban on all direct contributions to candidates by private corporations and labor unions, and it has also approved sweeping controls on gift-giving by private interest groups.[24] If the state's interest in corruption control justifies such restrictions, it should also authorize our much more modest restrictions.[25]

Nevertheless, nothing like the new paradigm has been proposed in the past. And it is always wise to move beyond precedent when dealing with the unprecedented. The basic issue is best elaborated through our master analogy: the secret ballot. After all, this practice also restricts associational freedom—by preventing representatives of parties and interest groups from accompanying their members into the voting booth and casting their ballot for them. Nor can these organizations observe their members as they vote behind the curtain. Regardless of these plain restraints on organizational freedom, nobody would suggest that there is anything unconstitutional going on!

The same should be true here—the restriction on the power of private PACs to vote with their members' dollars is grounded on the same rationale that historically justified the introduction of the secret ballot. Indeed, the threat of corruption is even greater in the case of nonanonymous donations. Vote-buying is perforce a retail operation, but a single instance of financial corruption can affect the entire election—with a candidate selling his position in exchange for big contributions that can be turned into thousands of votes through aggressive advertising campaigns. If the secret ballot is constitutional—and who would claim otherwise?—so is the donation booth.

REGULATIONS OF LAST RESORT

We are equally confident about the judicial reception of our limitation on the expenditure that any single person can make to individual candidates—$5,000 (House), around $15,000 (Senate), $100,000 (president)—as well as an annual limit on giving of $100,000 to all candidates. These large sums contrast with the $1,000 ceiling currently imposed on gifts to candidates—which will go up to $2,000 if McCain-Feingold is enacted into law.[26] To be sure, existing law allows a donor to give $5,000 to any individual PAC—and by proliferating gifts to many PACS, it is possible to give more than the $100,000 annual limit imposed by the model statute. But this theoretical conceit is overwhelmed by the very real power that the new paradigm accords to real people who wish to give substantial sums to a few candidates. Our new statute vastly enhances the effective power of citizens "to put their money where their mouth is"—provided they are willing to filter their support through the secret donation booth. Moreover, private donors retain the right to identify themselves when giving significant sums to the candidate's exploratory committees.

We concede that our more generous limits apply to a broader range of contributions than existing law. Donations to political parties count in our calculations, while they notoriously do not count under the status quo— which allows political parties to raise unlimited amounts of soft money for political education campaigns on behalf of candidates.[27] But *Buckley's* decision to uphold the $1,000 limit was not conditioned on the availability of this soft-money exemption. The Court's opinion entirely fails to anticipate the ingenuity of latter-day fund-raisers, and treats the $1,000 limit as if it were a far more effective constraint than it has turned out to be in practice.[28] If the Court was not offended by such a low limit in *Buckley*, it is far-fetched to suppose that it would be troubled by the vast expansion of donors' freedom envisioned by the model statute.

We pause to consider an ingenious objection. Our hypothetical critic concedes that our contribution limits are in fact less restrictive of property-owners' freedom than the $1,000 limit upheld by *Buckley*. But he seeks to negate the force of this concession by an overenthusiastic embrace of our main proposal, the secret donation booth. After all, *Buckley* upheld the $1,000 limit because of its role in insulating politics against the taint of corruption. But now that the statute provides for a secret donation booth, is there any significant need for other corruption-fighting techniques? Doesn't the very success of the donation booth condemn contribution limits—even the stratospheric ones we are suggesting?

No court would buy this argument. It is true, of course, that our secrecy algorithm will make things a lot tougher for big givers to get credit from candidates. But it does remain possible for a coordinated group of givers, or even a single enormous gift, to overwhelm the secrecy algorithm that serves as our main line of defense against check-bombing raids. It is prudent for Congress to take corrective action by imposing regulations of last resort—especially to reassure ordinary citizens who are skeptical of the power of mathematics to undermine the credibility of the biggest donors.

Was *Buckley* Right?

The previous section treated constitutional doctrine as if it were an obstacle course, and showed how partisans of the new paradigm could leap over the hurdles to the finish line. But constitutional law is something more than a series of roadblocks. It is a fund of collective ideals and anxieties, and comparisons with *Dred Scott* notwithstanding, *Buckley* has something valuable to teach.

We have already emphasized one large point: the wisdom of *Buckley*'s preference for subsidies over conventional command-and-control regulation. We now propose to defend another. Although the Court upheld a $1,000 limit on individual donations, it rejected any limit on the overall amount that candidates could spend. On its view of the Constitution, there is no such thing as a candidate who talks too much. The very idea is alien to the philosophy of the First Amendment.[29]

We agree. The problem is not too much speech but too little influence by ordinary Americans in campaign finance. The new paradigm responds by generating a vast new flow of Patriot dollars to dilute the influence of private money. There is no need to impose any limits on overall levels of candidate expenditure. We can have more speech and more equality at the same time. Once again, the new paradigm does not require the Court to retreat from its existing jurisprudence.

We want to make a stronger claim—not only is our initiative consistent with *Buckley*'s critique of overall spending limits, but the reform effort to challenge *Buckley* is positively misguided. If reformers ever succeeded in convincing the Court to change its mind, they would not improve our democracy but degrade it further—making it even easier for incumbents to assure their endless reelection without serious challenge. As we have already emphasized, sitting legislators are much better known to their constituents than almost all challengers. To make up for this serious disadvantage, challengers will generally need to spend lots of money.

Sitting legislators have a final advantage—they make laws, and so may be delighted by the prospect of "campaign reforms" that allow them to impose severe limits on overall expenditure. To be sure, they will not consider these restrictions an unmixed blessing—they also have many advantages when it comes to fund-raising. Nonetheless, they may find it worthwhile to tie their own hands if expenditure limits make it much tougher for challengers to overcome their advantage in informational capital.[30] By embracing such "reforms," incumbents will be creating a world in which theirs is the only name that voters can recall as they go into the voting booth.

When viewed from this angle, *Buckley*'s twin principles—against expenditure ceilings, for public subsidies—remind us that we have something to fear from entrenched politicians as well as entrenched wealth; and that reformers should not be eager to exchange one master for another in the struggle for democracy. In sounding this caution, *Buckley* is best viewed as following the great reapportionment cases of the Warren Court that insisted on the constitutional principle of one person, one vote.[31] These decisions also responded to efforts by incumbents to entrench themselves against the rigors of reelection—but in these cases, political insulation was achieved not by making it economically difficult for challengers to launch costly campaigns but by privileging incumbents with small and friendly constituencies. *Buckley* follows these cases in warning us of the democratic dangers involved in allowing the fox to guard the chicken coop.[32]

This point is ignored by thoughtless comparisons of *Buckley* to *Dred Scott*. But at the same time, we don't wish to create an equally thoughtless comparison to the reapportionment decisions—for the simple reason that *Buckley* defines a very different reversion point for subsequent legal development. The Warren Court struck down a classical form of legislative self-entrenchment—malapportionment—by affirming the principle of one person, one vote. *Buckley* responds to another form of legislative self-entrenchment—campaign expenditure limitation—by affirming the right of both legislators and their challengers to appeal endlessly to big donors (provided that they dole out funds in $1,000 chunks). Reformers are right to insist that *Buckley* fails to appreciate the plutocratic dangers lurking behind the Court's uncritical acceptance of the existing distribution of wealth as a normative baseline.

This is, at any rate, our diagnosis of *Buckley*'s central mistake, and we have fashioned our proposals to correct this blunder without repudiating the Court's enduring insights. We follow *Buckley* in refusing to allow self-entrenching legislators to suppress overall campaign expenditure in the name of reform. Our model statute places no ceiling on the amount of private money candidates can raise, nor does it require them to waive their right to raise private money in exchange for taking Patriot dollars. As long as they gain access to private funds through the secret donation booth, the sky is (almost) the limit. This provides an ultimate safety valve for the new paradigm—even if Congress tries to reduce the number of Patriot dollars flowing into each citizen's account, it cannot prevent challengers from appealing for private funds.

At the same time, Patriot gives real substance to *Buckley*'s gesture toward the democratic promise of subsidy programs. By funding Patriot at adequate levels, the statute dramatically shifts the system away from plutocracy and toward the ideal of equal citizenship expressed by the constitutional principle of one person, one vote. *Buckley* is right, in short, to insist that we are not spending too much on politics, and that a creative use of subsidy is just the technique we need for reconciling our commitment to free speech with our commitment to equal citizenship.

We have been praising *Buckley*'s refusal to allow sitting politicians to control the size of their opponents' campaign budgets. This praise, we should add, is entirely independent of the much-vexed question of whether money is "speech." Even if it isn't, the problem of incumbent advantage represents a central preoccupation of the modern judiciary. Indeed, as Professor John Ely has famously shown, much of constitutional law can be seen as a comprehensive effort to prevent sitting politicians from insulating themselves from fair electoral challenge by the "outs."[33] Our interpretation of *Buckley* simply carries these great constitutional themes into the field of campaign finance. Having come this far, it is time squarely to confront *Buckley*'s famous claim that money *is* speech for First Amendment purposes.[34] This perspective emphasizes the rights of individual contributors regardless of their cumulative effect on the overall vitality of the campaign. Here is one way to define this extra constitutional dimension: Quite apart from the problem of incumbent advantage, is there an expressive component to the simple act of contributing cash to a political campaign? If a person is forbidden from giving money to the candidate of his choice, does that prohibition stop him from saying something, as well as from doing something?

Most reformers say no, but this is a mistake.[35] Recall our treatment of the citizenship effect. We believe that the grant of 50 Patriot dollars will subtly change each American's relation to the candidates' media campaigns. As they turn on the television set, and glance at the candidates' advertising campaigns, voters will no longer understand themselves as passive consumers of Madison Avenue. They will begin to think of themselves as the potential authors of the candidates' themes: "Is this the sort of ad that I should sponsor with my 50 Patriot dollars? Or is the money better spent on some other sort of presentation?"

We don't reject *Buckley*'s emphasis on the expressive aspect of contributions. We simply seek to democratize the point by giving millions of ordinary Americans the chance to express their political commitments through patriotic contributions. Indeed, *Buckley*'s point emphasizes one of the new paradigm's great advantages over traditional modes of bureaucratic subsidy, which funnel money directly to candidates or parties without giving ordinary citizens the chance to express their views. When a bureaucrat hands a big check over to a leading candidate, the ritual is entirely devoid of expressive meaning. Little wonder, then, that partisans of the old agenda seem tone deaf to *Buckley*'s point about speech. In contrast, we not only affirm the Court's insight but make it a living reality in the lives of ordinary Americans.

Our praise of *Buckley* and its principles has its limits. The Court famously denies that a concern with equality has any constructive relation to the values of free speech, and this antiegalitarian stance has occasionally led it to embrace wrong-headed doctrine.[36] But it is a mistake for reformers to take these provocations too seriously and to demonize *Buckley*'s entire approach. On three large points—its preference for subsidies, its concern with the power of incumbents, and its emphasis on the expressive dimensions of campaign contributions—the Court has something important to say. And the new paradigm is stronger for incorporating these constitutional lessons into the fabric of its model statute.

11 | Patriotic Politics

We have been approaching our subject in a playfully provocative spirit—the spirit of realistic idealism. Realism first: We have staked our claim to real-world attention by brandishing a host of shiny technocratic tools. Fashioned over the past half-century in places like the Kennedy School and the Rand Corporation, they have become a central form of serious policy talk in Congress, the White House, and beyond. Modern policy analysis has many limitations, but it is the best the academy has to offer for the hardheaded appreciation of modern government. And it would be folly to throw these tools away when confronting the inevitable complexities of real-world reform.

And now for idealism: Unlike most policy analysts, we have not passively accepted the way existing political forces define our problem or contented ourselves with minor variations on the status quo. We aim to revive the great American tradition of popular sovereignty against the very real threats posed to its survival. There is undoubtedly something utopian about this enterprise. The ideological drift toward extreme forms of market capitalism may seem overwhelming at present, and it does take a certain idealism to suppose that ordinary Americans will make the political effort required to take back control over their destiny. Nonetheless, the ideal of popular sovereignty runs deep in our history, and it is far too soon to write its obituary.

Not that we are opposed to free markets.[1] To the contrary, we have used marketlike reasoning in the service of democratic ideals. Our whole idea is to carve out a vibrant sphere of politics by creating new forms of marketlike choice—forms that purify the practice of private giving while rejuvenating the reality of citizen control. We are, in short, responding to the current wave of market triumphalism with an exercise in intellectual jujitsu: We are calling on our own fellow Americans to rejuvenate their citizenship with the very same consumerist paraphernalia—credit cards and ATMs—that seem to threaten it most.

Some may find our embrace of these consumerist images disheartening, but Americans will never be persuaded to don tunics and return to some (idealized) version of the Athenian agora. The challenge is to enable twenty-first century people to build new forms of citizenship out of the ordinary materials of modern life—and from this perspective, there is no better place to look than the neighborhood ATM. By voting with their dollars, each American will be killing two birds with one flick of the credit card. Symbolically, he will be reaffirming his own commitment to citizenship—taking the time and trouble to pick out the candidates and groups that best represent his hopes for America. Practically, he will be contributing to a flow of citizen choices that will overwhelm the national drift to oligarchy. Merging symbol with practical power, he will be doing his bit to carve out a special space for democratic citizenship—in which ordinary people confront one another as equals as they hammer out the basic terms of their ongoing social contract.

We do not believe that Americans have given up on this dream, and we have shown that it is entirely realistic to hope for its fulfillment. This is enough to motivate our own commitment to the new paradigm. But we are sure that some readers have already tired of our sermonizing. They want to know whether and how our proposal would actually change the concrete terms of American politics. Who will win, and who will lose, in the brave new world of citizen finance? How will these changes affect the kinds of policies that might actually get enacted?

Crystal-ball gazing is a hazardous enterprise, and to diversify the risks, we approach these questions from several directions. We begin with a thought experiment that reruns the presidential election of 2000 on a racetrack designed by Ackerman and Ayres. How would George W. Bush have fared under the new paradigm? Who would have been his closest competitors?

We follow up with more abstract musings. We argue that the new paradigm will reduce, but not eliminate, pernicious forms of pork-barreling—to the point where the new public investment in Patriot dollars may earn big dividends when measured by the reduction in porkish projects. We conclude with some open-ended reflections on how the new playing field will reshape the terms of future political competition between parties, interest groups, and candidates. This is a game that both liberals and conservatives can play—with victory going to the side that shows greater entrepreneurial imagination in reaching out to the concerns of ordinary Americans.

And what is wrong with that?

The Money Primary

When nominating conventions were first invented during the age of Jackson, they were a great advance in the struggle for citizen sovereignty. During the earliest days of the republic, only members of Congress, meeting in party caucus, nominated candidates for the presidency.[2] The rise of the convention put an end to this reign of party leaders in a remote capital city. It marked a great outward turn to the rest of America—politicians from the whole country coming together for a fabulous week of democratic speechifying and repeated balloting, before the party finally settled on its standard bearer.

All this democratic hoopla could not disguise the elitist aspect of the affair. There really were smoke-filled rooms during the heyday of the convention. And the fate of competing candidacies was often determined by a small number of power brokers who controlled big state delegations. From this angle, the rise of the primary system represented yet another great outward turning toward the American People. Over the course of the twentieth century, the rule of party leaders was increasingly checked and balanced by the decisions of primary voters. There are still states where party leaders huddle together in (smoke-free) rooms and wheel and deal over a slate of nominees.[3] Yet these "leaders" are anxiously aware that their choices may be overturned by primary challengers who refuse to bow to their decisions.

But primaries cost money—and by the close of the twentieth century, the power leaching away from party leaders was taking on new oligarchic forms. A decade ago, nobody had heard of "the money primary."[4] But it is now the name of the game in American politics. Long before the first primary voter casts her ballot, there is a mad effort by candidates to make this vote meaningless by scaring contenders out of the race.

The trick is to become the first politician in your party to accumulate a big campaign war chest for a particular office. This early financial triumph, all by itself, gives the victor a first-mover advantage. Other candidates quickly recognize that they will have an uphill battle if they seek to contest the nomination. So will potential donors—especially those who view contributions as part of an ongoing process of gaining special privilege. For them, investments in "second movers" will predictably antagonize first movers—who will long remember acts of financial betrayal if they finally get elected. It therefore seems wiser, other things equal, to steer money to the first mover. This makes the task of second movers even more difficult, creating a snowball effect. An early lead in the money primary feeds on itself, leaving the voters with a sense that everything is over before they have had a chance to get into the act.

First-mover logic works differently for incumbents and challengers. Generally speaking, an incumbent already has a big first-mover advantage simply by virtue of his prior service. For years—perhaps decades—he has been in the news helping constituents, taking credit for popular programs, and so forth. As a consequence, the money primary will simply confirm the obvious—that he is the person to beat. But for the other side (and for both sides, when seats are open), the money primary is downright pernicious.

It operates at a time when the overwhelming majority of citizens aren't paying attention; and even if they were, many of the concrete issues that will become important later have not yet emerged over the horizon. It follows that any polling done by candidates can't be very predictive of their relative positions later in the race. In contrast to these squishy soft numbers, the money primary gives politicians a hard number with which to measure their credibility. Every competitor would love to say: "I've raised $250,000 while my leading opponent has only collected $10,000. So it's time for all other donors to get on board before the train leaves the station!"[5]

This dynamic gives enormous power to big givers who organize early and know what they want. They are in the perfect position to offer a candidate the chance to take an early lead in the money primary—but only if he endorses the key items on their agenda. The quid pro quo need not take the form of an explicit deal—to the contrary, hostile politicians might later get hold of any piece of paper, and use it with devastating effect later in the campaign, when voters are actually paying attention. Far better, then, to leave the most important things unspoken and let the dynamics of gratitude generated by the money primary carry the day. As a front-runner emerges from the pack, he will long remember the folks who helped him eliminate most serious rivals before the race had officially begun.

The general public will be less grateful. As a series of serious candidates drop out before the first vote is cast, the message will be clear: It is the money primary, not the people's primary, that counts in American politics.

A Thought Experiment

To see how far we have already come, consider the 2000 presidential campaign. Generally, the money primary will be less important in determining the nomination of the party in control of the White House. Bill Clinton was constitutionally barred from a third term, but he was determined to anoint his vice president as successor. This incumbency effect probably had more to do with Al Gore's success in scaring off competition than anything else. Consider the position of Richard Gephardt, Gore's most serious competitor. A skilled politician and the successful Democratic leader in the House of Representatives, he possessed the national network of contacts required to raise large sums in the money primary. He was also plainly interested in launching a left-of-center challenge to Gore's candidacy. But just as the primaries began in February 2000, Gephardt dropped out after a meeting with Bill Clinton: "Gephardt's Decision Wins Clinton's Praise" ran the front-page headline in the *St. Louis Post-Dispatch*.[6] A full year earlier, another serious competitor, Senator John Kerry, explained that he could not hope to compete successfully in the money primary: "My heart wants to talk about the issues I care about, but my head was telling me that the ten months I have to raise a huge amount of money for the now-accelerated primary schedule is difficult."[7] This meant that Gore had to face only Bill Bradley in the citizen primaries. A former sports hero and senator from New Jersey, Bradley had served eighteen years on the Finance Committee, and he used his Wall Street connections with great effect in competing for funds.[8] He also had another great advantage over the likes of Kerry and Gephardt. As a *former* senator, he could spend full time establishing his credibility in the money primary—ultimately equaling Gore's bankroll despite the vice president's incumbency advantage.

But did Bradley have the inner drive and fierce ambition of a winner? His dropout from Washington politics raised this question, which his lackluster primary campaign reemphasized. The fact that more ambitious and dynamic politicians did not take the plunge may be attributed, in part, to the rise of the money primary.

The effects were much plainer, and more pernicious, on the other side. Without a Republican in the White House serving as gatekeeper, a host of candidates charged into the field: Lamar Alexander, John Ashcroft, Gary Bauer, Pat Buchanan, Elizabeth Dole, Steve Forbes, John Kasich, Jack Kemp, Alan Keyes, Senator John McCain, Dan Quayle, Bob Smith, and Tommy Thompson.[9] A few were extremists, but many might have appealed to a broader public—if the money primary had not taken its toll.

As early as summer 1997, polls were identifying Governor George W. Bush as the leading Republican contender—though it is unclear how much of this lead was due to public confusion of the son with the father.[10] In any event, the son did make full use of his father's nationwide fund-raising network, with astounding success.

Federal law offers a choice to major party candidates like Bush: For the primary, he can accept a public subsidy and agree to spend no more than $40 million, or he can reject the subsidy and raise and spend unlimited amounts of hard money (albeit in $1,000 individual contributions).[11] For Bush this was a no-brainer. By July 1, 1999—seven months before the first primary vote in New Hampshire—he had already raised $36.3 million. This compared with $4.1 million for McCain, $3 million each for Dole and Quayle, and $2.2 million for Alexander.[12] Mr. Bush was "humbled by the response," and certainly his campaign wasn't publicly bragging about its fund-raising prowess, which played a key roll in generating a plethora of endorsements early in the electoral cycle.[13]

But privately his opponents (and other potential contributors) were quick to get the message. Congressman John Kasich had been running "an optimistic, door-to-door-to-door campaign in New Hampshire and Iowa that focused, as he put it, on 'building an army,' . . . hop[ing] to shock the political world with a surprisingly strong showing in those two early primaries." Nearly all of his $1.8 million in cash had been "transferred from his congressional campaign fund," but he dropped out on July 18 and endorsed Bush. As a campaign coordinator for Kasich explained: "Everyone always knew the strategy was to see if Bush stumbled, and the question was whether any one of the other candidates would have the resources to capitalize on that. But no one does."[14] Lamar Alexander and Dan Quayle were quick to follow, despite their success in raising very substantial sums—$3 million for Alexander (August 16, 1999) and $6.3 million for Quayle (September 27).[15]

They were soon followed by Elizabeth Dole, perhaps the most consequential dropout. Smart, seasoned, and the only woman in the race, Dole could compete strongly with Bush for moderate voters in the primaries, and given the Republicans' persistent "gender gap" with women, would have been an especially powerful candidate in the November election. But she dropped out on October 20, four months before the first primary: "Steve Forbes has unlimited resources. Governor Bush has raised over $60 million and has $40 million on hand. . . . It's kind of a Catch-22. Inadequate funding limits the number of staff at headquarters and in key states, it restricts your ability to communicate with voters. It places a ceiling on travel and travel staff. Over time it becomes nearly impossible to sustain an effective campaign."[16]

By the time New Hampshire voted on February 1, John McCain was the only serious rival left standing.[17] Bush's lead in the money primary was $72 million to $21 million, but the Republicans of New Hampshire voted for McCain over Bush by 49 percent to 31 percent.[18] This democratic upset had explosive consequences for money-raising. During February, McCain beat Bush by a margin of $14 million to $3 million.[19] But this did not remotely offset Bush's immense early lead. By the end of the month, Bush had spent $50 million to McCain's $21 million.[20]

Bush responded by pouring money into the next primaries and stepping up his fund-raising efforts. He managed a victory in South Carolina on February 19, with McCain declaiming against his opponent's financial advantage: "I mean, it was enormous. We were outspent about seven or eight—ten to one."[21] Three days later, McCain managed another upset in Michigan and carried his home state of Arizona—before hitting a wall on Super Tuesday in early March.[22] With thirteen states holding Republican primaries on the same day, Bush's preparation paid off.[23] McCain simply could not mount the advertising and field campaigns required to win in so many places at once.[24] Bush's broad victory on Super Tuesday doomed McCain's insurgency.

At this point, the money primary took a paradoxical turn. Up to this point, it was the race for private money that had shaped the campaign. But with the major-party candidacies settled by March, public funding gained a newfound importance as the race for third-party nominations heated up.

Because Ross Perot had won more than 5 percent of the presidential vote in 1996, his Reform Party was entitled to a federal subsidy of $12 million. Perot was no longer interested in running, and his party would have shriveled into insignificance had it not been for the pot of federal money attached to the Reform nomination. The prospect proved irresistible for Pat Buchanan, who deserted the fringe of the Republican Party to run as the Reform nominee. His hard-right candidacy threw the center-right party into turmoil, leading to its political disintegration. Buchanan did gain control of the federal subsidy—though his dismal showing at the polls means that Reform will no longer be a lucrative proposition for future candidates.

The prospect of federal subsidy had a different impact on left-wing politics. Ralph Nader succeeded where Pat Buchanan failed—becoming a beacon for voters dissatisfied with the two major parties. As the fall campaign proceeded, Nader had a fair chance of garnering 5 percent of the vote required to guarantee the Green Party a substantial subsidy in 2004.[25] But as the candidates reached the finish line, Nader's backers faced a tough choice. With Gore and Bush in a virtual dead heat, liberals had to reckon with the short-term consequences of a Green ballot—voting for Nader might get the Greens funding for the future, but it might tip the current election from Gore to Bush and push the country to the right.[26] The Naderites managed to get the worst of both worlds—not enough voted for Nader to obtain a federal subsidy for the Greens in 2004, but enough defected from Gore to cost him Florida and other states.

How would this horserace have been different if it had been run on our newly designed track?

Begin with Governor Bush. After jump-starting his race with a million-dollar exploratory fund raised from close friends, Bush would have approached his first big decision. Recall that the governor refused to limit his private fund-raising during the primaries in exchange for a federal subsidy of $20 million. Would he have done the same thing under the new paradigm?

Not likely. If Bush relied exclusively on private funding, he would leave the way clear for rivals like Elizabeth Dole and John McCain to pick up Patriot dollars that would otherwise go to him. At the same time, his private fund-raising prospects would decline dramatically—thanks to the secret donation booth. Bush's first-mover advantage would no longer operate to induce big givers to get on board quickly—because, by hypothesis, he would no longer be in a position to reciprocate if he gained the White House. Rather than hoping for special advantages, big givers would have a strong incentive to survey the field more impartially. They would give to Bush, rather than other moderate conservatives like Dole or McCain, only if they thought that he would be a stronger candidate against his likely Democratic opponent. Some undoubtedly would bet on Bush, but not nearly in the same proportion.

It follows that Bush would have had a lot to lose, and little to gain, by rejecting patriotic finance. Undoubtedly, the governor would have remained a formidable force in both private and patriotic markets. But deprived of his first-mover advantage, he would not have taken such a commanding lead early in the race.

What is more, his rivals would have had less incentive to drop out before the first vote was cast in New Hampshire. They all would realize that the early primaries marked the first time that millions of Americans start paying attention. A triumph in New Hampshire, or some other early race, could provoke a flood of patriotic currency into the victor's coffers—reducing the financial advantage obtained by the early front-runner. Even under the current system, John McCain's victory in New Hampshire generated a surge of financial support—within forty-eight hours, his campaign received a million dollars in small contributions over the Internet.[27] But this is a piddling sum compared to the likely response with patriotic finance.

Given the prospect of striking it rich, serious candidates like Elizabeth Dole would have had an overwhelming incentive to hang on—relying in part on the disproportionate (but still modest) private support of Republican women—until the early primaries determined whether she could appeal broadly to the party faithful.[28] With more moderate Republicans in the race, and a smaller lead in the money primary, George W. Bush would have had a much tougher time crushing his competition on Super Tuesday in March. Instead of cashing out his early lead, Bush would have had to test his mettle against both McCain and Dole—and perhaps other serious candidates— during the remaining primaries. If he emerged triumphant, he would have owed his victory to the considered judgment of all Republican voters in all of the primaries, not to the first-mover advantages he enjoyed before any ballots had been cast.

Bush might have stumbled in this more democratic contest. But would this have been bad for the Republican Party?

Dole and McCain brought distinctive assets to the table. As the first woman candidate of a major party, Dole could have compensated for the Republicans' yawning "gender gap," bringing millions of women voters into the fold. (In fact, Governor Bush won only 42 percent of the female vote in November.)[29] And John McCain was the only major party candidate who sparked genuine interest from the general public—both his heroic past as a prisoner of war and his emphatic commitment to campaign reform distinguished him from the bland personalities and poll-driven positions of his opponents. McCain would have had a new problem in our alternative universe—by hypothesis, our new paradigm for campaign finance would have deprived him of his leading issue. But never underestimate the ability of outstanding politicians to come up with issues that have some zing—and it was this precious capacity that set McCain apart.

Turning to the Democratic side of the equation, Al Gore's incumbency advantage gave him greater insulation from the sharper primary challenges that would have been permitted by the new paradigm. Given Bill Clinton's support and Gore's prominence during the last eight years, it was going to be hard for any rival to deny him the nomination—though Gore's wooden personality might well have been exploited by primary opponents more dynamic than Bill Bradley.

Even if the new paradigm had only a marginal impact on the primaries, its impact would have been more obvious in the general election. As we have seen, many left-leaning voters were facing a delicate strategic problem in deciding between Al Gore and Ralph Nader. Voting for Nader increased the chance of his gaining 5 percent of the national vote, thereby enabling the Greens to qualify for a federal subsidy in the next presidential election; but at the same time, a Nader vote made it more likely that Gore would lose to Bush, propelling government toward the right. As we have seen, the election result generated the worst of all possible worlds for these voters— with Nader falling below 5 percent, and Gore losing to Bush by a whisker.

In contrast, the new paradigm would have allowed these voters a more productive sense of political participation. Many of them would have voted their Patriot dollars for Nader, giving the Greens a large fund for an effective campaign. But more would have voted for Gore on election day, because

Nader did not need to make the 5 percent threshold for the Greens to qualify for subsidy the next time around.

The same is true for right-wing voters tempted to cast a ballot for Buchanan—they too would have been able to split the difference by sending Patriot dollars to the Reform Party but saving their vote for Bush in the final tally. The Buchanan vote was relatively small in this election—but a right-wing splinter candidate might well make a difference the next time.

Summing up all these imponderables, here is our call for the election of 2000 in an America governed by the new paradigm. As we peer into our crystal ball, we see Elizabeth Dole and John McCain destroying George Bush in the early primaries, then racing down the homestretch neck and neck—with the result depending on whether McCain comes up with a new and exciting issue to substitute for campaign finance. We assume that he doesn't, and that Dole wins the Republican nomination by a nose.

She then moves on to confront Al Gore in the general election. Gore manages to attract extra support from left-wing voters, because they no longer need worry about the impact of their ballots on campaign finance in 2004. But this small gain is hardly enough to offset Dole's massive appeal to millions of women who would otherwise vote Democratic. January 20 sees the inauguration of the first woman president of the United States.

We encourage you to engage in some crystal-ball gazing of your own. Have we discounted the special charisma of John McCain? Have we underestimated Bush or Gore? If put to a sharper democratic test, would these political dynasts have been more successful in reaching out to ordinary Americans?

As you struggle with these questions, it will be hard to avoid some awkward truths about the present condition of American democracy. Public commentary on the 2000 election has—understandably enough—been gripped by the shenanigans in Florida culminating in the decision by the Supreme Court halting the vote count.[30] But our thought experiment reveals deeper pathologies. Governor Bush is indebted not only to the Supreme Court for his current tenancy in the White House; he is no less indebted to his supporters in the money primary. Without their early and emphatic support, he might never have gotten the chance to race against Gore in the first place.

Sad but true: The most important events in the previous presidential race occurred before and after Americans went to the polls. Perhaps this unhappy truth about 2000 will prove to be an historical anomaly. But it is blind to ignore the danger signs. The time to rethink campaign finance is now.

Losers—and Winners

Look ahead a decade or two—to a time when the names of Bush and Dole and Gore and McCain are fading into the footnotes of history. How might the new paradigm reshape the broad outlines of American politics over the course of generations?

The future will be surprising—far beyond our powers to predict. As we have made plain throughout, we have built the case for reform on moral foundations, not social science predictions. It is a great and good thing for citizens of a democracy to confront their common problems together, under conditions of relative equality, and to seek solutions on the basis of democratic dialogue and decision. This simple point suffices to motivate the entire enterprise.[31]

Nevertheless, it won't hurt to peer into the shadows, and try to shed some light. One thing is pretty clear: The new paradigm will produce some big losers, and once they are identified, we can produce some (relatively) hard-edged predictions about the implications for public policy. Our crystal ball gets cloudier when we shift our gaze from big losers to big winners. The best we can do is to isolate some structural factors. We will leave it to you to guess whether liberals or conservatives will be more capable of seizing the opportunities opened up by the new paradigm.

WHITHER PORK?

Begin with the big losers—the political interests that currently push their agendas with large private contributions. The donation booth is likely to dry up a large portion of this giving and to diminish the influence of the lobbyists who remain.

This means that the big loser will be corporate America. Corporate PACs contributed 30 percent of all PAC donations in 2000, and PACs connected to "trade, membership, and health organizations" (such as the AMA and trial lawyers) chipped in another 22.5 percent.[32] Not only will big business provide a smaller share of private money, but private money will be diluted by a flood of Patriot dollars. As a consequence, special dealing with big business will be far less common—especially as pols learn that enhanced access no longer reliably translates into increased contributions.

In other words, less pork—or at least pork of a certain kind, in which a concentrated group of industrial producers use state power to exploit a large group of unorganized consumers. Partisans of sugar tariffs will be less powerful in their war for high sugar prices; organized groups of polluters will be less successful in externalizing their costs onto the consumers of clean air. As a matter of narrow cost-benefit analysis, the dollar savings on porkish legislation could easily dwarf the costs of running Patriot.

We are not proclaiming final victory. Reform will reduce the supply of industrial pork, but it won't have the same effect on another familiar variety. As long as congressmen are elected from particular geographic areas, they will have an enduring incentive to bring home the bacon. Call it the logic of localist pork, which proceeds from a deep asymmetry between the distribution of benefits and burdens created by our system. Quite simply, almost all local projects are financed by national taxes. This means that local constituents must pay only a small fraction of the national taxes necessary to finance their project. Because the locals get the lion's share of the benefit, they will predictably applaud whenever their senator or congressman announces the construction of a new highway or dam—even if the total costs of the project far outweigh the benefits.[33]

The new paradigm won't change this basic fact. But even here, it will change the kind of pork of maximal interest. Rather than pushing projects that reward a few big private givers, congressmen will look for those that could generate lots of patriotic cash from ordinary constituents. This means more neighborhood centers for the masses, fewer irrigation projects for desert agriculture.

Pandering is also likely to be more public. Burying pork in obscure provisions of the tax code is all that is currently required to curry favor with business lobbyists. But patriotic contributors to PACs will want to know what their PAC has accomplished—and anything that a $50 contributor knows, others will know as well. Greater publicity means less pork. A congressman's public decision to vote against his constituency's view of the public interest is likely to offend many voters—threatening to lose him more Patriot dollars than it gains.[34]

A final factor points in the same direction. Most patriotic PACs will tend to define themselves over issues that transcend local self-interest. The NRA might well persuade millions of its members to contribute to its patriotic PAC, and this may be lamentable if you favor gun control. But it is hard to argue that it is crass self-interest that motivates the contributors' commitment to the right to bear arms.[35]

The likely reduction and democratization of pork-barreling serves as our answer to readers who don't care a whit about democratic legitimacy or citizen sovereignty but are easily outraged by governmental inefficiency. Although our priorities are different, we don't mean to minimize the problem of waste, and we are happy to encourage the efficiency crowd to come aboard. The new paradigm promises something for (almost) everybody interested in better government.

FILLING THE VACUUM

So far, so easy: It doesn't take a rocket scientist to recognize that the new paradigm will reduce the influence of corporate lobbyists. We have simply sketched some political implications that flow from this basic point.

Now for the hard part. As the corporate lobbyists are pushed to the periphery, which interests and groups will occupy the power vacuum? Broadly speaking, folks who compete most effectively for Patriot dollars. But who precisely fits this description?

First, let us distinguish between two kinds of groups. Sociological interest groups will appeal for patriotic dollars on the basis of ongoing social relationships—based on work, family, religious communion, neighborhood association, and the like. As these associations go about their business of meeting and greeting, the question of campaign giving will undoubtedly come up—especially now that everybody has Patriot dollars, and will be wondering how to spend them.

Ideological groups rely on no such bond, but appeal to their contributors' commitment to common political ideals. They will make great efforts to create a psychological bond with their potential constituents—funding advertising campaigns that seek to tap into their constituents' self-concepts (much in the same way that commercial advertisers try to persuade consumers to think of themselves as "Marlboro Men").[36]

We are dealing in ideal types—particular organizations may mix sociological and ideological appeals in fascinating combinations. But we have said enough to raise a basic question: How will the two sorts of groups fare in competing for Patriot dollars? We can clarify this question through the notion of transactions costs. By definition, sociological groups are already interacting for some other purpose—as a consequence, they may experience relatively low marginal costs in organizing for campaign finance. The preexisting sociological relationship reduces the cost of solicitation.[37]

The size of this advantage depends on the cost of solicitation technologies available to ideological groups. This is why the Internet is important—because it dramatically reduces these costs. Other things being equal, the future promises a more level playing field between ideology and sociology.

But other things are never equal—actual results will vary with the extent to which ideological groups manage to crystallize compelling concerns for large publics. Sociological groups will predictably serve as defaults—if a Patriot holder isn't inspired by any of the noble causes trumpeted on television or the Internet, organizational efforts closer to home will seem more salient. To put the point positively, the new technologies will serve as a continuing provocation for ideological groups—encouraging them to find broad themes that might mobilize millions of citizens to direct Patriot dollars in their direction.

This is a game both liberals and conservatives will play, with implications for the future of political parties, movements, and interest groups. There was a time when political parties would have been the obvious recipient of vast sums of Patriot dollars. Not only did they provide broad ideological orientation, but they were powerful sociological realities—everybody knew somebody who held a patronage job or who got help from his local party organization at a time of need. Remnants of these face-to-face organizations remain scattered through the land, but the age of the "political machine" is long past.[38] And even the psychological bond of people to their parties is in decline.[39]

Nevertheless, Democrats and Republicans will come to the patriotic marketplace with a big head start. Over the past generation, they have gained vast experience in mass solicitation—both parties now consistently raise more than half of their hard money in contributions of less than $100.[40] They enter not only with expertise but with massive lists of regular contributors whom they can target for their patriotic appeals. Because future contributions will be anonymous, the value of these lists will rapidly depreciate. They will then be obliged to parlay their fund-raising experience into innovative ways of reaching their supporters.

They can expect fierce competition. Ideological organizations like the NRA and the Sierra Club have their own mailing lists and marketing experience. They will be eager to convince their members to send 50 Patriots to their PACS for distribution to the most promising candidates. Many of these groups have a sociological presence—with gun clubs or conservation groups reducing the costs of effective solicitation. These groups morph easily, moreover, into the category of social movements—consisting of a broader range of committed partisans willing to ring doorbells and solicit Patriot dollars in time-honored ways.[41]

We are content to leave the outcome of the ongoing struggle between parties, ideological groups, and social movements to the individual choices of millions of citizens. Only one thing is clear: The game isn't obviously biased in favor of liberals or conservatives. As far as political parties are concerned, the Republicans have generally been ahead of the Democrats in mass solicitation techniques.[42] A canvass of ideological organizations is more indeterminate: The National Wildlife Federation's roster of 4.4 million members compares favorably with the NRA's 2.8 million, but will the NWF's patriotic PAC mobilize as many members to contribute?[43] Turning to sociological groups, Democrats will gain from patriotic PACS established by labor unions, but Republicans will gain more from church-inspired PACS.[44] How all this will add up is anybody's guess.

But perhaps we are losing sight of the big picture. For the first time in history, the overwhelming majority of Americans will have a chance to make funding decisions. Fewer than twelve million Americans contributed to the last election campaign, but our initiative would be a failure if fewer than fifty million voted with their Patriot dollars.[45] Won't this result in a massive shift to the left?

Maybe, maybe not. For starters, poor people will make less frequent use of their Patriot accounts. This is certainly true of voting, and voting with dollars is not likely to be different.[46] It is a serious mistake, moreover, to suppose that the average American is a knee-jerk egalitarian.[47]

At most, the new paradigm opens up new possibilities for serious debate on issues of social justice. With corporate dominance removed and Patriot dollars diffused broadly, liberals have a chance to raise the question of economic equality with new seriousness. It is up to them to come up with a serious program that might persuade a skeptical public. If they fail, they will have nobody to blame but themselves.[48]

More modest changes are more likely. Representatives of major ethnic groups like the NAACP and La Raza will raise substantial funds for their patriotic PACS—as will mass organizations like the American Association of Retired Persons. But it is impossible to guess how these groups will divide the market with more conservative competitors.

Our crystal ball clouds over completely when we add in a final factor: Voters remain perfectly free to send their Patriots directly to candidates and ignore all pleas from patriotic PACS to serve as intermediaries. PACS do offer expertise in searching the field for candidates who offer the most ideological bang for the patriotic buck. But many Americans will prefer to do this job themselves—though how many depends on the ability of particular candidates to inspire broad confidence in themselves and their ideals.

By this point, it should be plain that hard-edged predictions are impossible.

Speaking broadly, the analytic situation begins to resemble one portrayed by John Rawls in his famous *Theory of Justice*.[49] As Americans look a generation or two ahead, they will find it impossible to predict whether the new paradigm will further their concrete interests. They are obliged to consider the problem from behind a veil of ignorance that deprives them of personal self-interest.

As Rawls rightly suggests, this condition invites all of us to focus on the more fundamental moral features of the proposal. Rather than looking upon the new paradigm as a mode of manipulating the future with precision, consider how it provides a flexible response to changing public views of the public agenda. No organization will have a monopoly on public opinion. Even dominant groups must constantly explore the space of public concern. Although they may have won yesterday's struggle for Patriot dollars, they can never take victory for granted. There will always be competition in the marketplace of ideas—new diagnoses for old problems, more ambitious efforts to redefine the very nature of the public good. Most exercises in political entrepreneurship will fail—and that is a good thing, because most new ideas are half-baked.

But in contrast to the old system, the new paradigm will place ordinary Americans firmly in the driver's seat. Rather than remaining passive spectators of the money primary, they will be actively shaping the terms of the ongoing competition. Rather than creating a new bureaucracy to dole out huge sums to entrenched parties and candidates, Americans will take charge of the future of politics in bite-sized chunks of $50, each citizen marching to the beat of a distant drummer.

We owe a lot to Senators McCain and Feingold. They have proved to cynics that Americans care about reform—care enough to reward politicians who put their careers on the line in the struggle against big money. But for enduring success, it isn't enough for a few gutsy leaders to push for serious legislation. Progressive change will prove enduring only if we reconstruct the reform agenda from the ground up.

The shift to the new paradigm won't happen overnight. It will take time for activists and policy wonks to think through our initiative, and more time for enterprising politicians to take up the cause and urge their fellow Americans to consider voting with Patriot dollars! As McCain and Feingold have shown, much more work would then be required before our model statute gained respectful attention in Congress.

It would be quixotic to expect assistance from the White House anytime soon. Given George W. Bush's dependence on the money primary, voting with dollars is the last thing he would find attractive. We are, to repeat, *realistic* idealists.

But we do hope that the new paradigm strikes a chord in the broader community. Even if McCain-Feingold makes it onto the statute books, nobody imagines that it marks the end of the line. Without further legislation, well-paid lawyers—many trained at the Yale Law School—will soon find ways around the new statutory limits on soft money. Within a decade or so, big givers and getters will have made the great campaign reform of the new millennium into Swiss cheese—and the influence-peddling business in Washington will continue with only minor variations.

There would be only one thing worse than a dismal repetition of disappointed hopes: an aggressive effort to throw in jail the campaign staffs found responsible for clever acts of evasion. Civilized democracy simply cannot function if losing candidates are regularly sent to jail after each election—and rest assured, there will be very few winning politicians among the jailbirds.

This is, in short, a very good time to break the cycle of reform and despair that looms before us. Senators McCain and Feingold have shown that the public is serious about serious change. The only question is to identify the reforms which deserve priority in the next major legislative initiative.

The answer will shape the future of American democracy for generations.

The Model Statute

The Model Statute

WITH DANTON BERUBE

In Part I we elaborated the foundations of our new paradigm. In Part II we worked up operational principles. Before presenting the model statute, we provide a road map of its main substantive provisions (with cross-references to the relevant sections) as an orienting guide.

Summary

1. EXPLORATORY COMMITTEE
   a. Candidates may raise funds for an exploratory fund from publicly disclosed contributions. § 12
   b. The maximum amounts that exploratory funds may receive are $50,000 for House candidates; $250,000 for Senate candidates (on average); and $1 million for presidential candidates. § 12(c)
   c. The maximum amounts that a (noncandidate) individual may contribute to an exploratory fund are $2,000 for House candidates; $10,000 for Senate candidates (on average); and $20,000 for presidential candidates. § 12(d)
   d. Candidates may contribute up to the overall exploratory cap to their own exploratory committee. § 12(g)

2. PATRIOT DOLLARS
   a. Registration
      i. All registered voters are eligible to register for Patriot card. § 14(a) Eligible individuals may register by mail, over the Internet, or at registrar's office or voting booth. §§ 14(e) & (g)
      ii. Registration is valid for only six years, but voting automatically reregisters an individual. § 14(d)

b. Dollar Amounts in Accounts

   i. Four separate subaccounts will potentially be associated with each Patriot card: $10 for House elections, $15 for senatorial elections; and $25 for presidential elections. If an incumbent president is eligible for reelection, then the Patriot cardholder will receive $10 for the presidential primary and $15 for the presidential general election. § 15

   ii. These amounts will be increased if the total private and Patriot contributions in the previous election fell below the prestatutory level of total funding for that level of elected office. § 27(c)

   iii. These amounts will be increased if the total private contributions in the previous election were more than 50 percent of the total Patriot contributions for that level of elected office. § 27(b)

   iv. The face value of the first 5 percent of Patriot dollars contributed to candidates for each level of elected office will be doubled. § 16(g)

   v. For the first eight years of the statute's operation, the face value of contributed Patriots may periodically be increased throughout an election cycle if the commission certifies that the total private and Patriot contributions for that level of elected office is less than half the amount that had been received up to the same point of the comparable election cycle in the prestatutory period. § 27(d)

   vi. The face value of prospective Patriot dollars contributed to a particular level of elected office will be discounted if an amount greater than twice the prestatutory level of funding has been received. The discounting formula will assure that the total value of Patriot dollars for a particular level of elected office shall never be more than four times the prestatutory amount of funding. § 27(e)

c. Contribution

   i. Patriot card holders can donate from an automated teller machine or at a Patriot office. § 14(f)

   ii. It is illegal for Patriot card holder to sell her Patriot contribution for any consideration. § 19(a)

iii. Depository institutions may not charge the commission more than the lowest unit charges made for comparable use of their ATMs by other users thereof. § 17(c)

d. Information

   i. All Patriot contributions from citizens (including citizen contributions to political organizations) must be made anonymously through the commission's blind trust. § 16(d)

   ii. But Patriot contribution transfers from political organizations to candidates, while made through the Blind Trust, will be publicly disclosed. § 16(d)

3. DONATION BOOTH REGULATION OF PRIVATE CONTRIBUTIONS

a. Contributions of private dollars must be made directly from individuals to the commission's Blind Trust. Candidates may not accept contributions. § 8(a)

b. If a contributor requests, the Blind Trust will publicly disclose the amount the contributor has given up to $200. § 8(h)(1)

c. The contributor may rescind any contribution within five days (or instruct the Blind Trust in advance to send a refund check). § 8(d)

d. Contributor identity is disclosed ten years after the election. § 8(h)(3)

e. Individuals who contribute more than $10,000 must make all of their contributions within a physical donation booth at a Patriot office. § 8(c)(2)

f. Blind Trust employees may not fraternize with candidates or party officials or their agents, nor may they work for candidates, parties, or major donors for a period of ten years. §§ 8(b)(2) & (3)

g. If the Blind Trust receives an unusually large amount of contributions from an unusually concentrated number of donors, it will report only a randomized amount of contributions (ranging from one standard deviation below to two standard deviations above the mean daily receipts) and will attribute excess amounts over a ten-day period. § 8(g)

h. Contributions to nonparty political organizations to fund express advocacy must be transmitted through the commission's Blind Trust. § 8(a)

i. Contributions to nonparty political organizations to fund political communications must be made through the Blind Trust unless the political organization is independent of any candidate, party, or organization that must raise funds through the donation booth. §§ 2(17), 8(j), 10(k)

j. All contributions to national political parties must be transmitted through the commission's Blind Trust. § 8(a)

k. Contributions to the federal accounts of state and local political parties must be transmitted through the commission's Blind Trust. § 8(a)

l. Contributions from political parties (including state and local parties) to candidates must be transmitted through the commission's Blind Trust, but the commission will publicly disclose the amount of these contribution. § 8(h)(2)

m. Loans to candidates are prohibited. § 8(k)

4. REGULATIONS OF LAST RESORT

a. Individuals may not contribute more than the following amounts to any candidate during an election cycle: $5,000 to a House candidate; $15,000 on average to a Senate candidate; $100,000 to a presidential candidate. § 10(e)

b. The Blind Trust will not attribute more than the following amounts from an individual contributor to any candidate during any contribution window: $2,500 to a House candidate; $7,500 on average to a Senate candidate; or $50,000 to a presidential candidate. § 10(c)

c. The contribution window during the last year of an election shall be two weeks and during previous years shall be four weeks. § 10(d)

d. Individuals may not contribute more than $100,000 to a national political party during any presidential political cycle, and not more than $50,000 will be attributed to a party account during any presidential contribution window. §§ 10(c) & (e)

e. Individuals may not contribute more than $5,000 per year to any political organization that is not a national political party and not more than an aggregate of $25,000 per year to political organizations other than national political parties. § 10(f)

f. Individuals may not contribute more than $100,000 per year to candidates or political organizations. § 10(g)

g. Notwithstanding these candidate-specific and aggregate contribution limits, candidates can contribute unlimited amounts to their own campaigns if they opt not to receive Patriot funding. § 11

h. Nonparty political organizations may not contribute private dollars to candidates nor engage in coordinated advocacy. §§ 2(17), 10(b) & (h)

i. National parties may contribute unlimited sums of private dollars to candidates. § 10(j)

j. National parties may not transfer funds to state and local parties. §§ 13(b) & (c)

k. Candidates and major purpose political organizations willfully violating the act may be barred from receiving Patriot funds for up to five years. §§ 20(e), 21(c)

5. COMMISSION STRUCTURE

a. The Federal Election Commission shall have five commissioners appointed by the president, and confirmed by the Senate, to serve staggered ten-year terms. §§ 6(a) & (b)

b. Only a retired justice or judge of the United States may be appointed. § 6(a)

c. The commission will supervise three subordinate divisions: an enforcement division, a blind trust division, and a Patriot account division. § 6(h)

d. The commission's budget (including the cost of Patriot vouchers, as well as the cost of administering the Patriot and blind trust programs) will be funded out of a continuing appropriation of the kind governing "entitlement" programs. § 28

6. MISCELLANEOUS

All dollar amounts in the statute are inflation indexed. § 26

Text: The Citizen Sovereignty Act

A Bill

To reform the financing of political campaigns by granting Patriot dollars to each citizen and requiring that all private contributions be made through a Blind Trust.

Be it enacted by the Senate and House of Representatives of the United States of America in Congress assembled,

Section 1. Short Title. [Original]
This Act may be cited as "The Citizen Sovereignty Act."

Section 2. Definitions. [Modeled on 2 U.S.C. § 431]
When used in this Act:
  (1) the term "election" means—
       (A) a general, special, primary, or runoff election;
       (B) a convention or caucus of a political party which has authority to nominate a candidate;
       (C) a primary election held for the selection of delegates to a national nominating convention of a political party; and
       (D) a primary election held for the expression of a preference for the nomination of individuals for election to the office of President.
  (2) The term "candidate" means an individual who seeks nomination for election, or election, to Federal office. Actions taken by agents or surrogates of a candidate are deemed to be actions by the candidate. For purposes of this paragraph, an individual shall be deemed to seek nomination for election, or election—
       (A) if such individual has received contributions aggregating in excess of $5,000 or has made expenditures on such individual's own behalf aggregating in excess of $5,000; or
       (B) if such individual has given his or her consent to another person to receive contributions or make expenditures on behalf of such individual and if such person has received such contributions aggregating in excess of $5,000 or has made such expenditures aggregating in excess of $5,000.

(3)   The term "Federal office" means the office of President or Vice President, or of Senator or Representative in, or Delegate or Resident Commissioner to, the Congress.

(4)   The term "political organization" means any committee, club, corporation, political party, association, or other group of persons which makes any expenditure or engages in any political communication.

(5)   The term "major purpose political organization" means any political organization the major purpose of which is the nomination or election of one or more candidates or the engagement in federal campaign activity. Any political organization may voluntarily designate itself as a major purpose political organization pursuant to section 4(d)(2). Any political party shall be treated as a major purpose political organization.

(6)   The term "political communication" means a communication— except as described in subsection (10)(A)—by means of any broadcast, cable, or satellite communication, newspaper, magazine, outdoor advertising facility, mass mailing, Internet or telephone bank to the general public, or any other form of general public advertising which refers to any candidate or political party or contains such other content of a political nature as the Commission by regulation shall designate.[1]

(7)   (A)   The term "House election cycle" means the two-year period consisting of the year in which regular elections to the United States House of Representatives are held and the year preceding said elections;

       (B)   The term "Presidential election cycle" means the four-year period consisting of the year in which the regular election for President of the United States is held and the three years preceding said election; and

       (C)   The term "Senate election cycle" means the six-year period consisting of the year in which a regular election for a specific seat in the Senate of the United States is held and the five years preceding said election.

(8)   The term "contribution" includes—

       (A)   any gift, subscription, loan, transfer, advance, or deposit of money or anything of value, including funds from Patriot accounts, made by any person to any candidate or political organization;

(B) the payment by any person of compensation for the services of another person which are rendered to a candidate or political organization without charge for any purpose; and

(C) a candidate's own money, property, asset, or other item of value with which the candidate intends to make any expenditure.

(9) The term "expenditure" includes—

(A) any purchase, payment, distribution, loan, transfer, advance, deposit, or gift of money or anything of value, made by any person for the purpose of influencing any election for Federal office; and

(B) a written contract, promise, or agreement to make any such expenditure.

(10) The terms "contribution" and "expenditure" do not include—

(A) any news story, commentary, or editorial distributed through the facilities of any broadcasting station, Internet, newspaper, magazine, or other periodical publication, unless such facilities are owned or controlled by any candidate or political organization;

(B) the use of a candidate's personal residence or automobile by that candidate;

(C) any purchase, payment, distribution, loan, transfer, advance, deposit, or gift of money or anything of value, made by any person for the purpose of indirectly influencing any election for Federal office, provided that there is no endorsement or identification of any candidate and that the person did not coordinate the action directly or indirectly with any candidate;

(D) the value of services provided without compensation by any individual who volunteers on behalf of a candidate or political organization; or

(E) the use of real or personal property, including a church or community room used on a regular basis by members of a community for noncommercial purposes, and the cost of invitations, food, and beverages, voluntarily provided by an individual to any candidate or political organization in rendering voluntary personal services on the individual's residential premises or in the church or community room for a candidate or political organization's activities, to the extent that the cumulative value of such invitations, food, and beverages provided by such individual on behalf of any candidate or political organization does not exceed $1,000 during any two-year period corresponding to a House election cycle.

(11) The term "Commission" means the Federal Election Commission.

(12) The term "person" includes an individual, partnership, committee, association, political organization, corporation, labor organization, or any other organization or group of persons, but such term does not include the Federal Government or any authority of the Federal Government.

(13) The term "political party" means an association, committee, or organization which nominates a candidate for election to any office whose name appears on the election ballot as the candidate of such association, committee, or organization.

(14) The term "national political party" means the organization which, by virtue of the bylaws of a political party, is responsible for the day-to-day operation of such political party at the national level, as determined by the Commission.

(15) The term "Act" means the Citizen Sovereignty Act.

(16) The term "depository institution" is used as it is defined in 12 U.S.C. § 461(b)(1)(A)(i)–(vi).

(17) The term "affiliated political organization" means any political organization other than a political party which—

 (A) is under the direct or indirect control of any candidate;

 (B) is a parent, subsidiary, branch, division, department, or local unit of any political organization which must raise its contributions through the Blind Trust;

 (C) along with one or more other political organizations—at least one of which must raise its contributions through the Blind Trust—is established, financed, maintained, or controlled by—

(i) a single corporation and/or its subsidiaries;

(ii) a single national or international union and/or its local unions or other subordinate organizations;

(iii) an organization of national or international unions and/ or all its State and local central bodies;

(iv) a membership organization, including trade or professional associations, and/or related State and local entities of that organization or group;

(v) the same person or group of persons; or

(vi) substantially the same group of persons;

(D) is otherwise so closely connected to a candidate or other political organization which must raise its contributions through the Blind Trust as to constitute a de facto affiliated political organization pursuant to regulations to be established by the Commission; or

(E) coordinates within any two-year period any expenditure or political communication with any candidate or other political organization which must raise its contributions through the Blind Trust, including—

(i) making said expenditure or political communication at the request or suggestion of a candidate or other political organization which must raise its contributions through the Blind Trust;

(ii) submitting the control or decision-making authority for said expenditure or political communication to a candidate or other political organization which must raise its contributions through the Blind Trust;

(iii) engaging in substantial discussions or negotiations regarding said expenditure or political communication with a candidate or other political organization which must raise its contributions through the Blind Trust;

(iv) making said expenditure or political communication through the use of the same political consultant, advertising agency, or other agent as a candidate or other political organization which must raise its contributions through the Blind Trust; or

(v) engaging in other such acts defined by the Commission
in regulations with respect to an expenditure or political
communication such that it constitutes a de facto
coordination with a candidate or other political
organization which must raise its contributions through
the Blind Trust.

Section 3. Treasurer Requirement. [Modeled on 2 U.S.C. § 432]
(a) Every candidate and political organization shall have a treasurer.
During any period in which the office of treasurer is vacant, the
candidate or political organization may not make any contribution
or expenditure and may not receive any distribution from the
Federal Election Commission's Blind Trust.
(b) The treasurer for a candidate or political organization shall keep
an account of—
(1) all expenditures made by the candidate or political
organization, including the name and address of the payee for
the expenditure, the date, amount, and purpose of the
expenditure, and a canceled check for the expenditure;
(2) all administrative expenses paid by the candidate or political
organization, including the name and address of the payee for
the expense, the date, amount, and purpose of the expense,
and a canceled check for the expense;
(3) all expenses paid by the political organization for any political
communications or other political activities, including the
name and address of the payee for the expense, the date,
amount, and purpose of the expense, and a canceled check for
the expense; and
(4) all distributions to the candidate or political organization from
the Federal Election Commission's Blind Trust.
(c) The treasurer shall preserve all records required to be kept by this
section for seven years.
(d) No candidate or political organization may maintain an account at
a depository institution. Funds expended by any candidate or
political organization must be by draft against the account at the
Federal Election Commission's Blind Trust—unless the political

organization does not make any expenditures and is not an affiliated political organization or major purpose political organization, in which case it may maintain an account at a depository institution.

Section 4. Registration of Candidates and Political Organizations. [Modeled on 2 U.S.C. § 433]

(a) Each candidate shall file a statement of organization with the Commission within ten days of becoming a candidate within the meaning of this Act.

(b) Each political organization shall file a statement of organization within ten days of becoming a political organization within the meaning of this Act.

(c) The statement of organization of a candidate or political organization shall include—

   (1) the name and address of the candidate or political organization;

   (2) the name, address, and position of the custodian of books, records, and accounts of the candidate or political organization; and

   (3) the name and address of the treasurer for the candidate or the political organization.

(d) The statement of organization for each political organization shall also

   (1) designate the name and address of any person who is authorized by the political organization to make contributions or expenditures on its behalf;

   (2) include a statement as to whether the organization is or desires to be treated as a major purpose political organization;

   (3) include a statement as to whether it is an affiliated political organization and if so, the identity of all candidates and political organizations with which it is affiliated.

(e) If a candidate, the spouse of a candidate, or the parent, sibling, or child of a candidate or of the candidate's spouse is designated as a person who is authorized by the political organization to make contributions or expenditures on its behalf, then no contributions to or expenditures on behalf of that candidate may be made by the political organization.

(f) The statement of organization for a candidate shall also include a statement as to whether the candidate wishes to receive transfers from Patriot accounts pursuant to Section 11.

(g) Any change in information previously submitted in a statement of organization shall be reported to the Commission no later than ten days after the date of the change.

(h) All statements of organization shall be published by the Commission via the Internet.

Section 5. Reporting Requirements. [Modeled on 2 U.S.C. § 434]

(a) The treasurer for a candidate or political organization shall file quarterly reports with the Commission within fifteen days of the end of each calendar quarter. The treasurer shall sign and verify each such report under penalty of perjury.

(b) Each report under this section shall disclose the following for the preceding calendar quarter—

(1) all expenditures made by the candidate or political organization, including the name and address of the payee for the expenditure, the date, amount, and purpose of the expenditure;

(2) all administrative expenses paid by the candidate or political organization, including the name and address of the payee for the expense, the date, amount, and purpose of the expense;

(3) all expenses paid by the political organization for any political communications or other political activities, including the name and address of the payee for the expense, the date, amount, and purpose of the expense;

(4) all distributions to the candidate or political organization from the Federal Election Commission's Blind Trust;

(5) the amount of funds available to the candidate or political organization at the beginning and the end of the reporting period; and

(6) the amount, date, and recipient of all contributions or transfers of Patriot funds made by the political organization.

(c) Said reports shall be published by the Commission via the
     Internet.

Section 6. Federal Election Commission. [Modeled on 2 U.S.C. § 437c]
  (a) There is established a commission to be known as the Federal
       Election Commission. The Commission is composed of five
       members appointed by the President, by and with the advice and
       consent of the Senate. Only a justice or judge of the United States
       appointed to hold office during good behavior who has retired
       from office pursuant to 28 U.S.C. § 371 shall be eligible to be a
       member of the Commission.
  (b) (1) Members of the Commission shall serve for a single term of
            ten years, without the possibility of reappointment, except
            that of the members first appointed—
            (A) one of the members shall be appointed for a term
                 ending two years after the date of enactment;
            (B) one of the members shall be appointed for a term
                 ending four years after the date of enactment;
            (C) one of the members shall be appointed for a term
                 ending six years after the date of enactment; and
            (D) one of the members shall be appointed for a term
                 ending eight years after the date of enactment.
       (2) A member of the Commission may serve on the Commission
            after the expiration of his or her term until his or her
            successor has taken office as a member of the Commission.
       (3) An individual appointed to fill a vacancy occurring other
            than by the expiration of a term of office shall be appointed
            only for the unexpired term of the member he or she
            succeeds.
       (4) Any vacancy occurring in the membership of the
            Commission shall be filled in the same manner as in the case
            of the original appointment.
       (5) Each member of the Commission shall be paid at the rate of
            basic pay in effect for level III of the Executive Schedule. Said
            pay shall be in addition to any other pension the member
            may receive.

(c) The Commission shall elect a chairman and a vice chairman from among its members for a term of four years. A member may serve as chairman only once during the term of office to which such member is appointed. The vice chairman shall act as chairman in the absence or disability of the chairman or in the event of a vacancy in such office.

(d) (1) The Commission shall administer, seek to obtain compliance with, and formulate policy with respect to, this Act. The Commission shall have exclusive jurisdiction with respect to the civil enforcement of this Act except as provided in section 20(g).

(2) Nothing in this Act shall be construed to limit, restrict, or diminish any investigatory, informational, oversight, supervisory, or disciplinary authority or function of the Congress or any committee of the Congress with respect to elections for Federal office.

(e) All decisions of the Commission with respect to the exercise of its duties and powers under the provisions of this Act shall be made by a majority vote of the members of the Commission. A member of the Commission may not delegate to any person his or her vote or any decision-making authority or duty vested in the Commission by the provisions of this Act.

(f) The Commission shall meet at least once each month and also at the call of any member.

(g) The Commission shall prepare written rules for the conduct of its activities, shall have an official seal which shall be judicially noticed, and shall have its principal office in or near the District of Columbia (but it may meet or exercise any of its powers anywhere in the United States).

(h) The policies and activities of the Commission shall be implemented with the assistance of the following three subordinate divisions which shall be subject at all times to the authority of the Commission:

(1) The Enforcement Division shall be responsible for conducting all audits and for the civil and criminal enforcement of this Act, including continuous contemporaneous internal audits to

ensure that all contributions are properly forwarded to the candidates and political organizations to which they are directed;

(2) The Trust Division shall be responsible for operating the Federal Election Commission's Blind Trust; and

(3) The Patriot Account Division shall be responsible for establishing and maintaining all Patriot accounts and donation booths.

(i) The Commission shall appoint the director of each division. The director of the Enforcement Division shall also serve as the general counsel to the Commission. Each director shall be paid at the rate of basic pay in effect for level IV of the Executive Schedule. With the approval of the Commission, each director may appoint and fix the pay of such additional personnel as he or she considers desirable without regard to the provisions of title 5 governing appointments in the competitive service. Each director shall be hired for a term of six years and may not be dismissed except for good cause shown as determined by at least four members of the Commission.

(j) With the approval of the Commission, each director may procure temporary and intermittent services to the same extent as is authorized by section 3109(b) of title 5, but at rates for individuals not to exceed the daily equivalent of the annual rate of basic pay in effect for grade GS-15 of the General Schedule.

(k) In carrying out its responsibilities under this Act, the Commission shall, to the fullest extent practicable, avail itself of the assistance, including personnel and facilities, of other agencies and departments of the United States. The heads of such agencies and departments may make available to the Commission such personnel, facilities, and other assistance, with or without reimbursement, as the Commission may request.

(l) Notwithstanding the provisions of subsection (j), the Commission is authorized to appear in any action instituted under this Act, either (A) by attorneys employed in its office, or (B) by counsel whom it may appoint, on a temporary basis as may be necessary for such purpose, without regard to the provisions of title 5 governing appointments in the competitive service, and whose compensation it may fix without regard to the provisions of chapter 51 and subchapter III of chapter 53 of such title. The compensation of counsel so appointed on a temporary basis shall be paid out of any funds otherwise available to pay the compensation of employees of the Commission.

(m) The Commission shall maintain and publish via the Internet a running archive of all reports and other information which it is required to publish under this statute.

Section 7. Powers of Commission. [Modeled on 2 U.S.C. § 437d]

(a) The Commission and its Divisions have the power—

(1) to require by special or general orders, any person to submit, under oath, such written reports and answers to questions as the Commission or a Division may prescribe;

(2) to administer oaths or affirmations;

(3) to require by subpoena, signed by the chairman, the vice chairman, or the general counsel, the attendance and testimony of witnesses and the production of all documentary evidence relating to the execution of its duties;

(4) in any proceeding or investigation, to order testimony to be taken by deposition before any person who is designated by the Commission or a Division and has the power to administer oaths and, in such instances, to compel testimony and the production of evidence in the same manner as authorized under paragraph (3);

(5) to pay witnesses the same fees and mileage as are paid in like circumstances in the courts of the United States;

(6) to initiate civil actions for injunctive, declaratory, or other appropriate relief in the name of the Commission to enforce the provisions of this Act, to defend civil actions filed pursuant to section 20(g), and to appeal civil actions in which it is a party;

(7) to file petitions for certiorari with and otherwise to appear in its own name before the United States Supreme Court, through its general counsel, the United States Supreme

Court's decision in *Federal Election Commission v. NRA Political Victory Fund,* 513 U.S. 88 (1994) notwithstanding;

(8) to develop such prescribed forms and to make, amend, and repeal such rules and regulations, pursuant to the provisions of chapter 5 of title 5, as are necessary to carry out the provisions of this Act, including preserving the secrecy of the Blind Trust and ensuring the integrity of Patriot accounts;

(9) to conduct investigations and hearings expeditiously, to encourage voluntary compliance with this Act, and to report apparent violations to appropriate law enforcement officials;

(10) to require sellers and providers of political communications to provide regular and prompt reports of the identities of purchasers and users thereof, as well as the date and dollar value of said purchases or uses; and

(11) to enter into contracts or other agreements with any of the several States or any private entity or person in order to execute its responsibilities under this Act in the most efficient and effective manner possible.

(b) Upon petition by the Commission, any United States district court within the jurisdiction of which any inquiry is being carried on may, in case of refusal to obey a subpoena or order of the Commission issued under subsection (a) of this section, issue an order requiring compliance. Any failure to obey the order of the court may be punished by the court as a contempt thereof.

(c) No person shall be subject to civil liability to any person (other than the Commission or the United States) for disclosing information at the request of the Commission.

(d) Whenever the Commission submits any legislative recommendation, or testimony, or comments on legislation, requested by the Congress or by any Member of the Congress, to the President or the Office of Management and Budget, it shall concurrently transmit a copy thereof to the Congress or to the Member requesting the same. No officer or agency of the United States shall have any authority to require the Commission to submit its legislative recommendations, testimony, or comments on legislation, to any office or agency of the United States for approval, comments, or review, prior to the submission of such recommendations, testimony, or comments to the Congress.

(e) The power of the Commission to initiate civil actions under subsection (a)(6) of this section shall be the exclusive civil remedy for the enforcement of the provisions of this Act, except as provided in section 20(g).

Section 8. Blind Trust. [Original]

(a) The Commission shall establish a blind trust which will receive all contributions for candidates and political organizations. No person may collect, pass on, bundle, or otherwise transmit contributions from any other person to the blind trust. The amount or status of specific contributions or the identity or any other information about any contributor or contribution to the blind trust shall not be revealed except as provided in subsection (h).

(b) The Commission shall implement procedures to ensure that the number of employees with knowledge of the amount or status of specific contributions or the identity or any other information about any contributor or contribution is kept to a minimum.

(1) No employee may disclose the amount or status of specific contributions or the identity or any other information about any contributor or contribution except as provided in subsection (h).

(2) A Commission employee with knowledge of the amount or status of specific contributions or the identity or any other information about any contributor or contribution may not accept employment with any candidate or political organization or any donor who has contributed more than $10,000 in any two-year period corresponding to a House election cycle for a period of ten years following the conclusion of his or her employment with the Commission.[2]

(3) Current Commission employees with knowledge of the amount or status of specific contributions or the identity or any other information about any contributor or contribution are prohibited from fraternizing with any candidate, the officers of any political organization, or any donor who has

contributed more than $10,000 in any two-year period corresponding to a House election cycle.

(4) A current Commission employee with knowledge of the amount or status of specific contributions or the identity or any other information about any contributor or contribution shall immediately disclose to the Commission any information which could create an actual or apparent conflict of interest or raise even the appearance of impropriety with respect to his or her duty to keep said knowledge absolutely secret.

(5) No records related to contributions shall be discoverable in any civil proceeding unless they have previously been published pursuant to subsection (h).

(c) All contributions to the blind trust must be by check made payable to the "Federal Election Commission's Blind Trust" and should be accompanied by separate instructions identifying the candidate or political organization to which it should be distributed. Said check must include the donor's social security number on its face. Any contribution without distribution instructions shall be returned to the contributor.

(1) Contributions of less than $10,000 must be personally mailed or hand-delivered to a Patriot office by the person making the contribution.

(2) All individuals making contributions of $10,000 or more during any calendar year must make additional gifts in person at a Patriot office and within the confines of the donation booth after the contributor's identity has been confirmed by an official at the Patriot office.

(d) At any time prior to making the contribution or within five days of the delivery of any contribution to the blind trust, the contributor may deliver a written request for the revocation of all or part of the contribution. Upon receipt of such a request and after the funds for the contribution have cleared to the blind trust, the blind trust shall refund as requested all or part of the contribution to the contributor. Refunds to a political organization shall be in the form of a credit within the blind trust, subject to the limitation in subsection (g). All other refunds shall be by check. The revocation status of any contribution shall be subject to the same secrecy provisions set forth in subsections (a) and (b). A revocation shall be deemed to have been requested for any contribution or part thereof which would exceed the contribution limitations set forth in section 10, except as provided in section 10(d).

(e) The blind trust shall publish via the Internet the following information for every candidate and political organization on a daily basis:

   (1) the date, identity, and amount (up to $200) of all nonanonymous contributions and transfers during the past two years;

   (2) the current available balance of Patriot and non-Patriot contributions and transfers;

   (3) the total of Patriot and non-Patriot contributions and transfers during the past two years;

   (4) the ratio of Patriot to non-Patriot contributions and transfers during the past two years; and

   (5) for every candidate—the date, source, and amount of all transfers of Patriot funds from major purpose political organizations during the past two years.

(f) The available balance for any candidate or political organization will be the total of contributions to the blind trust directed to the candidate or political organization for which funds have cleared and the five-day revocation period has expired, less any refunds to contributors and prior distributions, subject to the limitation in subsection (g).

(g) The balance amount that is reported as being available shall be limited temporarily based on a formula to be promulgated by the Commission with the intent of obscuring the identity of large concentrated gifts.

(h) (1) All contributions shall be anonymous unless the contributor specifically requests attribution. If the contributor specifically requests attribution at the time of making the contribution to the blind trust, for every contribution for which funds have cleared and the five-day revocation period has expired, the Commission shall publish via the Internet the fact that a contribution was made by the donor to the recipient and the amount of the contribution, provided however that the amount of a contribution of $200 or more shall be reported as "$200+."

(2) The recipient and the entire amount (after any refund) of a transfer made by a major purpose political organization shall immediately following the five-day revocation period be published via the Internet notwithstanding any request for anonymity.

(3) Ten years after every relevant election cycle the Commission will conduct a public audit of all contributions made during said election cycle to ensure that all contributions were properly forwarded to the candidates and political organizations to which they were directed. In the course of said audit, the Commission shall publish via the Internet the amount, donor, and recipient of all contributions. The identity of the donor shall be disclosed at the time of the audit notwithstanding any prior request for anonymity. Said audit shall be completed within six months.

(i) When funds are expended by a candidate or political organization from the blind trust, all private dollars shall be spent before Patriot dollars are spent.[3]

(j) Any political organization may establish a special blind trust account to receive funds to be used solely for political communications which do not constitute expenditures. Contributions to said accounts shall be processed and reported in the same manner as other contributions under this section. Contributions to political communications blind trust accounts, however, are not subject to any contribution limitations contained within this Act, including aggregate contribution limitations, and may be made by any nonforeign person, group, committee, club, association, union, corporation, or other entity.

(k) Absolutely all loans to candidates and political organizations are prohibited.

(l) Notwithstanding the provisions of subsection (c), the Commission may adopt by regulation alternative mechanisms for contributions to the blind trust which it concludes are more efficient and effective; provided, however, that any such mechanism must include equivalent safeguards to maintain anonymity and deter fraud or abuse.

Section 9. Claims of Contributions to Blind Trust Not Prohibited. [Original] It shall not be a violation of this Act for any person to display canceled checks or otherwise claim to have made a contribution to a candidate or political organization through the Federal Election Commission's Blind Trust, regardless of whether such a contribution was actually made or whether any refund of the contribution was requested during the five-day revocation period.

Section 10. Restrictions Upon Contributions. [Original]
   (a)   No person may directly or indirectly make any contribution to a candidate or political organization unless said contribution is made through the Federal Election Commission's Blind Trust.
   (b)   No candidate or political organization may directly or indirectly receive any contribution unless said contribution is made through the Federal Election Commission's Blind Trust.
   (c)   No contribution in excess of the following amounts may be credited to any candidate or national political party during any contribution window as defined by subsection (d):
      (1) $2,500 to any candidate seeking nomination for election, or election, to the office of Representative in, or Delegate or Resident Commissioner to, the Congress;
      (2) $5,000 plus $40 per 100,000 adult residents of the State to be represented to any candidate seeking nomination for election, or election, to the office of Senator in Congress;
      (3) $50,000 for any candidate seeking nomination for election, or election, to the office of President; and
      (4) $50,000 to any national political party.
   (d)   The contribution window during the last year of every House election cycle, Senate election cycle, and Presidential election cycle shall be 2 calendar weeks and for every other year during said cycles, it shall be 4 calendar weeks. The contribution window for

contributions to national political parties shall be the same as the contribution window for the Presidential election cycle. The excess of any contribution beyond the limitations set forth in subsection (c) shall be treated as a contribution made during the next contribution window; subject to the limitations set forth in subsections (e) and (g).

(e) No person may make contributions in excess of the following:

    (1) $5,000 to any candidate seeking nomination for election, or election, to the office of Representative in, or Delegate or Resident Commissioner to, the Congress during any House election cycle;

    (2) $10,000 plus $80 per 100,000 adult residents of the State to be represented to any candidate seeking nomination for election, or election, to the office of Senator in Congress during any Senate election cycle;

    (3) $100,000 for any candidate seeking nomination for election, or election, to the office of President during any Presidential election cycle; and

    (4) $100,000 to any national political party during any Presidential election cycle.

    (5) The contribution limitations in subsections (e)(1)–(3) shall be tripled for candidates of parties which have not received at least 5 percent of the popular vote in any election during the past six years in the district, State, or States the candidate seeks to represent.

(f) No person may contribute more than $5,000 per year to any political organization other than a national political party or more than an aggregate of $25,000 per year to political organizations other than national political parties.

(g) No person may contribute an aggregate of more than $100,000 per year to candidates or political organizations, except as provided in sections 8(j) and 10(k).

(h) Only an adult natural person who is a citizen of the United States may make a contribution. All contributions must be made by said person in his or her own name and using only his or her own personal funds. Any labor union, corporation, or any other

person, group, committee, club, association, or other entity which
is not an adult natural person and citizen of the United States is
expressly prohibited from making a contribution.

(i) In addition to all other civil or criminal remedies, the
Commission may seek civil forfeiture of any contribution made
in violation of this Act.

(j) Any national political party may transfer funds through the blind
trust to any candidate in any amount without limitation.

(k) Notwithstanding any other provision of this section or this Act,
however, any political organization other than a political party
which does not make any contributions or expenditures and is
not an affiliated political organization or major purpose political
organization may accept funds outside of the blind trust without
any limitations from any nonforeign person, group, committee,
club, association, union, corporation, or other entity.

(l) All contributions to affiliated political organizations and
candidates shall be aggregated and subject to the lowest applicable
contribution limitations for any member of the affiliated group.

(m) If the Commission, after proper investigation and upon clear and
convincing evidence, concludes that contribution limits in
subsections 10(c) and (e) must be decreased in order to preserve
the anonymity of contributions to the blind trust or may be
increased without jeopardizing the anonymity of contributions to
the blind trust, it is hereby authorized to modify said limits; provided, however, that under no circumstances may the contribution
limits in subsections 10(c) and (e) be reduced by more than
fifty percent or increased by more than one hundred percent.

Section 11. Self-Funded Candidates. [Original]

(a) Notwithstanding Section 10, any candidate may make
contributions to the candidate's own campaign in any amount.[4]
Contributions by a candidate to other candidates or political
organizations, however, remain limited to the amounts set forth in
Section 10.

(b) No candidate shall be eligible to receive transfers directly or
indirectly from any Patriot account unless said candidate has

made an election to voluntarily waive the right under subsection (a) to make unlimited contributions to the candidate's own campaign. Candidates who make such an election may not contribute more than the amounts set forth in Section 10 to any candidates or political organizations, including their own campaign.

Section 12. Exploratory Committee. [Original]
(a) Any person may form an exploratory committee and accept what would otherwise constitute contributions, not to exceed the limits in subsections (c) and (d), outside of the blind trust without being considered a candidate for the purpose of this Act; provided, however, that if the person is or becomes a candidate, the identity of all contributors and the amount each contributed to the exploratory committee shall be reported to the Commission within ten days. The Commission shall then publish the identity of all contributors and the amount each contributed to the candidate's exploratory committee via the Internet.
(b) No person may form more than one exploratory committee during any two-year period.
(c) No exploratory committee may accept aggregate funds in excess of the following:
  (1) if the office being considered is Representative in, or Delegate or Resident Commissioner to, the Congress, $50,000;
  (2) if the office being considered is Senator in the Congress, $0.0442 per resident of the State to be represented; provided, however, that in no case shall the limit be less than $50,000 or more than $1,000,000; or
  (3) if the office being considered is President of the United States, $1,000,000.
(d) No person other than the person for whom the exploratory committee was formed may contribute to an exploratory committee in excess of the following:
  (1) if the office being considered is Representative in, or Delegate or Resident Commissioner to, the Congress, $2,000;
  (2) if the office being considered is Senator in the Congress,

$0.00176 per resident of the State to be represented; provided, however, that in no case shall the limit be less than $2,000 or more than $20,000; or

(3) if the office being considered is President of the United States, $20,000.

(e) Funds may be given to an exploratory committee only by an adult natural person who is a citizen of the United States. The funds must be given by said person in his or her own name and using only his or her own personal funds. Funds given to an exploratory committee do not count toward the contribution limitations set forth in subsections 10(c), (e), and (f). Exploratory contributions reported to the Commission are, however, included for the purpose of the $100,000 annual aggregate contribution limitations set forth in subsection 10(g).

(f) The Commission shall establish regulations to ensure that every exploratory committee shall substantially comply with the treasurer, registration, and reporting requirements set forth in sections 3, 4, and 5.

(g) Any potential candidate may contribute any amount to his or her own exploratory committee subject to the aggregate limitations in subsection (c).

(h) A candidate's exploratory committee must be closed to additional contributions before any other private contributions may be received through the Blind Trust.

Section 13. Restrictions on the Use of Distributions. [Original]

(a) A candidate may use non-Patriot funds from the Federal Election Commission's Blind Trust only for the purpose of making expenditures on the candidate's behalf and paying reasonable administrative expenses related to the candidacy.

(b) A political organization (other than a national political party) may use non-Patriot funds from the Federal Election Commission's Blind Trust only for the purpose of making expenditures, engaging in or funding political communications or other lawful political activities, and paying reasonable administrative expenses incurred by the political organization. Transfers of non-Patriot funds to other political organizations or candidates are not permitted, except as provided in subsection (c).

(c) A national political party may transfer non-Patriot funds in the Federal Election Commission's Blind Trust to candidates.[5]

Section 14. Creation of Patriot Accounts. [Original]

(a) Every United States citizen who is registered to vote in an election for any federal office shall be eligible for a Patriot account. In any state which does not require registration to vote in an election for any federal office, every resident who is legally entitled to vote in an election for any federal office and who has voted in such an election at least once within the past four years shall be eligible for a Patriot account.

(b) The several States of the United States shall promptly and regularly provide to the Commission all necessary information requested by it for the purpose of implementing this section.

(c) In order to have a Patriot account, an eligible citizen must register with the Commission.

(d) Patriot account registrations shall be valid for a period of six years, but may be renewed for subsequent six-year periods in any manner sufficient for initial registration. The registration for any Patriot account holder shall automatically be renewed by the act of voting in an election for any federal office.

(e) Any citizen may register for a Patriot account in person at any Patriot office or at any polling place during any federal election by presenting proof of identity and residence. The Commission shall ensure that the citizen is eligible for an account under subsection (a).

(f) During registration, the registrant must elect to make transfers from his account either via automatic teller machines (ATMs) at depository institutions or via a donation booth located at a Patriot office. To be eligible for the ATM option, the account holder must present a valid credit card, debit card, EBT (electronic benefits transfer), or ATM card in his or her own name to be electronically linked to his or her Patriot account with a PIN (personal identification number). A registrant who selects the donation booth option will be given a Patriot card bearing his or her name and Patriot account number.

(g) Any citizen selecting the ATM option may also register for a Patriot account via the Internet or by mail by providing his or her credit card, debit card, or EBT or ATM card number to the Commission. The Commission shall ensure that the citizen is eligible for an account under subsection (a). The Commission shall further confirm the identity and residence of the citizen by mailing a confirmation to the address associated with the tendered credit card, debit card, EBT, or ATM card account and requiring that the confirmation be returned to the Commission within thirty days. Registration will not be complete until the confirmation is received by the Commission.

Section 15. Credits to Patriot Accounts. [Original]

(a) A credit of $10 shall be made to every Patriot account on the first day of the year prior to the general election for the office of Representative in, or Delegate or Resident Commissioner to, the Congress.

(b) An additional credit of $15 shall be made on the first day of the year prior to any general election for the office of Senator in Congress to every Patriot account held by the residents of the State to be represented.

(c) An additional credit of $25 shall be made to every Patriot account on the first day of the year prior to the general election for the office of President of the United States. If the President then in office is eligible for reelection, then said credit shall be allocated as follows: $10 for use in the primary campaign and $15 for use in the general election campaign; but this restriction shall terminate immediately if the President informs the commission, in writing, that he is not a candidate for reelection. Primary-campaign Patriot funds must be expended by candidates before July 15 of the year of the general election for the office of President of the United States. General-election campaign Patriot funds may not be expended by candidates before July 15 of the year of the general election for the office of President of the United States.

(d) In the event that a special election is called, then an additional credit shall be made immediately to every Patriot account held by residents of the district, State, or States in which the special election is to be held. The amount of the credit shall be the following:

(1) If the election is for Representative in, or Delegate or Resident Commissioner to, the Congress, then $10;

(2) If the election is for Senator in Congress, then $15; or

(3) If the election is for President, then $25.

(e) In the event that a candidate withdraws, or otherwise becomes ineligible for election, after receiving Patriot dollars, then any unexpended Patriot dollars held by the candidate which have not been previously transferred to other candidates shall be returned to the Patriot accounts from which they came, pro rata.

Section 16. Transfer and Distribution of Funds in Patriot Accounts. [Original]

(a) The holder of a Patriot account may transfer all or part of the current balance of the account to any candidate or major purpose political organization which is in compliance with sections 4 and 5, subject to the limitations in subsection (b). The Commission shall continually publish a list of eligible candidates and major purpose political organizations via the Internet. No other types of transfers from a Patriot account are permitted.

(b) (1) Funds originally credited to a Patriot account pursuant to Section 15(a) may be transferred only to a major purpose political organization or to a candidate seeking nomination for election, or election, to the office of Representative in, or Delegate or Resident Commissioner to, the Congress.

(2) Funds originally credited to a Patriot account pursuant to Section 15(b) may be transferred only to a major purpose political organization or to a candidate seeking nomination for election, or election, to the office of Senator in the Congress.

(3) Funds originally credited to a Patriot account pursuant to

Section 15(c) may be transferred only to a major purpose
political organization or to a candidate seeking nomination for
election, or election, to the office of President of the United
States.

(4) Funds originally credited to a Patriot account pursuant to
Section 15(d) may be transferred only to a major purpose
political organization or to a candidate seeking nomination for
election, or election, to the office which is the subject of the
special election.

(c) Transfers from Patriot accounts shall be made through the Federal
Election Commission's Blind Trust and, except as otherwise
provided by this Act, shall be treated the same as any other
contribution under section 8.

(d) All transfers from a Patriot account must be anonymous, and a
refund of a transfer from a Patriot account shall be credited back
to that account. All transfers of Patriot funds from a major
purpose political organization to a candidate, however, are not
anonymous.

(e) Any Patriot funds which have not been transferred to and spent
by a candidate by the date of the general election shall be
forfeited.

(f) Only a candidate can take a distribution of funds which originated
from a Patriot account from the Federal Election Commission's
Blind Trust. A major purpose political organization may not take
a distribution of funds which originated from a Patriot account
from the Federal Election Commission's Blind Trust. Said major
purpose political organization is limited to transferring the funds
to a candidate consistent with subsection (b).

(g) The first 5 percent (calculated on the basis of the total number of
current Patriot accounts) of all funds available in a House election
cycle, Senate election cycle, or Presidential election cycle which are
transferred to candidates (directly or via a major purpose political
organization) shall be matched in equal amount (i.e., doubled) by
the Commission.

(h) Candidates may transfer Patriot dollars they receive to other
candidates. Said transfers shall be treated in the same manner, and

subjected to the same restrictions, as those made by major purpose political organizations to candidates.

Section 17. Mechanism for Transfers from Patriot Accounts. [Original]

(a) The Patriot Account Division of the Commission shall establish Patriot offices within every congressional district in the United States of sufficient number to service the needs of the residents of the district and geographically distributed to enhance the accessibility of the offices. Patriot offices shall be established in a cost-effective manner and may be located within preexisting federal offices or operated by contract or agreement with any State agency or suitable private entity.

(b) The donation booths at Patriot offices shall contain a computer or other device programmed to permit secure transfers from Patriot accounts to eligible candidates and major purpose political organizations, as well as the cancelation and refund of any prior transfer within five days of that transfer. The booths shall be screened so that all transactions are private. Before entering the booth, the account holder must present his or her Patriot card and proof of identity. The donation booth shall operate in the same basic manner as described in subsection (d).

(c) The Patriot Account Division of the Commission, in conjunction with the Board of Governors of the Federal Reserve System, shall make arrangements for the use of the automatic teller machines at depository institutions to facilitate transfers from Patriot accounts to candidates or major purpose political organizations via the Federal Election Commission's Blind Trust for those account holders who have elected to use the ATM option. The Commission is authorized to provide compensation to the depository institutions for the use of their ATMs and shall prescribe appropriate rules and regulations to require that said charges shall not exceed the lowest unit charges made for comparable use of such machines by other users thereof.

(d) Upon insertion of the credit card, debit card, EBT card, or ATM card that is electronically linked to his or her Patriot account and the entry of the appropriate personal identification number, the holder of the Patriot account shall be—

(1) advised of the current balance of the Patriot account and each subaccount;

(2) permitted to request a refund of all or part of a transfer from the Patriot account to a candidate or major purpose political organization which was initiated within the prior five days;

(3) given access to a listing of all candidates and major purpose political organizations currently eligible to receive transfers from the Patriot account;

(4) permitted to make new transfers of all or part of the current balance of the Patriot account to eligible candidates and major purpose political organizations; and

(5) advised of the number of days until the general election for the relevant office and of the fact that any funds not transferred by that date will be forfeited.

(e) The Enforcement Division of the Commission, in conjunction with the Board of Governors of the Federal Reserve System, shall take all feasible measures to detect and prevent unlawful use of Patriot accounts, including but not limited to monitoring transfers from Patriot accounts for suspicious activity and reviewing video records from automatic teller machines suspected as vehicles for unlawful transfers.

Section 18. Development of New Patriot Account Technology. [Original]
The Patriot Account Division of the Commission shall engage in research regarding the use of Internet or other technologies for the administration of Patriot accounts and transfers from said accounts to eligible candidates and major purpose political organizations. Notwithstanding the provisions of Section 17, the Commission may adopt by regulation any mechanism for the administration of Patriot accounts and transfers from said accounts to eligible candidates and major purpose political organizations which the Commission concludes is more efficient and effective; provided, however, that any such mechanism must include adequate safeguards to deter fraud or abuse.

Section 19. Prohibition Against Improper Transfers. [Original]
(a) It shall be unlawful for any person to give or any individual to accept any consideration whatsoever in exchange for the transfer

of funds from a Patriot account to any candidate or major purpose political organization.

(b) It shall be unlawful for any person to make or revoke transfers from any other individual's Patriot account.

(c) It shall be unlawful for any person to possess any credit card, debit card, EBT card, ATM card, or Patriot card with the intent of making or revoking transfers from any other individual's Patriot account.

Section 20. Civil Enforcement. [Modeled on 2 U.S.C. § 437g]

(a) Any person who believes a violation of this Act has occurred may file a complaint with the Enforcement Division of the Commission. Such complaint shall be in writing, signed and sworn by the person filing such complaint, shall be notarized, and shall be made under penalty of perjury and subject to the provisions of section 1001 of title 18. Within five days after receipt of a complaint, the Commission shall notify, in writing, any person alleged in the complaint to have committed such a violation. Before the Commission conducts any vote on the complaint, other than a vote to dismiss, any person so notified shall have the opportunity to demonstrate, in writing, to the Commission within fifteen days after notification that no action should be taken against such person on the basis of the complaint. The Commission may not conduct any investigation or take any other action under this section solely on the basis of a complaint of a person whose identity is not disclosed to the Commission.

(b) If the Commission, upon receiving a complaint under subsection (a) or on the basis of information ascertained in the normal course of carrying out its supervisory responsibilities, determines, by an affirmative vote of three of its members, that it has reason to believe that a person has committed, or is about to commit, a violation of this Act, the Commission shall, through its chairman or vice chairman, notify the person of the alleged violation. Such notification shall set forth the factual basis of the alleged violation. The Enforcement Division of the Commission shall make an investigation of the alleged violation, which may include a field investigation or audit, in accordance with the provisions of this section.

(c) If the Commission concludes that there has been a violation of this Act, the Commission may, upon an affirmative vote of three of its members, institute a civil action for relief, including a permanent or temporary injunction, forfeiture, restraining order, or any other appropriate order (including an order for a civil penalty which does not exceed $5,000) in the district court of the United States for the district in which the person against whom such action is brought is found, resides, or transacts business.

(d) In any civil action instituted by the Commission under subsection (c), the court may grant a permanent or temporary injunction, forfeiture, restraining order, or other order, including a civil penalty which does not exceed $5,000, upon a proper showing that the person involved has committed, or is about to commit (if the relief sought is a permanent or temporary injunction or a restraining order), a violation of this Act.

(e) In any civil action for relief instituted by the Commission under subsection (c), if the court determines that the Commission has established that the person involved in such civil action has committed a knowing and willful violation of this Act, the court may impose a civil penalty which does not exceed $25,000. If the person is a candidate or major purpose political organization, the court may also bar that person from receiving any transfers from Patriot accounts for a period of up to five years.

(f) In any action brought under this section, subpoenas for witnesses who are required to attend a United States district court may run into any other district.

(g) Any party aggrieved by an order of the Commission dismissing a complaint filed by such party under subsection (a), or by a failure of the Commission to act on such complaint within a 120-day period beginning on the date the complaint is filed, may file a petition with the United States District Court for the District of Columbia within sixty days after the date of the dismissal or the expiration of the 120-day period. In any proceeding under this subsection the court may declare that the dismissal of the complaint or the failure to act is contrary to law, and may direct the Commission to conform with such declaration within thirty days, failing which the complainant may bring, in the name of such complainant, a civil action to remedy the violation involved in the original complaint.

(h) Any judgment of a district court under this section may be appealed to the court of appeals, and the judgment of the court of appeals affirming or setting aside, in whole or in part, any such order of the district court shall be final, subject to review by the Supreme Court of the United States upon certiorari or certification as provided in section 1254 of title 28.

(i) If the Commission determines after an investigation that any person has violated an order of the court entered in a proceeding brought under this section, it may petition the court for an order to hold such person in civil contempt, but if it believes the violation to be knowing and willful, it may petition the court for an order to hold such person in criminal contempt.

(j) Any notification or investigation made under this section shall not be made public by the Commission or by any person without the written consent of the person receiving such notification or the person with respect to whom such investigation is made.

Section 21. Criminal Enforcement. [Modeled on 2 U.S.C. § 437g]

(a) If the Commission by an affirmative vote of three of its members or the general counsel of the Commission—subject to a veto by three members of the Commission—determines that there is probable cause to believe that any person has committed a knowing and willful violation of this Act, the Commission's general counsel shall bring a criminal prosecution against said person, subject to the limitation in subsection (b).

(b) The Commission's general counsel is hereby authorized to prosecute in the name of the United States any person pursuant to subsection (a) after giving fifteen days' notice to the Attorney General of the United States; subject, however, to the power of the Attorney General to order that the Commission's general counsel terminate said prosecution within thirty days of the notification. If the Attorney General of the United States terminates such a prosecution, the factual and legal bases for that decision must be explained publicly and in writing.

(c) Any person who knowingly and willfully commits a violation of any provision of this Act shall be fined, or imprisoned for not more than five years, or both. The amount of this fine shall not exceed the greater of $25,000 or three times the illegal contribution or expenditure at issue. If the person is a candidate or major purpose political organization, the court may also bar that person or organization from receiving any transfers from Patriot accounts for a period of up to five years.

(d) Notwithstanding subsection (a), the Commission may not order the general counsel to bring a criminal prosecution arising out of an affiliated political organization's failure to raise funds for political communications through the Blind Trust unless the Commission determines on the basis of credible evidence that there has been a substantial increase in the ratio of political communications to private contributions, as monitored by the Commission pursuant to section 27(f).

Section 22. Judicial Review. [Modeled on 2 U.S.C. § 437h]

The Commission or any United States citizen may institute such actions in the appropriate district court of the United States, including actions for declaratory judgment, as may be appropriate to construe the constitutionality of any provision of this Act. The district court immediately shall certify all questions of constitutionality of this Act to the United States court of appeals for the circuit involved, which shall hear the matter sitting en banc.

Section 23. Partial Invalidity. [Modeled on 2 U.S.C. § 454]

If any provision of this Act, or the application thereof to any person or circumstance, is held invalid, the validity of the remainder of the Act and the application of such provision to other persons and circumstances shall not be affected thereby.

Section 24. State Laws Affected. [Modeled on 2 U.S.C. § 453]

The provisions of this Act, and of rules prescribed under this Act, supersede and preempt any provision of State law with respect to any election for Federal office.

Section 25. Period of Limitations. [Modeled on 2 U.S.C. § 455]
No person shall be prosecuted, tried, or punished for any violation of this Act unless the indictment is found or the information is instituted within five years after the date of the violation.

Section 26. Inflation Indexing. [Original]
All dollar figures in this Act shall be annually adjusted for inflation by the Commission using the Consumer Price Index for all-urban consumers published by the Department of Labor.

Section 27. Modifications to the Amount of Patriot Credits. [Original]
(a) After proper investigation, the Commission shall determine the following "prestatutory" amounts:

(1) the aggregate contributions to candidates in House races during the two campaigns preceding the implementation of this Act;

(2) the aggregate contributions to candidates in Senate races during the two campaigns preceding the implementation of this Act;

(3) the aggregate contributions to candidates in the Presidential race during the campaign preceding the implementation of this Act; and

(4) in addition to the aggregate totals for each of the preceding, the Commission shall also determine the cumulative monthly subtotals of each group of contributions for the twelve months preceding the respective elections.

(b) In addition to adjustments for inflation pursuant to section 26, the Commission shall adopt regulations providing that in the event that the total Patriot credits transferred to candidates in House races, Senate races, and/or Presidential races in a given election cycle are not at least double the sum of non-Patriot contributions to said candidates through the Blind Trust, the amount of credits to Patriot accounts set forth in section 15 for the next comparable election cycle shall be increased by whatever percentage would have been necessary to ensure that the Patriots transferred in the prior election cycle were double the sum of non-Patriot contributions.[6]

(c) In addition to adjustments for inflation pursuant to section 26, the Commission shall adopt regulations providing that the amount of credits to Patriot accounts set forth in section 15 for House races, Senate races, and/or Presidential races shall be automatically increased by the same percentage as would have been necessary to ensure that the total Patriot contributions to candidates plus private contributions to candidates through the Blind Trust for each set of elections transferred during the preceding comparable election cycle are equal to the level of "prestatutory" contributions for the comparable elections as determined by the Commission in subsection (a).

(d) In addition to adjustments for inflation pursuant to section 26, during the first eight years following the implementation of this Act, the Commission shall adopt regulations providing that the amount of credits to Patriot accounts set forth in section 15 for House races, Senate races, and/or Presidential races shall be automatically and immediately increased whenever the number of Patriot dollars distributed to candidates plus private contributions to candidates through the Blind Trust to date during said elections are less than one half of the level of "prestatutory" contributions for the comparable elections at the same point in time as determined by the Commission in subsection (a)(4). The amount of increase shall be that percentage by which the number of Patriot dollars distributed to candidates plus private contributions to candidates through the Blind Trust to date during said elections must be increased in order to equal one half of the level of "prestatutory" contributions for the comparable elections at the same point in time as determined by the Commission in subsection (a)(4).

(e) Notwithstanding subsections (b)–(d), the Commission shall adopt regulations providing that the value of credits to Patriot accounts set forth in section 15 for House races, Senate races, and/or Presidential races shall be marginally reduced once they exceed twice the level of "prestatutory" contributions for the comparable elections as determined by the Commission in subsection (a) such that under no circumstances shall their value exceed four times the level of "prestatutory" contributions for the comparable elections as determined by the Commission in subsection (a).

(f) The Commission shall regularly monitor and report the cost of political communications made during campaigns and the ratio of political communications to private contributions and the ratio of political communications to Patriot dollars. For the purpose of this section, the Commission may develop regulations which factor the value of political communications, regardless of whether they were funded through the Blind Trust or not, into its determination of the level of private contributions to candidates.

Section 28. Appropriations. [Modeled on 42 U.S.C. § 441 and related provisions]

(a) There is hereby established on the books of the Treasury of the United States a fund to be known as the "Patriot Fund."

(b) Out of any money in the Treasury of the United States not otherwise appropriated, for the fiscal year in which this Act is adopted there is appropriated for payment to the Patriot Fund the amount of $6,000,000,000.

(c) Out of any money in the Treasury of the United States not otherwise appropriated, for the second fiscal year after the year in which this Act is adopted there is appropriated for payment to the Patriot Fund such sum as is necessary to make the balance of the Patriot Fund equal to $6,000,000,000.

(d) For each subsequent second fiscal year after the second fiscal year following the year in which this Act is adopted, out of any money in the Treasury of the United States not otherwise appropriated, there is appropriated for payment to the Patriot Fund such sum as is necessary to make the balance of the Patriot Fund equal to three times the amount of total Patriot credits transferred during the second prior two-year period.

(e) All transfers from Patriot accounts shall be funded out of the Patriot Fund.

(f) All administrative and other expenses incurred by the Commission shall be paid out of the Patriot Fund. To that end, out of any money in the Treasury of the United States not otherwise appropriated, for the fiscal year in which this Act is adopted there is appropriated for payment to the Patriot Fund the additional amount of $4,000,000,000. For each subsequent second fiscal year after the second fiscal year following the year in which this act is adopted, out of any money in the Treasury of the United States not otherwise appropriated, there is appropriated for payment to the Patriot Fund to cover administrative and other expenses incurred by the Commission an additional $1,000,000,000.[7]

Section 29. Independent Audits. [Original]
The Government Accounting Office shall conduct an independent audit of all administrative expenditures by the Commission eight years after the year in which this Act is adopted and then every subsequent five years. It shall at the same time review the levels of appropriations to the Patriot Fund to determine whether they are sufficient for the purposes of this Act. It shall report the results of said audits and reviews with any recommendations for changes to Congress and the Commission.

The Stabilization Algorithm

Our statute directs the FEC to promulgate regulations to ensure that (1) total (private and Patriot) contributions on presidential and off-year elections do not fall below their previous levels; and (2) Patriot contributions are at least twice as great as private contributions. But to add some meat to the bones of that mandate, this appendix details how the FEC might intervene to reduce the risks of financial droughts and private swamping discussed in Chapter 6.

Financial Droughts

THE LAGGED RESPONSE

The primary response of the commission to financial droughts should be lagged. The commission should calculate the greatest amount that was raised (expressed in today's real dollars) by federal candidates, national parties, and the federal accounts of state and local parties, together with the amounts expended on independent or coordinated express advocacy in any of the last three presidential elections before passage of our statute. Call this amount of status quo total contributions TC_{SQ}.[1]

Once our statute is up and running, the commission is charged with the task of determining whether there should be a lagged response to a financial drought that occurred in the previous election. The commission thus must calculate both the total amount of contributions (as defined above, together with expenditures on express advocacy) and the total amount of Patriot contributions made in the last presidential election. Call these total contributions and Patriot contributions (again expressed in today's real dollars) TC_L and PC_L, respectively.

If $TC_L \geq TC_{SQ}$, then the amount of Patriot dollars, P, distributed to registered recipients should remain unaffected (i.e., $50 in today's real dollars). However, if $TC_L < TC_{SQ}$, then the amount of Patriot dollars should increase to:

$$P' = P\left[\frac{PC_L + \min(0, TC_{SQ} - TC_L)}{PC_L}\right]$$

Thus if P = $50, PC_L = $1 billion, TC_L = $2 billion, and TC_{SQ} = $3 billion, then in real terms the Patriot distribution for the next election should increase to $100 (= P′ = $50 × [(1 + (3 − 2))/1]).

THE NONLAGGED (PROACTIVE) RESPONSE

During the first eight years of the statute's operation, we also propose a proactive (or nonlagged) intervention to ensure against severe shortfalls of more than 50 percent from the status quo. As with the previously defined TC_{SQ}, the commission would calculate the status quo total contributions that had been contributed on a monthly basis starting twelve months before the election. Let these amounts be denoted TC_{SQ}^t, where, for example, TC_{SQ}^{12} would equal the average total contributions that had been given more than twelve months before a particular election. TC_C^t and PC_C^t would be analogously defined amounts with regard to total and Patriot contributions in the current election that have been received more than t months before the current election.

As long as $TC_C^t \geq (0.5) \times TC_{SQ}^t$ for any given time period t, then the amount of Patriot dollars, P, initially distributed to registered recipients should remain unaffected. However, if $TC_C^t < (0.5) \times TC_{SQ}^t$, then the amount of Patriot dollars that have already been contributed should automatically increase by the multiplier, M:

$$M = \left[\frac{PC_C^t + \min\left(0, \left(\frac{TC_{SQ}^t}{2} - TC_C^t\right)\right)}{PC_C^t} \right]$$

Thus if a year before the election $PC_{C^{12}}$ = $500 million, $TC_{C^{12}}$ = $250 million, and TC_{SQ}^{12} = $1 billion, then the FEC should proactively intervene and increase the value of all Patriot dollars that have been contributed to that date by 50 percent (M = 3/2 = (0.5 + 0.25)/(0.5)).

PRIVATE SWAMPING

The stabilization algorithm response to private swamping involves only a lagged response. The commission under the algorithm might increase over the last Patriot disbursement, P, if total private contributions in the previous election (VC_L) turn out to be more than one-half the total Patriot contributions in the previous election (PC_L).[2] If $2VC_L > PC_L$, then the swamping algorithm would increase Patriot disbursement to:

$$P'' = P\left[\frac{(PC_L) + \min(0, 2VC_L - PC_L)}{PC_L}\right]$$

Thus if $P = 50$, $PC_L = \$3$ billion, and $VC_L = \$2$ billion, then the Patriot distribution for the next election should increase to \$66.66 ($P'' = \$50 \times [(3 + (4 - 3))/3]$).

CAPPING THE SWAMPING RESPONSE

But this Patriot adjustment for swamping leaves the federal fisc at risk of spending a virtually unlimited amount of money on Patriot funding. To cap this risk we propose both a lagged and a nonlagged response. The lagged response modifies the foregoing swamping adjustment so that the formula (1) attempts to maintain a one-to-one ratio of private to Patriot contributions only on marginal dollars that drive the expected Patriot contributions to more than twice the status quo total contributions and (2) caps expected Patriot expenditures at three times the amount of status quo total contributions. In mathematical terms, this means that if $VC_L > TC_{SQ}$, then the Patriot disbursement should only increase to:

$$P'' = P\left[\frac{\min(3TC_{SQ}), (2TC_{SQ} + VC_L - TC_{SQ})}{PC_L}\right]$$

Thus if $P = 50$, $PC_L = \$3$ billion, $VC_L = \$4$ billion, and $TC_{SQ} = \$3$ billion, then the Patriot distribution for the next election should increase to \$116.66 ($P'' = \$50 \times [(6 + (4 - 3))/3]$)—whereas the undampened disbursement amount would have been \$133.33 (\$50 \times [(3 + 8 - 3)/3]$). This overall cap on expected Patriot expenditures of three times the status quo total contributions is reached only if lagged private contributions (in the shadow of the donation booth) become more than twice the status quo total contributions (in real terms). Because the Patriot disbursement might be increased by an adjustment for either drought or swamping, the final disbursement P^* should be the greater of either of the two individual adjustments:

$$P^* = \max[P', P'']$$

A problem with the forgoing response—which attempts to cap the expected Patriot contributions at three times the status quo contributions—is that it implicitly assumes that the rate of Patriot contributions will remain constant in the following election. If the rate at which citizens contribute their Patriot disbursements increases appreciably, it is possible that the public fisc will be liable for several times the cost of current elections. To place a firmer cap on the cost of Patriot, we also propose a nonlagged capping mechanism (see section 27(e) of our statute). If more than twice the maximum total contributions in the prestatutory period, TC_{SQ}, have been contributed in a particular election, the commission will begin to discount increasingly the value of any further Patriot contributions. The discount will be a function of the following variables:

G = the number of Patriot dollars that have previously been given less $2(TC_{SQ})$;

T = the total potential number of undiscounted Patriot dollars that might be contributed (equaling the per capita Patriot disbursement, P, multiplied by the number of registered Patriot recipients) less $2(TC_{SQ})$;

C = the absolute cap on the number of discounted Patriot dollars less $2(TC_{SQ})$.

With these variable definitions, the discount can be expressed as:

$$D = \left(\frac{T - G}{T} \right)^{(T - C)/C}$$

where Patriot dollars received in excess of $2(TC_{SQ})$ would be multiplied by the discount factor D. This functional form has the appealing properties that it varies between 1 (for $G = 0$) and 0 (for $G = T$) and that if all T Patriot dollars are given, the total discounted value of the contributions will be C. Thus, for example, if T = $24 billion, C = $6 billion, and G = $5 billion, then the marginal Patriot dollar subsequently contributed would be discounted at 50 percent. If G grows to $12 billion, the marginal Patriot is worth 12.5 cents on the dollar.

APPENDIX B
The Secrecy Algorithm

The secrecy algorithm translates the actual daily amounts contributed into a daily amount that the blind trust reports to each candidate (or political intermediary) as the total available for immediate disbursement.[1] Let:

$A(t)$ = the actual total private dollar receipts (excluding any exploratory committee contributions) for the tth day

$R(t)$ = the amount reported to the candidate as being contributed on the tth day,

where $t = 1$ is defined to be the first day of the campaign.[2]

Whether the secrecy algorithm is triggered turns on the size of three underlying variables. First, we calculate the mean and standard deviation of daily contributions for the previous thirty days:[3]

$$\mu_t = \sum_{i=1}^{30} \frac{A(t - i)}{30}$$

and

$$\sigma_t = \left\{ \sum_{i=1}^{30} \frac{[A(t - i) - \mu_t]^2}{30} \right\}^{(1/2)}$$

Second, we calculate the total amount of the ten largest contributions on day t (where all of the contributions from political intermediaries are considered as being one contribution), which we define to equal $A_{10}(t)$. This last calculation is our central measure of the daily concentration of contributions.

As described in the text, the randomization procedure is triggered only if daily contributions are both unusually high and unusually concentrated. Otherwise, the amount reported by the blind trust is set equal to the amount actually received.

We are now prepared to make this proposal concrete. The amount reported will equal the amount actually received under the following conditions.

$R(t) = A(t)$, if either (i) $A(t) \leq \mu_t + \sigma_t$ or (ii) $A_{10}(t) \leq \sigma_t$. However, if the total amount actually received is greater than one standard deviation above the average daily receipts $(A(t) > \mu_t + \sigma_t)$ and if the ten largest contributions represent more than a standard deviation of daily receipts $(A_{10}(t) \geq \sigma_t)$, then the sum reported by the blind trust would be a random amount ranging between the average daily receipt and two standard deviations above the daily receipt:

$$R(t) = \min[A(t), \mu_t + u(\mu_t - \sigma_t, \mu_t + 2\sigma_t)]$$

where $u(\mu_t - \sigma_t, \mu_t + 2\sigma_t)$ is a uniformly distributed random variable that is equally likely to take on any valuation between one standard deviation below the mean daily receipt $(\mu_t - \sigma_t)$ and two standard deviations above the mean daily receipt $(\mu_t + 2\sigma_t)$.

If the randomization algorithm is triggered, there may be excess unreported sums that will be reported in some future day's balance by the blind trust. We define the excess unreported amount to be $E(t) = A(t) - R(t)$.

We propose dividing this excess amount into a random number of unequal parts and treating each part as if it were received randomly sometime in the next ten days. To be specific, the mechanism multiplies the excess by a fraction between zero and one-half and assigns the product to a day between one and eleven days hence. Both the fraction and the day are randomly drawn from uniform distributions. What remains of the excess amount after this product has been subtracted is again multiplied by a positive fraction less than one-half, redistributed forward, and so on, until the residual excess is less than one-quarter its original size. This final share of the excess is randomly assigned forward using the same methodology. Thus, on average, the excess amount will be broken into four equally sized parts, which will be reported an average of 5.5 days after being received.[4]

Unreported excess amounts that are attributed to a future day would be counted as part of the actual receipts of that day and then subjected to the same secrecy algorithm (meaning that if the total received that day—including the unreported excess attributed to that day's receipts—was too large and too concentrated, it would be subject to randomized reporting). For example, if the randomization algorithm dictated that $100,000 of receipts on a particular day should go unreported, a randomly selected fraction between $0 and $50,000, say $30,000, would be reassigned to a randomly selected day between one and eleven days later, say five days hence. The remaining $70,000 might be further divided into two chunks of $5,000 and $41,000, which could appear two and ten days later, for example. Because the residual $24,000 would be less than one-quarter of the original $100,000, it would not be further subdivided but rather reassigned in toto to another randomly selected day, perhaps the same day as the first chunk.

We estimated the impact of this algorithm using actual daily contributions to seven presidential candidates in the 1996 and 2000 election cycles and to thirty-eight House and forty Senate candidates in 1998 and 2000, as well as soft money contributions to the two major parties in 1996 and 2000.[5] Before reporting our results, a few methodological points are in order. First, we eliminated periods of time at the beginning and end of an election cycle during which the candidate reported very few, if any, positive contributions. For the three presidential candidates who withdrew before the general election (Forbes, McCain, and Bradley), we ignored contributions made more than one week after they withdrew. Throughout the periods covered, we

TABLE 1. Percentage of Days Randomized and Percentage of Cumulative Contributions Reported by Race and Year (1,000 Simulations Per Candidate)

Race	1996	1998	2000	Cumulative
% Days Randomized				
House		22.8%	23.6%	23.2%
Senate		22.5%	24.6%	23.5%
President	22.0%		23.2%	22.7%
Soft Money	21.4%		25.1%	23.2%
% Contributions Reported				
House		96.3%	94.9%	95.6%
Senate		97.0%	95.2%	96.1%
President	96.0%		97.5%	96.8%
Soft Money	98.4%		97.7%	98.1%
Number of Candidates				
House		18	20	38
Senate		20	20	40
President	3		4	7
Soft Money	2		2	4

Figure 1. Cumulative Contributions for Dole '96

limited our analysis to weekdays, even though some candidates reported a few Saturday (and even Sunday) contribution figures. Otherwise, zero values on weekends would artificially skew the thirty-day mean and standard deviation. In addition, we reported figures in $50 increments because candidates rarely receive contributions in odd amounts.

For each candidate's daily totals, we applied the secrecy algorithm one thousand times, allowing our random number generator to pick different values in each iteration. The results of these Monte Carlo simulations are reported in table 1. As reported in Chapter 7, the average randomization rate was 23.3 percent of days, and the average percentage of cumulative contributions reported five days later was 96.0 percent. Each reassignment of contributed dollars generates an average reporting delay of 5.5 days. On average, the sum of dollars reassigned was 40.5 percent of total contributions received, implying that each dollar waited to be reported an average of only 2.23 days beyond the five-day recission period.

Overall, the deviation between actual and reported contributions is slight. Randomization will not unduly burden a candidate's ability to run her campaign. Take, for example, Robert Dole's presidential run in 1996. Figure 1 charts cumulative actual and reported contributions over the course of his campaign under one iteration of the secrecy algorithm, including the five-day recission delay. Still, the gap between actual and reported contributions is small.

APPENDIX C
Designing Contribution Limits

In this appendix we discuss how we designed regulations of last resort to defend the donation booth from "contributor bombing": Candidates will be tempted to verify donors' promises of large contributions by checking their daily account balance with the blind trust and determining whether it has jumped abnormally.

The candidate's inferential process is strikingly similar to the position of a financial economist undertaking an event study of "abnormal" return in stock prices. The financial economist examines unusual changes in stock prices to assess whether material information became available to market participants on a particular day. The candidate examines abnormal changes in her trust balance to assess whether an unusually large gift (claimed by a particular contributor) became available on a particular day. As with event studies, an abnormal change in the account balance is one that exceeds the average expected daily contributions.

As the size of this abnormality grows relative to the standard deviation of daily contributions, the candidate can with greater confidence reject the hypothesis that the abnormality was merely a product of random chance—and accept the alternative hypothesis that a contributor has made an unusually large gift. For example, in the absence of the secrecy algorithm, if the size of abnormality (the amount by which total daily contributions exceeds the expected daily contributions) is more than two standard deviations, the candidate will have more than 95 percent confidence that the abnormality was not produced by normal volatility in contributions. In statistical terms, a finding that the abnormal change in the trust balance is more than two standard deviations is "statistically significant" evidence that something non-random has occurred.[1]

The secrecy algorithm complicates the candidate's inferential process. The algorithm is tailored to operate when an abnormal increment is larger than one standard deviation. Abnormally large daily contributions cause the trust to report a randomized amount that one-third of the time will actually represent an abnormally *low* amount of contributions for that day. Randomization will substantially disrupt the candidate's ability to make inferences based on trust balance changes on a single day.

The candidate is likely to respond by determining whether the cumulative contributions over a two-week period are abnormally large.[2] If an unusually large contribution triggers randomization, the algorithm randomly distributes unreported amounts over the following two-week period (extended to four weeks during noncampaign years).[3] Decoding is complicated because the algorithm breaks up the excess into a random number of unequal amounts. Candidates will also have imperfect information about the precise size of the mean and standard deviation of actual daily contributions (because they observe only reported amounts), and hence will have difficulty— even putting aside computational problems—implementing fancier inferential estimates. Most of the decodable information will be derived by comparing the cumulative abnormal contributions for the two-week period to the two-week standard deviation of contributions.

This comparison parallels a second kind of stock market study that focuses on cumulative abnormal changes in stock prices over multiple days. Finance economists prefer multiple-day event studies when they suspect that it takes a good deal of time for a particular piece of information to be reflected in the market price. They define an event window—say ten days— to assess whether the cumulative abnormal change in stock price is large relative to the multiple-day standard deviation. Candidates analogously are likely to revert to a multiday analysis when, because of the secrecy algorithm, they believe that it may take more than one day for the full value of a particular contribution to be reflected in their blind trust balance.

The key here is to recognize that the cumulative standard deviation for a candidate's total contributions over several days increases in the square root of the number of days:[4]

Cumulative (Multiday) Standard Deviation = Single-Day Standard Deviation
$$\times \ (\text{\# of Days})^{(1/2)}$$

This formula means that the standard deviation increases at a less than linear rate. For example, as shown in table 2, if the single-day standard deviation in a candidate's contributions is $10,000, then we would expect the standard deviations of total contributions over several days to increase—but not at $10,000 per day. As shown in the table, the cumulative standard deviation for two days would be only about $14,000. And the cumulative standard deviation for ten days is just over three times larger ($31,623).

TABLE 2. Standard Deviations for Cumulative (Multiday) Contributions
(assuming $10,000 single-day standard deviation)

# of Days	1	2	3	4	5
Std. Dev.	$10,000	$14,142	$17,321	$20,000	$22,361
# of Days	6	7	8	9	10
Std. Dev.	$24,495	$26,458	$28,284	$30,000	$31,623

We are now in a position to show both how the secrecy algorithm compli-cates the candidate's inference and the extent to which the algorithm's "noisy signal" can still be penetrated. If the standard deviation of a candidate's daily contributions is $10,000, then in the absence of the secrecy algorithm, a contributor must give at least $20,000 (two standard deviations) to provide the candidate with a 95 percent confidence that the abnormal jump in her balance on a particular day was not merely an artifact of random fluctuation. But the secrecy algorithm, by increasing the time period for assessing abnor-mal returns, increases the cost of giving the candidate equal confidence that an unusually large contribution was made. In the shadow of the algorithm, a contributor now has to give more than $63,200 (two standard deviations for ten days) to provide the same 95 percent level of confidence that a $20,000 contribution could have provided without the algorithm.

Setting caps at a lower number of standard deviations reduces the candi-date's confidence that a particular abnormality is caused by an abnormally large gift. Table 3 shows the relation between setting the donation limit at a particular number of standard deviations and the confidence level obtained by the candidate. The left-hand column expresses the contribution cap in terms of the ten-day standard deviation: It shows, for example, that a ceiling set at two standard deviations gives the candidate a confidence level of 95.4 percent that a nonrandom contribution has occurred. The middle column expresses any ten-day cap in terms of a one-day standard deviation by multi-plying the left-hand column by 3.16.[5] For example, if the contribution limit were set 3.16 times larger than a single standard deviation of daily contribu-tions, then the secrecy algorithm (which spreads a maximum contribution over ten days), will allow the candidate a confidence level of only 68.3 per-cent. And so forth.

We have set our individual campaign contribution limits very cautiously.

TABLE 3. Relationship Between Standard Deviation
and Candidate Confidence

Contribution Cap in Terms of 10-Day Standard Deviation	Contribution Cap in Terms of 1-Day Standard Deviation	Maximum Expected Candidate Confidence Level
0.00	0.00	0.0%
0.13	.40	10.0%
0.25	.79	20.0%
0.39	1.23	30.0%
0.50	1.58	38.3%
0.67	2.12	50.0%
1.00	3.16	68.3%
1.65	5.22	90.0%
1.96	6.20	95.0%
2.00	6.32	95.4%
2.50	7.91	98.8%
2.56	8.10	99.0%

Our aim is to deprive the candidate of more than a 20 percent confidence that he has received an unusually large contribution. As the table suggests, this goal can be achieved by setting contribution limits so that the cumulative abnormality is never larger than one-quarter of one standard deviation.[6]

To set the actual ten-day periodic limits, we must empirically estimate the expected daily-contribution standard deviation for specific offices. As shown in table 3, a limit of a 20 percent confidence level over ten days is achieved if the contribution limit is set at 0.79 times the standard deviation of daily contributions—an amount that represents one-quarter of one standard deviation of cumulative contributions over a ten-day period. There is no theoretically correct confidence level, and in choosing this amount we are guided by untested intuitions about how much uncertainty is sufficient to disrupt candidate inferences and hence is likely to deter bombing. Readers who prefer a higher or lower estimate can easily translate their own intuition into hard numbers by substituting a different multiple from the middle column of table 3.

TABLE 4. Estimation of Office-Specific Contribution Limits

Office	Estimated Standard Deviation of Daily Contributions	One-Quarter of One Estimated Standard Deviation of Cumulative (10-Day) Contributions	Proposed Office-Specific Contribution Limits
House	$3,181	$2,548	$2,500
Senate	$9,840	$7,882	$7,500
President	$117,453	$94,097	$50,000

Table 4 takes the final analytic step—translating our procedure into particular numerical limits. Our estimates of standard deviations in daily contributions are extremely crude. They are based on an analysis of actual contributions to the four major party presidential candidates in 1996 and 2000, and to thirty-eight House and forty Senate candidates in 1998 and 2000.[7] They are averages of the standard deviations over the entire election cycle which, as noted above, tended to decrease as the election drew near.[8] Most important, they are based on private giving under a system of mandated disclosure and without our proposed massive infusion of Patriot dollars. Private giving patterns are likely to change substantially under our proposed statute: We expect both the mean and the standard deviation to decline. Although the table provides a useful starting point, the commission should reassess contribution limits in the light of actual experience under the new paradigm.

With these important caveats, table 4 shows how we derive our race-specific contribution limits. The left-hand column reports our (crudely) estimated one-day standard deviations. The middle column reports the ten-day equivalent that will produce a 20 percent confidence interval (this is 0.79 times the left-hand column). For example, we estimate that a House contribution limit of $2,548 average implies, on average, that a candidate has no more than 20 percent confidence that an abnormally large contribution had been received. Because these calculations are based on data from the 1996 and 2000 elections and will change significantly under the new paradigm, we have erred on the side of caution and rounded down the figures in the right-hand column.[9] In the case of presidential giving, we have rounded down further to $50,000. This still allows donors to give fifty times as much money during any two-week period as they can currently give over the entire election cycle. In the end, we prohibit individual contributors from giving more than $2,500 to a House candidate, $7,500 (on average) to a Senate candidate, and $50,000 to a presidential candidate in any two-week period.[10]

During nonelection years, we double the length of the contribution window from two to four weeks. Because the standard deviation of contributions is substantially lower, this expansion is necessary to achieve the same ten-day standard deviations shown in table 4.

The secrecy algorithm should be sufficient to prevent single-day bombing, and the periodic contribution limit should be sufficient to prevent single-period bombing. But contributors and candidates eager to defeat the algorithm might try more complex stratagems—involving multiple periods or multiple candidates. For instance, a contributor might be able to credibly flag her contributions (1) by giving the maximum periodic amount in multiple periods (and asking the candidate to look at cumulative abnormal contributions for multiple periods) or (2) by giving the maximum periodic amount to multiple candidates (and asking those candidates to look at the cumulative abnormal contributions for the group as a whole).

We consider the problem posed by bombing multiple candidates, but the same analysis applies to multiperiod bombing of a single candidate's account. Even though the cumulative abnormal standard deviation grows with the number of campaigns, the cumulative (multicampaign, multiday) standard deviation increases only in the square root of the number of campaigns:

$$\text{Cumulative (multicampaign, multiday) Standard Deviation}$$
$$= \text{Cumulative (single-campaign, multiday) Standard Deviation}$$
$$\times \ (\text{\# of Campaigns})^{(1/2)}$$

Because this rate of increase is less than linear, a contributor can enhance candidates' confidence by giving the maximum allowable candidate-specific amount to multiple candidates at the same time.

Table 5 shows how the standard deviation for the multicampaign, multiday cumulative abnormal contributions increases with the number of campaigns. As we saw in table 2, the standard deviation of abnormal contributions for a single campaign over a ten-day period is $31,623. But the standard

TABLE 5. Standard Deviations for Cumulative (Multicampaign, Multiday) Contributions (assuming $10,000 single-day standard deviation and a 10-day analysis)

# of Campaigns	1	2	3	4	5
Std. Dev.	$31,623	$44,721	$54,772	$63,246	$70,711
# of Campaigns	6	7	8	9	10
Std. Dev.	$77,460	$83,666	$89,443	$94,868	$100,000

deviation for abnormal contributions for two campaigns is less than double this amount—increasing only to $44,721. If the maximum race-specific contribution amount is $31,600, a contributor can increase the confidence of two candidates by simultaneously giving this maximum to each campaign. Even though this hypothetical maximum race-specific limit represents less than one standard deviation of volatility for each blind trust balance, giving simultaneously will generate an expected abnormality that is larger than a single standard deviation for cumulative abnormal contributions to both accounts ($31,600 × 2 = $63,200 > $44,721)—and hence provide a higher confidence level to both candidates.

This analysis permits a final parallel to corporate finance event studies. Finance economists often run "event studies" to assess how similar occurrences (such as the announcement of a tender offer) affect multiple firms. It is often possible to detect a statistically significant price change when looking at a variety of firms even though none of the individual firm price changes is statistically significant.

Contributors and candidates can exploit a similar phenomenon. A contributor can increase the credibility of her promises by announcing that she has simultaneously given the maximum allowable race-specific donation, say, to ten Democratic Senate candidates. To be sure, these multicandidate strategies are more difficult to implement—both in the sense of requiring more dollars and in the sense of entailing larger costs of coordination. But if a donor is willing to pay a big enough price, he can still defeat both the secrecy algorithm and our race-specific contribution limits.

To a significant extent, these shenanigans are self-limiting. First, there are a limited number of periods and a limited number of candidates for a potential contributor to bomb—for example, there are only thirty-nine periods per House electoral cycle. Second, serious problems of attribution will inevitably arise when many donors claim to have contributed in the same period. As a candidate's temporal dance card begins to fill up, it becomes more likely that a maximum contribution will be made during any given two-week period—thereby encouraging others to lie and tell candidates that they too have just given the maximum amount. Just as faux terrorist groups claim credit for the Hezbollah's bombings, faux donors can do the same for the financial bombings of others. When a candidate receives multiple claims, she will have great difficulty attributing the inevitable shortfall in contributions to any particular contributor.

The severe attribution problem created by multiple claimants is the most important way that our regime protects the blind trust. But to be extra cautious, we also impose overall limits on the amount that a contributor can give to an individual candidate and on the amount that a contributor can give to multiple candidates. Because the possibility for such signaling is really a function of the number of campaigns to which a contributor gives (or the number of periods in which a contributor gives to a single campaign), we could impose a more complex schedule of contribution ceilings that varied with the number of campaigns or periods to which a contributor gives.

Table 6 provides an example. A contributor (independently constrained by the periodic $7,500 contribution limit) might be allowed to give a total of $10,606 if she were contributing in only two periods but could give up to $23,717 if she were giving in ten different periods. This kind of flexible cap would suffice to prevent contributors engaged in complex donation strategies from creating an abnormal change in the cumulative blind trust balances of more than one-quarter of a standard deviation. Such a "flexible cap" is more finely tailored to the core constitutional concern with corruption, but it seems too complex for sound administration, and so we have rejected it for flat numerical ceilings on the overall amount that individuals can give.

To restrain the possibility of multiple-period bombings, we have pro-

TABLE 6. Example of Multicampaign, Multiperiod Contributions Schedule

# of Periods or Campaigns	1	2	3	4	5
Contribution Limit	$7,500	$10,606	$12,990	$15,000	$16,770
# of Periods or Campaigns	6	7	8	9	10
Contribution Limit	$18,371	$19,843	$21,213	$22,500	$23,717

posed in Chapter 8 an overall candidate-specific limit that is twice the single-period limit. Because of the functional form of standard deviations (the square root of four is two), this limit is the amount that might be given over four periods without increasing candidate confidence to more than 20 percent. For simplicity's sake, we allow contributors to give the entire amount in just two periods, allowing candidates to infer an abnormality with slightly more confidence. If nobody else claimed to give a big check during two periods, a $15,000 contribution could generate a 26 percent confidence level. But candidates with reasonable prospects of success are almost certain to receive many big promises during such an extended period (equal to one month during the campaign year, two months at other times)—and in this standard case, confidence levels will sink very rapidly indeed.

To restrain more complex bombing scenarios, we place an overall limit on the amount that contributors can give to all candidates. Our limit of $100,000 per year allows contributors to give the maximum amount either to forty House candidates or to forty senate candidates, on average.[11] We give contributors much flexibility because the attribution problem is likely to be severe in multicandidate cases. Under the new regime, the FEC will let everybody know how much all candidates' trust balances have increased, but individual candidates will have a hard time determining whether other candidates have received many promises of big contributions from other donors.

We do not promise perfection. Given the pervasive attribution problems, we are quite confident that our periodic and overall contribution caps provide a powerful backup to the secrecy algorithm. And if further problems prove serious, the commission has the authority to respond appropriately.[12]

Costs of Administration

Using extremely conservative assumptions, we estimate the total annual cost of operating the new paradigm at approximately $300 million. Costs may well be much less, but even this conservative estimate suggests that popular sovereignty won't be exorbitantly expensive.

We break the expenses into five major components: Patriot registration, blind trust overhead, Patriot processing fees, private donation processing fees, and start-up and Web-maintenance fees.

Patriot Registration Expenses

The first and most significant category will be Patriot program registration. This requires voter identification verification and the linking of voters' personal credit and bank card accounts to Patriot accounts. The collection and inputting of the necessary data, the verification of identifications, and the necessary constituent service responsibilities are projected to reach about $100 million in annual expense. Table 7 shows that this figure is based on a number of conservative assumptions, including that one hundred million people register every four years and that half register via the polling place or post office (the most expensive venues).

Blind Trust Overhead Expenses

The second category funds the general and administrative staff necessary to oversee the Patriot registration program, to oversee Patriot donations, to oversee donation booth processes for private donations, to process free-floating Patriot contributions, and to provide executive-level management and strategic direction. All the costs, excluding the operation of the donation booth, will be approximately $78 million annually. As table 8 indicates, this figure assumes that there will be one line supervisor for every twenty employees, as well as a reasonable number of executive, accounting, legal staff and physical (and computer) accommodations.

TABLE 7. Patriot Registration Expenses

	Telephone	Mail	Internet	Poll/Post Office	Assumptions & Notes
% of Patriot Donors	12.5%	12.5%	25%	50%	100,000,000 Total Patriot Donors
Channel Registrants	12,500,000	12,500,000	25,000,000	50,000,000	
Registration Frequency	4	4	4	4	Years/registration
Annual Registrants	3,125,000	3,125,000	6,250,000	12,500,000	
Marketing Costs	$20.00	$20.00	$20.00	$20.00	Cost Per Thousand Impressions
Number of Impressions	10	10	10	10	Per Donor
Total Marketing Costs	$2,500,000	$2,500,000	$5,000,000	$10,000,000	
Registry Administration	5.0	10.0	N/A	13.0	Minutes per registrant
Employee Minutes	126,240.0	126,240.0	126,240.0	126,240.0	
Employee Registration Capacity	25,248.0	12,624.0	N/A	9,710.8	Registrants/employee
Necessary Headcount	123.8	247.5	N/A	1,287.2	
Employee Expense	$42,000	$42,000	$42,000	$42,000	$35,000 Salary Base + 20% Benefits
Total Registry Admin. Costs	$5,198,432	$10,396,863	N/A	$54,063,688	
Mail Verification Notices	$0.25	$0.25	$0.25	$0.25	$0.25 price per piece at bulk production and mailing
Mail Verification Phone Administration	3.0	3.0	3.0	N/A	3 Minutes/registrant
Employee Minutes	126,240.0	126,240.0	126,240.0	126,240.0	
Employee Registration Capacity	42,080.0	42,080.0	42,080.0	N/A	Registrants/employee
Necessary Headcount	74.3	74.3	148.5	N/A	
Employee Expense	$42,000	$42,000	$42,000	$42,000	$35,000 Salary Base + 20% Benefits
Total Mail Verification Costs	$3,900,309	$3,900,309	$7,800,618	N/A	
	$11,598,740	$16,797,172	$12,800,618	$64,063,688	

Total Annual Registration Exp: $105,260,219

TABLE 8. Blind Trust Overhead Expenses

	General	Telephone	Mail	Internet	Poll/Post Office	Assumptions & Notes
Executives Managers	10.0	5.0	5.0	5.0	5.0	
Accounting Staff	20.0	15.0	15.0	15.0	15.0	
Legal Staff	6.0	1.0	1.0	1.0	1.0	
Line Supervisory Headcount	N/A	9.90	16.09	7.43	64.36	1 for every 20 30K-employees
Administrative Asst. Headcount	12.0	10.3	12.4	9.5	28.5	1 for every 3 executives; 40 K salary +20%
Average Salary	$96,000	$96,000	$96,000	$96,000	$96,000	$80,000
Office Expense	$96,000	$96,000	$96,000	$96,000	$96,000	Equal to salary for administrative employees
	$8,064,000	$6,921,997	$8,308,246	$6,367,498	$19,120,984	
Total Blind Trust Overhead Cost:			$48,782,725			
Post Office Donation Booth Construction		$8,718,455.70				2000 Donation Booths at $50,000 amortized over 20 years at 6%
Computer Equipment			$11,869,820.02			$50 million amortized over 5 years at 6%
Administrative Building Expense		$8,718,455.70				$100 million amortized over 20 years at 6%
Total Blind Trust Overhead Cost:			$78,089,456			

Patriot Processing Fees

To estimate the costs of processing Patriot contributions, we assume that the agency will pay a market rate to the credit and bank card network owners for the rights to use their system for Patriot "spending." The range for merchant access to proprietary credit card networks is 0.75–1.35 percent of transaction value. We use the low-end rate of 0.75 percent, which is mandated by our statute to avoid monopolistic overcharges by the ATM system provider. In the two years preceding a presidential election, we assume that one hundred million Patriot contributors will give $45 ($10 for House + $10 on average for Senate (2/3 × $15) + $25 for president); in the non–presidential election cycle, we assume that seventy million Patriot contributors will contribute $20 ($10 for House + $10 on average for Senate (2/3 × $15)).

To the best of our knowledge, the marginal cost of gaining access to credit card systems is vanishingly small. Companies calculate access charges so as to cover total system costs. We may be wrong on this important issue, because cost data is proprietary information. We have constructed our "super-conservative" annual estimate of $300 million by assuming that companies could justify a minimum ATM charge of twenty-five cents per transaction, regardless of the number of Patriot dollars transferred.

As table 9 shows, this implies a much higher cost of operation: $54 million during cycles corresponding to presidential elections and $18 million during nonpresidential cycles. (We assume that the average Patriot card holder will make three transactions during presidential election years and 1.5 transactions during off-years.) If we eliminate the fixed transaction fee (but retain the 0.75 percent rate charge), annual Patriot transaction costs would fall to $17 million and $5 million, respectively, for cycles corresponding to presidential elections and off-year elections.

Private Donation Processing Fees

To be conservative, we assume that the donation booth will not deter any private giving, and we thereby estimate the highest plausible cost of processing transactions. In other words, our estimates suppose that the blind trust will receive $3 billion during the two-year cycle corresponding to the

TABLE 9. Summary of Annual Expenses

Annual Expense Summary	Start-up	Year 1	Year 2	Year 3	Year 4	Assumptions & Notes
Web Development & Maintenance	$20,000,000	$5,000,000	$3,000,000	$3,000,000	$3,000,000	Based on liberal estimates of the expenses required for acquisition of the necessary hardware and software to fulfill the database need of the conceived web site.
Patriot Transaction Fees	N/A	18,375,000	18,375,000	54,375,000	54,375,000	.75% rate plus 25 cents/transaction. $45/donor pres. years; $20/donor off years. 100 million donors pres. years; 70 million donors off year. 3 trans./donor pres. years; 1.5 trans./donor off years.
Private Donation Processing & Acctg.	N/A	37,500,000	37,500,000	75,000,000	75,000,000	5% rate. $3 billion donated pres. years; $1.5 billion donated off years.
Registration Expense	N/A	$105,260,219	$105,260,219	$105,260,219	$105,260,219	
G&A Expense	N/A	$78,089,456	$78,089,456	$78,089,456	$78,089,456	
Total Program Cost:	$20,000,000	$244,224,675	$242,224,675	$315,724,675	$315,724,675	
Average Annual Cost:	284,474,675					

presidential election, and $1.5 billion during the off-year election cycle. We have also assumed that the marginal cost of processing these contributions will be approximately 5 percent—a particularly conservative assumption compared with the current costs that presidential candidates incur in their General Election Legal, Accounting, and Compliance (GELAC) spending. In 2000 George W. Bush's GELAC spending, through January 31 of 2001, equaled 1.5 percent of his total receipts (including private contributions used in the primary campaign and public funds used in the general election). As table 9 shows, our very conservative assumptions generate marginal annual processing costs of $75 million during the presidential election and $37.5 million during the off-year cycle. Again, these estimates are no better than the crude assumptions upon which they are made. But both our no-deterrence assumption and our 5 percent processing cost serve to inflate the likely cost of the system.

Start-up and Web-Maintenance Fees

Finally, we have budgeted $20 million in start-up expenses used in creating the agency's online registration system. We calculate this figure based on market averages for Web development, and we expect that $20 million will be more than sufficient to create an Internet registration system that uses innovative database management tools to capture, store, and forward necessary registrant information. We also budget $3 million in annual maintenance expenses necessary to maintain the Web platform's software and hardware as its needs and system constraints evolve.

The sum of all these expenses for the first four years of operations are reported in table 9. The total annual cost of administering our new paradigm—based on our very conservative assumptions—is less than $300 million annually. These cost estimates are, however, a by-product of the underlying assumptions. If Patriot and private giving were 50 percent higher than previously assumed, the annual average expected administrative costs would increase to $331 million. (If these donations were 20 percent lower than expected, the costs would decline to $266 million.)

NOTES

1. REFORMING REFORM

1. See Doug Bandow, Best Campaign-Finance Reform Is No Limits, *USA Today*, Aug. 11, 2000, at 15A; James Bopp, Jr., Campaign Finance "Reform": The Good, the Bad and the Unconstitutional, Heritage Foundation, Backgrounder no. 1308, July 19, 1999, pp. 3, 20, 21–22 (found on www.heritage.org); Pete du Pont, Campaign Finance Defies a Complicated Solution, *Tampa Trib.*, Sept. 7, 1997, at 6. This theme is taken up by Justices Kennedy and Thomas in their separate opinions—both dissenting—in *Nixon v. Shrink Missouri Government PAC*, 528 U.S. 377, 408, 428–29 (2000). Representative John Doolittle has proposed "The Citizen Legislature and Political Freedom Act," which essentially repeals all limits on contributions and requires their immediate disclosure to the public. H.R. 1922, 106th Cong. §§ 2 and 4 (1999).

2. See, e.g., Kathleen M. Sullivan, Political Money and Freedom of Speech, 30 *U.C. Davis L. Rev.* 663, 688–89 (1997); Samuel Issacharoff and Pamela S. Karlan, The Hydraulics of Campaign Finance Reform, 77 *Tex. L. Rev.* 1705, 1736–37 (1999); Testimony of Ira Glasser, Executive Director of the American Civil Liberties Union, before the United States Senate Committee on Rules and Administration, Mar. 22, 2000, FDCH Congressional Testimony; Kathleen Sullivan, Against Campaign Finance Reform, 1998 *Utah L. Rev.* 311, 326–27; Joel M. Gora, *Buckley v. Valeo:* A Landmark of Political Freedom, 33 *Akron L. Rev.* 7, 35–36 (1999).

3. See www.fec.gov/finance (contributions to federal candidates and parties of federal "hard" monies were in excess of $2.9 billion). See also Don Van Natta, Jr., Dough Gets Little Rise Out of Voters: The 2000 Campaigns for President and Congress Might Cost a Record $3 Billion, but People Don't Seem to Care, *Portland Oregonian*, Jan. 30, 2000, at D-3 ("Never have so many given so much in so little time. . . . [C]ampaign finance experts estimate that the 2000 elections for president and Congress will end up costing a total of $3 billion, an amount that would dwarf the $2.1 billion spent in 1996").

4. There is one obvious constitutional problem generated by a regime of mandatory disclosure. Publicity may have a chilling effect on contributions to unpopular groups. See, e.g., *NAACP v. Alabama*, 357 U.S. 449 (1958) (finding production order issued in connection with litigation over qualification of NAACP to do business in state unconstitutional to extent it required disclosure of members within the state, because of potential chilling effect on affiliation with NAACP). *Buckley* accordingly exempts from the disclosure requirement minor parties that can show "a reasonable probability that the compelled disclosure of a party's contributors' names will subject them to threats, harassment, or reprisals from either Government officials or private parties."

Buckley v. Valeo, 424 U.S. 1, 73. See also *Brown v. Socialist Workers '74 Campaign Comm. (Ohio)*, 459 U.S. 87, 93–98 (1982) (finding that Ohio could compel the disclosure of neither campaign contributors nor recipients of campaign disbursements when the people so identified would likely be subject to harassment).

This is a very serious problem, but it need not detain us because we will be arguing against the entire notion of mandatory disclosure.

5. See, e.g., Jack C. Heckelman, The Effect of the Secret Ballot on Voter Turnout Rates, 82 *Pub. Choice* 107, 119 (1995) (estimating a 6.9 percent drop in voting in states utilizing the secret ballot and attributing drop to the elimination of bribery).

6. Ideological giving raises the question of democratic fairness, because ideologies favored by the rich will have an obvious advantage. In Chapter 3 we shall suggest ways of ameliorating this problem—it can never be magically "solved"—within the framework of a free society.

7. See, e.g., Samuel Issacharoff and Pamela S. Karlan, The Hydraulics of Campaign Finance Reform, 77 *Tex. L. Rev.* 1705 (1999), and Kathleen M. Sullivan, Political Money and Freedom of Speech, 30 *U.C. Davis L. Rev.* 663, 688–89 (1997).

2. PATRIOT

1. See Chapter 1, note 3. Of these contributions, soft-money accounted for $410 million and public contributions (federal matching funds in the presidential primary and public funds in the general election) accounted for $195 million. See www.fec.gov/finance.

2. Even without Patriot, presidential campaigns have been found to "reinforce and update political socialization"—a social-scientific way of describing the "citizenship effect." See Bruce Buchanan, Regime Support and Campaign Reform, in *Campaign Reform: Insights and Evidence* 173 (Larry M. Bartels and Lynn Vavreck eds., 2000).

3. See Bruce Ackerman, *We the People: Foundations* 235–43, 272–75 (1991); John Rawls, *Political Liberalism* 217 (1993).

4. See John H. Wigmore, *The Australian Ballot System as Embodied in the Legislation of Various Countries* 1–57 (2d ed. 1889) (describing the progress of the Australian ballot movement in Australia and as adopted in Europe, Canada, and the United States); see also Lionel E. Fredman, *The Australian Ballot: The Story of an American Reform* 10 (1968) ("[It] virtually terminated bribery, lavish treating, and disorder at elections.").

5. This two-level treatment is much in evidence in the Presidential Election Campaign Fund Act, 26 U.S.C. § 9001. Major political party candidates receive general election funding of $20 million plus a COLA adjustment. In 1996 the flat grant to each party was in the amount of $62 million. See Federal Electoral Commission: The FEC and the Federal Campaign Finance Law, www.fec.gov/pages/fecfeca.htm (last visited Sept. 24, 2000). In contrast, minor-party candidates must have polled at least 5 percent in the preceding election to qualify for anything. And those that reach this

threshold receive an amount based on the ratio of the party's popular vote to the average popular vote of the two major-party candidates—a formula that invariably gives them much less than the major parties. 26 U.S.C. § 9004.

6. Although Buchanan gained the support of the Reform Convention, John Hagelin emerged as a favorite of some Reform Party officials, who seceded and reassembled down the street to nominate Hagelin as a rival Reform Party candidate. See Michael Janofsky and B. Drummond Ayres, The 2000 Campaign: The Reform Parties, *N.Y. Times*, Aug. 12, 2000, at A10; B. Drummond Ayres and Michael Janofsky, The 2000 Campaign: The Reform Party; Rift on Buchanan Leads to Split, *N.Y. Times*, Aug. 11, 2000, at A1.

This split put into question who would receive the $12.5 million in federal campaign funds. An FEC rule required a candidate to appear as the party nominee in at least ten states to qualify—touching off a chaotic scramble for ballot access that Buchanan won. See Cathy Newman and Ben White, States Left to Pick Reform Party Ticket, *Wash. Post*, Aug. 27, 2000, at A5. But Perot entered the fray, saying that Hagelin was "the only proper candidate to receive public funding, based on the votes [Perot] received in the 1996 election." See Peter Carlson, Buchanan Awarded U.S. Funds for Reform Party, *Wash. Post*, Sept. 13, 2000, at A13.

Nevertheless, the FEC voted unanimously to give the entire $12.6 million to the Buchanan campaign. Hagelin initially threatened to challenge the FEC decision in federal court, but he dropped the challenge within days and returned to campaign under the banner of the Natural Law Party. See Ben White, Politics, *Wash. Post*, Sept. 15, 2000, at A20; Peter Carlson, Buchanan Awarded U.S. Funds for Reform Party, *Wash. Post*, Sept. 13, 2000, at A13; Ben White, FEC Recommends Funds Go to Buchanan, *Wash. Post*, Sept. 9, 2000, at A7; FEC Aides to Back Federal Funds for Buchanan, *Wash. Post*, Sept. 8, 2000, at A5. See also Federal Election Commission, Sept. 14, 2000, Press Release, FEC Certifies General Election Public Funds for Buchanan-Foster Ticket (explaining decision of commission to provide Reform Party funds to Buchanan campaign).

To our knowledge, this is the first time in American history that the fate of a political party was determined by a federal agency—an unforeseen, but predictable, consequence of the old paradigm's approach to the threshold problem.

7. Under the current presidential public funding scheme, a presidential candidate must show "broad-based public support" to be eligible for primary matching payments. This is established by raising $5,000 in $250 contributions in at least twenty states. See 26 U.S.C.S. § 9003.

8. Me. Rev. Stat. Ann. tit. 21-A, §§ 1121–28 (2000). Candidates for state senator qualify by raising only 150 contributions of $5, and candidates for the state assembly need to raise only 50 contributions of $5. Id. See Michael E. Campion, The Maine Clean Election Act: The Future of Campaign Finance Reform, 66 *Fordham L. Rev.* 2391 (1998). Three other states have passed similar laws. See Arizona Rev. Stat. tit. 16, §§ 940–61; Mass Gen. Laws Ann. ch. 55-A, §§ 1–18; Vermont Stat. Ann. tit. 17, §§ 2851–56.

9. A final problem generated by the traditional approach: What happens if a candidate refuses the subsidy and successfully outspends his subsidized opponents by raising larger sums in the private marketplace? As Chapter 10 suggests, Patriot solves this problem better as well, but we shall defer treatment of the problem until we have developed more tools for its solution.

10. See Maurice Duverger, *Political Parties: Their Organization and Activities in the Modern State* (1955). See also Bruce Ackerman, The New Separation of Powers, 113 *Harv. L. Rev.* 633, 657 n. 153 (2000).

11. Voter turnout over the past ten years is summarized in the following table compiled by the Federal Election Commission (available at www.fec.gov/pages/htmlto5.htm):

Election Year	% Turnout of Voting Age Population
2000	51.1
1998	36.4
1996	49.1
1994	38.8
1992	55.1
1990	36.5

3. THE DONATION BOOTH

1. This section takes its title from Saul Levmore, The Anonymity Tool, 144 *U. Pa. L. Rev.* 2191, 2222 (1996).

2. Researchers have yet to find an election between candidates in which information about funding actually made a difference in the outcome. But there have been cases of referenda in which voters have punished the side with unsavory funding. See Elisabeth R. Gerber, *The Populist Paradox: Interest Group Influence and the Promise of Direct Legislation* (1999).

3. For example, some Republican candidates refuse to accept contributions from Log-Cabin Republicans (who support gay rights). Ruth Marcus, "Pink Money" Flowing to Democrats; Gay Contributions Now Major Source, *Wash. Post*, Aug. 18, 2000, at A25. But the contributions are relatively trivial. It is extremely rare for a candidate voluntarily to return substantial gifts. Notorious exceptions include Hillary Clinton's returning $50,000 from a Muslim group and the Democratic Party's giving back $140,000 improperly raised at a Buddhist temple. Editorial, Our Money Is Not Good Enough, *Wash. Post*, Oct. 30, 2000, at A27; American Political Network, Gore Met Previously with Buddhist Sect Leader, 10 *Hotline* 69 (Dec. 24, 1996).

4. See William N. Eskridge, Jr., Privacy Jurisprudence and the Apartheid of the Closet,

1946–1961, 24 *Fla. St. U. L. Rev.* 703, 772 (1997) (discussing "mutually protective closet"). See also Samuel May, *The Fugitive Slave Law and Its Victims* (1861) (free blacks at times pretended to be runaway slaves).

5. See Lawrence Lessig, The Regulation of Social Meaning, 62 *U. Chi. L. Rev.* 943, 1010–11 and n.225 (1995) (citing *Jewish Museum, Kings, and Citizens: The History of the Jews in Denmark, 1622–1983* (Jorgen H. Barfod, Norman L. Kleebatt, and Vivian B. Mann eds., 1983)).

6. See, e.g., Jack C. Heckelman, The Effect of the Secret Ballot on Voter Turnout Rates, 82 *Pub. Choice* 107, 119 (1995) (estimating a 6.9 percent drop in voting in states utilizing the secret ballot and attributing said drop to the elimination of bribery); see also Geoffrey Brennan and Loren Lomasky, *Democracy and Decision: The Pure Theory of Electoral Preference* 219–20 (1993) ("Arguably, some of the point went out of voting once voting ceased to involve an open declaration of one's political convictions"). But see John R. Lott, Jr., and Larry Kenny, How Dramatically Did Women's Suffrage Change the Size and Scope of Government? tbl. 2 (unpublished manuscript, noting that the secret ballot reduced voter turnout by 2 to 4 percent).

7. Imagine what would happen to Yale's large contributions if the university announced that it would accept only anonymous donations, and that big givers could no longer expect their names to be memorialized on the front of buildings and the publications of professors holding endowed chairs. See also Amihai Glazer and Kai A. Konrad, A Signaling Explanation for Charity, 86 *Am. Econ. Rev.* 1019, 1021 (1996) (noting that fewer than 1 percent of the donations to Yale Law School, Harvard Law School, and Carnegie Mellon University are anonymous).

8. Hard data are tough to come by. Surveys by Gallup, the Survey Research Center, and the Center for Political Studies between 1952 and 1996 suggest that givers range between 4–12 percent of the national adult population. In 1996 that number was closer to 6 percent, with a polling error of up to 4 percent. See Herbert Alexander, Spending in the 1996 Election, in *Financing the 1996 Election* 11, 27–28 (John C. Green ed., 1999).

A "Citizen Participation Project" study, conducted by Sidney Verba, Henry Brady, Norman Nie, and Kay Lehman Schlozman, reported that 18 percent of 15,000 individuals said that they had given money to a political campaign at one time or another. The Citizen Participation Study was conducted in two parts. The first stage consisted of a random telephone survey of 15,503 members of the American voting age population. The second stage consisted of an in-person interview with 2,517 of the original 15,503 persons. Of those 2,517 individuals the mean contribution was $58 per year. Among politically active respondents the mean was $247. See Sidney Verba, Kay Lehman Schlozman, and Henry E. Brady, *Voice and Equality: Civic Voluntarism in American Politics* 54 (1995).

In 1996, 630,000 donors gave $200 or more to any federal election candidate. These donors constituted less than 0.325 percent of the voting population. Two hun-

dred thirty-five thousand people, just over one tenth of 1 percent of the voting population, gave $1,000 or more (The Big Picture: 1996, www.opensecrets.org/pubs).

9. In all 1996 federal campaigns, candidates received $597 million from individuals who
contributed $200 or more and $734 million from individual donors who contributed
less than $200. See The Big Picture: 1996, www.opensecrets.org/pubs.

   See also www.opensecrets.org/pubs/bigpicture/overview/bpoverview.htm: "For
members of Congress, small donors typically make up about 20 percent of their
campaign funds. (The exact averages were 19 percent in the House and 22 percent
in the Senate.) . . . Indeed, if you look solely at those who gave $1,000 or more, you
find that the number of donors is something under 235,000—about 1/10th of 1 percent of the American public. In all, they gave an estimated $477 million to candidates
and political parties in 1995–96, and a total of $638 million if you include contribu-
tions to PACs and soft money accounts as well." In the 1998 congressional campaigns,
candidates received $464 million from individuals who contributed $200 or more
and $351 million from individuals who contributed less than $200 (The Big Picture:
1998, www.opensecrets.org/pubs).

10. A national survey of more than 1,100 donors who gave $200 or more to congressional
candidates in the 1996 election contains data on their annual family income:

Annual Family Income	% of Donors
$500,000 or more	20
$250,000–499,999	26
$100,000–249,999	35
$50,000–99,999	14
$49,999 or less	5

"Why Do Donors Give?" a report by the Center for Responsive Politics (available at
www.opensecrets.org/pubs).

11. For a fine recent study, see Michael Schudson, *The Good Citizen: A History of American Civic Life* (1998).

12. Robert Putnam, *Bowling Alone: The Collapse and Revival of American Community* 48–
53 (2000). Professor Putnam greatly prefers other forms of face-to-face engagement as
modes of creating the social capital needed to sustain a Tocquevillean culture. But
we do not read him to suggest that check-writing is culturally insignificant. He is
simply saying—and we agree—that it is not nearly enough to sustain the civic culture
as a vital force in the twenty-first century.

13. We shall respond in Chapter 5 to this serious problem with an additional device. It
proposes a special regime for "exploratory committees" designed to enable candidates
to raise an initial pot of money quickly and easily at the earliest stages of their campaigns. Although this device plays an important role in our overall scheme, we prefer
to leave the text uncluttered at this foundational stage of our argument.

14. See Maurice Duverger, *Political Parties: Their Organization and Activities in the Modern State* 230–31 (1955) ("[E]very Centre party is by its very nature divided").

15. John R. Lott, Jr., Explaining Challenger's Campaign Expenditures: The Importance of Sunk Nontransferable Brand Name, 17 *Pub. Fin. Q.* 108 (1989) (arguing that spending in previous years builds "brand loyalty" among voters and thus deters challengers from running); John R. Lott, Jr., The Effect of Nontransferable Property Rights on the Efficiency of Political Markets: Some Evidence, 32 *J. Pub. Econ.* 231 (1987) (finding that property rights of incumbency make successful challenges expensive and unattractive); James M. Snyder, Jr., Long-Term Investing in Politicians, or Give Early, Give Often, 35 *J. Law & Econ.* 15 (1992).

16. Incumbents also have the franking privilege. As Ralph Winter has noted: "In 1974, the year in which the limits were passed, over $38 million was spent on the congressional frank—the heaviest use of the frank at that time being near the dates of primary and general elections. In the same year, the total spent by challengers in all primary and general election campaigns was barely over twenty million dollars. The incumbents who passed the 1974 Act, therefore, spent almost twice as much on franked mail alone as challengers spent on all of their political activities in both primary and general elections. In addition to the frank, incumbents have other perks which are useful for political purposes. These include a staff, a variety of offices, access to inexpensive broadcast facilities, paid trips to the district, and so on. These resources are enormously useful for communicating with voters in order to generate electoral support. The Act's limitations on expenditures, therefore, fell vastly more heavily upon challengers than upon incumbents." Ralph K. Winter, The History and Theory of *Buckley v. Valeo*, 6 *J.L. & Pol'y* 93, 102 (1997).

17. Although Democrats are at a relative fund-raising disadvantage under the existing system, this may not be true under the secret donation booth. For example, if Republican private-dollar contributions are more likely to be motivated by enhanced access or influence than ideological conviction, mandated anonymity could give Democrats the private-dollar advantage. Our point, however, transcends the specifics of party politics.

18. See Justice Harlan's dissent in *Harper v. Virginia State Board of Elections*, 383 U.S. 663 (1966).

19. The Twenty-Fourth Amendment to the Constitution explicitly bans poll taxes in federal elections, and the Supreme Court's decision in *Harper*, supra note 18, effectively achieves the same result for state elections.

20. We have focused on a progressive matching-grant scheme because of its obvious attractions to progressive reformers. There are many other mixed systems, but we don't think that further analysis will contribute much genuine understanding of the basic principles at stake.

21. One of us was sufficiently impressed by the force of this question that he took the abolitionist side when he first proposed Patriot. See Bruce Ackerman, *Crediting the Voters: A New Beginning for Campaign Finance*, American Prospect 71–80 (Spring 1993).

4. REGULATIONS OF LAST RESORT

1. 2 U.S.C. § 441 (a). Under current law, an individual may give:

   $1,000 per election to a federal candidate or the candidate's campaign.
   Primaries, runoffs, and general elections are considered separate campaigns;
   $5,000 per calendar year to a PAC;
   $20,000 per calendar year to a national party;
   $25,000 maximum on all federal campaign giving (including candidates,
   parties, PACs, etc.). (Id.)

2. FECA does not limit the dollar amounts given to national parties, designated as non-federal dollars. These contributions are known as soft money and, under FEC rules, may be spent by parties on such nonfederal campaign activities as:

   The nonfederal portion of the party's administrative overhead;
   Voter registration;
   Voter mobilization;
   Infrastructure improvements;
   Electioneering communications (also known as issue advocacy). (Id.)

   See Stephen Ansolabehere and James M. Snyder, Jr., Soft Money, Hard Money, Strong Parties, 100 *Colum. L. Rev.* 598, 600 (2000) ("In 1998, the Democratic and Republican national party organizations raised $445 million in federal (hard money) accounts and $224 million in non-federal (soft money) accounts"). In 1998 party money accounted for about 45 percent of all campaign money raised at the national level. Nonfederal contributions accounted for 15 percent of all money raised that year at the national level. Id. at 607.

   Soft money contributions have been highly concentrated, with eighteen thousand donors giving $196 million in 1998. Eleven percent of these contributions were more than $20,000 (the limit on hard dollar contributions). But this 11 percent (approximately 2,000 donors) gave 78 percent of the soft money, $153 million (an average of just over $75,000). Id. at 607. Three hundred ninety donors gave more than $100,000, and twenty-six gave more than $500,000. Richard Briffault, The Political Parties and Campaign Finance Reform, 100 *Colum. L. Rev.* 620 (2000).

3. McCain-Feingold does not attempt a clean-money solution to the problem by injecting new forms of public money into the process, and so it would be churlish to criticize its failure to consider Patriot. The only subsidies in the bill are extremely indirect. See, e.g., S. 27, 107th Cong. Sec. 305 (mandating lowest media rates for candidates and parties).

4. S. 27, 107th Cong. Sec. 102 (2001).

5. Id. at Sec. 316.

6. Id. at Sec. 201.

7. Id. at Sec. 203 & 201(f)(E).

5. MIXING PARADIGMS

1. During this early period of the campaign, large contributions will typically trickle in over a four-week period. See Chapter 8 and Appendix B.
2. See www.fec.gov. The $1 million presidential limit also pales in comparison with the $91.3 million raised by President Bush in the 2000 primary season and with the $40.1 million clean-money expenditure limit that applied to candidates who accepted public matching funds in the primary season. Indeed, the $1 million amount is much less than the $7.1 million that the Governor George W. Bush Presidential Exploratory Committee raised in the three months between January and April 1999. It should be noted, however, that Bush's exploratory committee spent only $854,000 during this period.
3. It would be foolish to counter the problem of gamesmanship via a complex hearing mechanism designed to determine whether a politician filling his exploratory fund had already "intended" to become a candidate. Such a proceeding would divert public attention from the main issues of the campaign to a question of subjective intention that is almost impossible to prove. Worse yet, the hearing would be overtaken by events before it could be concluded—with the "explorer" making the requisite declaration after filling her war chest, or deciding to withdraw from the competition.
4. Forbes spent $37.4 million of his own money in 1996 (The Big Picture: 1996, www.opensecrets.org/pubs), and $76 million in 2000 (www.tray.com). Corzine lent $33 million to his own campaign in 2000 (www.tray.com). Huffington contributed $16.3 million plus $12 million in loans in 1994 (www.tray.com). Perot contributed almost $10 million plus $188,000 in loans to his campaign in 1996, and $60.8 million plus $4.5 million in loans in 1992 (www.tray.com).

   In 1998 all federal candidates contributed $91.8 million to their own elections—out of a total of $1.5 billion donated during this off-year election (this aggregate sum includes soft money and PAC contributions). FEC Reports on Congressional Fundraising for 1997–98, www.fec.gov/press/canye98.htm.

6. DESIGNING PATRIOT

1. Some states will be obliged to adapt registration procedures for Patriot to conform to their special systems for registering voters. For example, North Dakota does not require registration before election day, and might rely exclusively on registering voters at the polls. See Federal Election Commission, State Voter Registration Requirements, www.fec.gov/pages/Voteinst.htm (visited Feb. 17, 1999). Everybody votes by mail in Oregon (see Priscilla L. Southwell and Justin Burchett, Vote-by-Mail in the State of Oregon, 34 Willamette L. Rev. 345 (1998) (describing Oregon's experience with a vote-by-mail system)), and so the state might rely more heavily on initial

voter registration procedures and might also develop an innovative system of Internet registration.

2. Sixty-six percent of the voting-age population (193 million) were registered in 1996. *Statistical Abstract of the United States, 1999,* table 488. The Census Bureau projects that 157 million Americans will be credit card holders by 2000. Id., at table 825. See also David Laibson et al., A Debt Puzzle (unpublished manuscript, Jan. 1, 2000) (79 percent of households surveyed in the 1995 Survey of Consumer Finances reported having a credit card). There are now more than 140 thousand ATMs in the country. In addition, some of the 875,000 point-of-sale (grocery store, gas station, etc.) machines might be adapted for use by Patriot. Id. at table 829.

3. A "transactions account" is a "category comprising checking, savings, and money market deposit accounts, money market mutual funds, and call accounts at brokerages. The families without such accounts in 1998 were disproportionately likely to have low incomes; to be renters; to be in the bottom quarter of the distribution of net worth; to be headed by a person younger than 35 or at least 75; to be headed by a person neither working nor retired; and to have a nonwhite or Hispanic respondent." Arthur B. Kennickell et al., Recent Changes in U.S. Family Finances: Results from the 1998 Survey of Consumer Finances, *Federal Reserve Bulletin* 8 (Jan. 2000).

4. The Department of Treasury mandated the use of EBT (electronic benefits transfer) for "all Federal payments made by a [federal] agency." 31 C.F.R. §§ 208.1, 208.2, 208.3, 208.5, 208.6. Thirty-nine states currently have EBT programs. BUYPASS EBT, Where Is EBT? at www.neteps.com/pages/ebt/where.html (last visited Oct. 17, 2000) (displaying a map that shows where EBT is available across the country). All states are required to implement food stamp EBT systems by October 1, 2002. 65 Fed. Reg. 49719–26 (Aug. 15, 2000). See also American Public Human Services Association, Electronic Benefit Transfer Systems (EBT), www.aphsa.org/reform/ebt.htm (1999) (describing the new regulations on the use of EBT for welfare benefits). Connecticut, for example, has already shifted to a Digital Imaging/Biometric Identification Project for its welfare benefits distribution. This card is a "tamper-proof, secure photo identification card," containing "the applicant's photo, welfare identification number, a 2D bar-code containing fingerprint minutiae data for fast 1:1 identification verification, and a[n] ISO standard mag stripe that can carry everything from EBT financial transaction codes for use in ATMs and POS (point of sale) devices to medical eligibility data for medical service providers." Connecticut Department of Social Services, Digital Imaging: DSS's Biometric Identification Project, at www.dss.state.ct.us/digital/project.htm (last visited Dec. 6, 2000) (describing the mandatory identification card for welfare recipients in Connecticut).

5. *Statistical Abstract of the United States* (1999), table 635.

6. Patriotic contributions could also be made through the Internet—as long as the account is tied to a bank or credit card number. To prevent fraudulent sales of Patriot dollars for cash, account holders must be deterred from revealing their credit card number (and personal identification number, or PIN) to the fraudster. As a matter

of fact, cardholders are already aware of the dangers involved in unauthorized Internet use, and have become reluctant to reveal this information to others.

7. A briber might return to the machine five days later and require the bribee to show that the money is missing from her Patriot account. This is a lot of trouble to take in order to assure that $50 has gone into the account targeted by the briber. Moreover, even if the bribee's Patriot account is empty, the briber can't know whether she has redirected her Patriots to another candidate. And unless the briber returns to the ATM at the very moment that the recission period lapses, there is still a chance for a subsequent repudiation of the deal.

8. A special problem arises with credit or ATM cards whose credit line has been exhausted. Holders of "maxed out" cards might be willing to sell them for a few dollars because the fraudster will not be able to use the cards to go on a spending spree. Nick Souleles, a professor of finance at the Wharton School, estimates that about 15 percent of credit cards are maxed out (defined as using more than 90 percent of their credit limit). See Nick Souleles, Consumer Response to Changes in Credit Supply: Evidence from Credit Card Data (unpublished manuscript, 2000).

    This problem is serious but not unsolvable. Holders of maxed out cards have reason to worry that fraudsters might evade the control system and successfully use the card to purchase goods or services, doing serious damage to the cardholder's credit rating. It is also quite possible to link electronic systems so that access to Patriot dollars is denied whenever a card is maxed out.

9. Imagine Jane Doe logging on to a Patriot registration Web site. She types in the number of the ATM card with which she wishes to link her account, along with her PIN and a voter registration number provided by her local election board. Patriot Co. then verifies that she is a registered voter, that she has not registered any other cards, and that she does in fact have this ATM card with this PIN. It can then send her a confirmation by mail (to the same mailing address as her regular bill), which she must sign and return to complete her registration. Such a system might well be technologically manageable long before political conditions were ripe for the enactment of our model statute.

10. For a more elaborate effort, see Bruce Ackerman, *We the People* (vol. 1: *Foundations* 1991, vol. 2: *Transformations* 1998).

11. For a further discussion of the significance of voting for citizenship, see Bruce Ackerman, *We the People: Foundations* 236–43 (1991).

12. Theoretically, it is possible to divulge the names of the contributors while keeping the amounts of their gifts confidential. But given the small sums involved, we opt for total anonymity.

13. To further PAC accountability, our statute requires the public disclosure of the names of officers of the PAC (and anybody else who will determine the PAC's beneficiaries). Courts have upheld such disclosure requirements, distinguishing them from coerced publication of the names of rank-and-file members. See, e.g., *NAACP v. Alabama*, 357 U.S. 449, 464 (1958). If a PAC could show a "reasonable probability" of reprisals

or harassment, the Constitution might demand a waiver of this requirement, even as it applies to officers. See *Brown v. Socialist Workers '74 Campaign Committee (Ohio)*, 459 U.S. 87 (1982) (striking down application of statute mandating disclosure of recipients of funds spent by Socialist Workers party).

14. Even if we purge the system of the influences of disproportionate wealth, there still may remain a problem of disproportionate organizing technologies. Milk producers may have an easier time raising Patriot dollar contributions than milk consumers. But the very concentrated numbers of milk producers limits the number of Patriot dollars they have available to contribute.

15. Another potential application concerns access to television. We generally oppose mandates on television stations to provide free or subsidized time. These proposals suffer from the standard pathologies of command-and-control regulation—most notably, the multiple embarrassments involved in designing threshold requirements that discriminate amongst the innumerable politicians who yearn for subsidized speech rights (see Chapter 2). Special dangers arise whenever agents of the state are given the power to control media decisions. During the last weeks of a hard-fought campaign, will bureaucrats tilt against challengers when handing out television time?

   Better to give the candidates patriotic cash and let them bargain their way onto TV. If we were going to insist on a special regime regulating television access, we would prefer the distribution of special TV vouchers into each patriotic account, which individuals could then direct to candidates of their choice. If 130 million registered voters were given vouchers worth 1/2,000 of a second of network time each, say, it would translate into roughly nineteen hours of candidate speech.

16. Our restriction on the use of Patriot dollars will, alas, generate some bad incentives on the margin. A Ralph Nader or a Pat Buchanan will know that if he simply stays on the sidelines, he cannot obtain patriotic funding for his issue advocacy. He will therefore have an extra incentive to become a declared candidate to obtain public funding. But given the many other incentives for spoilers to enter the race, this one seems unlikely to be decisive.

   Moreover, expanding the voucher to include all "First Amendment" communications has problems of its own. Your bowling league or church might start a pseudo–First Amendment organization to raise public money for its next social event. We leave these problems for some future book.

17. There have been numerous efforts to limit out-of-state contributions. An early version of McCain-Feingold contained provisions restricting out-of-state contributions to a certain percentage (such as 40 or 60 percent) of a candidate's total. See S. 25, 105th Cong., 1st Sess. (1997); H.R. 493, 105th Cong., 1st Sess. (1997); S. 1219, 104th Cong., 2d Sess. (1996); H.R. 2566, 104th Cong., 1st Sess. (1995); see also Jeff Barker, Most of Sarbanes's Funding Comes from Outside Maryland, *Baltimore Sun*, Oct. 14, 2000, at A1 (describing how McCain-Feingold's limit on out-of-state contributions was dropped for lack of support).

   Reformers often deplore the large role played by wealthy out-of-staters. See Colloquium, Constitutional Implications of Campaign Finance Reform, 8 *Admin. L.J. Am. U.* 161, 181–82 (1991) (Professor Jamin Raskin). This complaint generates the inevitable reply that restricting out-of-staters improperly insulates incumbents from political challengers. ABA Election Law Committee Panel Discussion, 13 *J.L. & Pol.* 163, 169–70 (1997) (Professor Lillian BeVier).

Courts have been generally hostile to statutory attempts to limit out-of-state contributions. See *Vannatta v. Keisling,* 151 F.3d 1215 (9th Cir. 1998) (striking down an Oregon constitutional amendment restricting out-of-district contributions to state candidates); *Whitmore v. FEC,* 68 F.3d 1212 (9th Cir. 1995) (rejecting as "frivolous" claim for an injunction to bar congressional candidates from accepting out-of-state contributions); *Landell v. Sorrell,* 118 F. Supp. 2d 459 (D. Vt. 2000) (striking down provision of the Vermont Campaign Finance Reform Act limiting out-of-state contributions to 25 percent of a state candidate's total contributions); *Krislov v. Rednour,* 226 F.3d 851 (7th Cir. 2000) (striking down Illinois law requiring "signature gatherers"—individuals who gathered signatures necessary for a House or Senate candidate to be placed on the ballot—to be registered voters of the relevant political subdivision). But see *State of Alaska v. Alaska Civil Liberties Union,* 978 P.2d 597 (Alaska 1999) (rejecting constitutional challenge to Alaska's restriction on nonresident contributions to state and local candidates).

18. Our $10/$15 split corresponds roughly to the division of receipts and expenditures between the primary and general election in recent presidential elections:

Year	Candidate	Primary receipts	General receipts	Primary percentage
1996	Clinton (D)	$42,536,628	$61,820,000	40.8
	Dole (R)	$44,911,596	$61,820,000	42.1
1992	Clinton (D)	$37,534,972	$55,240,000	40.5
	Bush (R)	$38,014,005	$55,240,000	40.8
1988	Bush (R)	$31,798,284	$46,100,000	40.86
	Dukakis (D)	$28,504,017	$46,100,000	38.2
TOTALS		$223,299,502	$326,320,000	40.6

Federal Electoral Commission Web site: The FEC and the Federal Campaign Finance Law (visited December 7, 2000) www.fec.gov/pages/fecfeca.htm. The percentage does not vary greatly for incumbents and nonincumbents.

Our formula does depart from the one prevailing under the existing subsidy program for presidential candidates, which gives only half as much money to a candidate during the primary as it does during the general election. See 26 U.S.C. § 9008 (1999) and Comm'n on Campaign Finance Reform, Ass'n of the Bar of the City of New York, *Dollars and Democracy: A Blueprint for Campaign Finance Reform* 29 (2000).

19. In addition to the president who has already served his allotted two terms, an incumbent may refuse to run (Calvin Coolidge in 1928) or halt his reelection campaign in midstream (Lyndon Johnson in 1968). In the latter case, we would remove the subaccount limitation immediately upon the President's withdrawal from the race.

20. While an incumbent vice president has sometimes won his party's nominations, such a candidate has always encountered serious opposition requiring large campaign expenditures—and therefore obviating the structural unfairness that motivates the subaccount solution.

21. The following table summarizes Senate and House incumbents' reelection success rates (as percentages of those seeking reelection):

Year	Senate incumbents' reelection success rate	House incumbents' reelection success rate
1990	96.9	96.0
1992	82.1	88.3
1994	92.3	90.2
1996	90.5	94.0
1998	89.7	98.3

Norman J. Ornstein, Thomas E. Mann, and Michael J. Malbin, *Vital Statistics on Congress* 57–58 (2000).

22. The following table summarizes the percentages of Senate and House incumbents seeking reelection:

Year	Percentage of Senate incumbents seeking reelection	Percentage of House incumbents seeking reelection
1990	91.4	93.8
1992	80.0	85.0
1994	74.3	89.0
1996	61.8	88.8
1998	85.3	92.4

Id.

23. Almost all incumbents are challenged, but they often face very weak opponents. See, e.g., Jeffrey S. Banks and D. Roderick Kiewiet, Explaining Patterns of Candidate Competition in Congressional Elections, 33 *Am. J. Pol. Sci.* 997, 1000 (1989).

24. What is more, incumbents will also be in a position to enter the export trade by shipping the money to favored candidates running elsewhere.

25. The following table displays the percentages of open House and Senate seats from 1990 to 1998:

Year	Percentage of Senate seats that were open	Percentage of House seats that were open
1990	8.6	6.2
1992	20.0	15.0
1994	25.7	11.0
1996	38.2	11.2
1998	14.7	7.6

The data are from Norman J. Ornstein, Thomas E. Mann, and Michael J. Malbin, *Vital Statistics on Congress* 57–58 (2000).

26. More than $2.3 billion in private funds were contributed to federal campaigns in the 2000 election cycle (excluding PAC contributions after October 18, 2000). Publicly financed contributions paled in comparison at $235.2 million (including matching funds to multiple primary candidates and grants made to the two major parties and the Reform Party for presidential nominating conventions and the general election). See www.fec.gov.

27. See Report of the Task Force on Campaign Reform, in Larry Bartels and Lynn Vavrek, *Campaign Reform: Insights and Evidence* 226 (2000) (Pew study group of fourteen leading experts concludes that "one of the primary problems . . . is not too much spending, but too little").

28. *N.Y. Times*, Section IV: Week in Review, Apr. 30, 2000 at 6 (Table: If You're Tired of Political Ads, What About Those Cars and S.U.V.'s, citing source as "Competitive Media Reporting"). As a nation we spend about $250 billion a year on advertising and marketing (including nonbroadcast advertisements). Advertising: Weak Retail and Dot-Coms Take a Toll, *N.Y. Times*, Dec. 11, 2000, at C1. The top eight automobile manufactures spent over $8.9 billion in 1998 on broadcast spots. See Ad Age 100 Leading National Advertisers in 1998, at adage.com/cgi-bin/adage.cgi. Other advertisers whose annual individual spending rivals that spent on all political speech include Proctor and Gamble, $2.6 billion; McDonald's, $1.5 billion; Pepsico, $1.3 billion; and the U.S. government, $792 million. Id.

29. A fine recent compendium contains a wealth of empirical work supporting this conclusion from a variety of angles. See Bartels and Vavreck, note 27 supra, collecting essays by Larry M. Bartels, at 1, John G. Geer, at 62, Lynn Vavreck, at 79, Marion Just, Tami Buhr, and Ann Crigler, at 122. See also John Coleman and Paul Manna, Congressional Campaign Spending and the Quality of Democracy, 62 *J. of Pol.* 757 (2000); Filip Palda, *How Much Is Your Vote Worth?* (1994) (campaign spending in-

creases the quality of democracy by increasing the amount of useful information); Christopher Kenny and Michael McBurnett, An Individual-Level Multiequation Model of Expenditure Effects in Contested House Elections, 88 *Am. Pol. Sci. Rev.* 699 (1994) (individuals with relatively low levels of education, a relatively weak interest in campaigns, and relatively weak political convictions are strongly influenced by candidate spending); R. Michael Alvarez, *Information and Elections* 168, 188 (1997) (less-educated and less politically engaged voters do learn in the course of a campaign either from media coverage or candidate expenditures).

30. Similar feedback adjustments come into play if off-year elections occur under drought conditions. When the presidency is not at stake, our statutory formula instructs the commission to make appropriate adjustments for the lower citizen participation rates that prevail.

31. We are concerned only with conditions of nationwide drought. Although particular races may look underfunded, we rely on out-of-district donors to correct serious problems by sending Patriots to deserving candidates.

32. Note that the decline in percentages was offset by the increase in taxpayer filings. In 1996 there were 118,832,995 individual filings, compared with 84,536,000 filings in 1976. See Tax Statistics, Internal Revenue Service, www.irs.gov/tax_stats/index (visited on Apr. 10, 2001). See also Herbert Alexander, Spending in the 1996 Election, in *Financing the 1996 Election* 11, 30 (John C. Green ed., 1999) (discussing percent of voting population that contributes). See also *Statistical Abstract of the United States, 1978.*

33. Between 1972 and 1986 federal law also permitted taxpayers to deduct one-half of political contributions up to $50. In contrast to the check-off, this gave Americans an incentive to support particular candidates. But in even sharper contrast, tax deductions only make it cheaper to contribute, not costless, and so impose a much greater burden than would Patriot. In any event, about 7 percent of taxpayers claimed the deduction before it was eliminated as part of the general tax reform of 1986. See California Tax Commission on Campaign Financing, *The New Gold Rush: Financing California's Legislation Campaigns* (Los Angeles: Center for Responsive Government, 1985), at 15.

Tax deductions and tax credits are also used in a variety of states to spur contributions. See Campaign Finance Law 2000, chart 4: States with Special Tax or Public Financing Provisions, www.fec.gov/pages/cf100chart4.htm (visited Feb. 9, 2001); Elizabeth Daniel, *Subsidizing Political Campaigns* (1997).

Minnesota's innovative program comes closest to Patriot. The state offers refunds of $50 for individuals and $100 for joint filers, for contributions to candidates. See Burt Neuborne, *A Survey of Existing Efforts to Reform the Campaign Finance System* 19 (1997). This program is like Patriot both in permitting gifts to favored candidates and in making these gifts costless. But it requires contributors to take the trouble to obtain a special refund form, file it with the state's Department of Revenue, and wait for reimbursement. See also www.cfboard.state.mn.us/bdinfo/nrckoff.html. Paperwork seems to have reduced the effectiveness of the system. In 1994 only 60,000 Minnesotans managed to complete the necessary forms to obtain their checks. Id. This contrasts with the 335,000 Minnesotans who participated in a second state program which, like its federal counterpart, allows state taxpayers to check off a box on their tax returns providing $5 to a Minnesota Elections Campaign Fund. As the text explains, citizens should be far less motivated to contribute to such a campaign fund than to give to candidates directly. The fact that five times more Minnesotans chose to check off a box than file a special form indicates the deterrent effect of a paperwork requirement. Here, of course, Patriot is different, allowing citizens countless opportunities to use their Patriot dollars at their ATMs without bureaucratic hassle.

An excellent undergraduate thesis at Harvard has recently reported on the experience with tax credit systems in the four states that have adopted them (Arkansas, Minnesota, Ohio, and Oregon) as well as the short-lived federal experiment. Guy Lincoln Smith V, A Third Way in Campaign Finance Reform: Political Contribution Credits and Their Role in Increasing Political Equality (unpublished manuscript, March 2001). Smith finds that state programs have generated low participation rates (less than 4 percent—often substantially less). Worse yet, poor people were especially unlikely to participate. But Smith points out that the tax-credits systems were often poorly advertised and that poor people would be especially deterred by the paperwork and costs involved in lending the government money between the time of contribution and the time of refund.

A Kennedy School study of the 2000 election provides the basis for a more optimistic assessment. A sample of American citizens older than eighteen were asked whether they had read about, thought about, or talked about the ongoing campaign. The study developed an "involvement index" on the basis of these soundings, which indicated that about 20 percent of Americans were "significantly involved" in the campaign a year before the election and that the involvement level increased to 40 percent at the height of the campaign season, declining over the summer to 20 percent before ascending to 50 percent on election day. See Shorenstein Center Report at www.vanishingvoter.org.

34. There were 806,340 contributors in the 2000 election cycle who gave more than $200 to candidates, parties, and PACs. Interview with Randy Haney, The Center for Responsive Politics, Feb. 9, 2001. Because candidates are not required to report contributions under $200, it is much more difficult to estimate their total number. Gore's campaign has disclosed, however, that between Nov. 7, 2000, and Dec. 13, 2000, there were approximately four contributions under $200 for every contribution over $200. See Recount Funds for Bush, Gore Fall Between Election, Tax Law, *Political Finance & Lobby Reporter,* Dec. 13, 2000. If this 4-to-1 ratio held more broadly, approximately 4 million people gave to campaigns. There are more than 130 million Americans who are currently registered to vote and in all probability would register for Patriot as well. U.S. Census Bureau, *Current Population Reports,* P20-453 (1999).

35. The same consideration condemns another approach to swamping. Under this alter-

native, the statute would authorize the commission to limit private fund-raising by candidates who accept Patriots—restricting private fund-raising to some multiple of the amount that a candidate raises publicly. This approach would require the commission to undertake controversial enforcement actions in midcampaign, and in a manner certain to generate heated charges of partisanship.

36. Because most administrative costs will be fixed, not variable, it is not realistic to expect large reductions here. And it is dangerous to make it is easy for Congress to undermine the program by a low-visibility attack on these costs. See Chapter 10.

37. *Buckley v. Valeo,* 424 U.S. 1, 48–49 (1976).

7. DESIGNING THE DONATION BOOTH

1. The most famous skeptic about the secret ballot was John Stuart Mill. John Stuart Mill, *Considerations on Representative Government* 205–28 (1862).

2. Hard data on the amount of time spent raising funds are elusive, but supportive anecdotes abound. See, e.g., Philip M. Stern, *Still the Best Congress Money Can Buy* 147 (rev. ed. 1992) (Congressman Edgar is quoted "[E]ighty percent of my time, 80 percent of my staff's time, 80 percent of my events and meetings were fundraisers. . . . Rather than going to a senior center, I would go to a party where I could raise $3,000 or $4,000"); Martin Schram, Speaking Freely, Center for Responsive Politics, www.opensecrets.org/pubs/speaking/speaking03 (1995) (Sen. Dennis DeConcini is quoted "When I was running, I was spending about two hours a day on the phone raising money. Minimum. Six days a week. . . . Sometimes I'd get really crackin' and I'd stay and do more"; Senator Durenberger is quoted "The fund-raising, when you're in Washington, is, on the average, three evenings each week, somebody is having a fund-raiser. Whether for you or somebody else—the [National Republican Senatorial] Committee, the Republican National Committee. In even-numbered years, after mid-February, you can count on three nights a week, spending 45 minutes to an hour at a fund-raiser. In addition, in your own race, you'd add another 10 or 12 hours a week to that from February through the primary or through August").

3. The 2000 presidential election provides a vivid example of why mandated disclosure does not produce informational parity between the candidate and the public. See Andrew Wheat, Legalized Bribery, 21 *Multinational Monitor* (March 2000), www.essential.org/monitor/mm2000/00march/wheat.html. See also Michael Isikoff, The Money Machine, *Newsweek* 46 (Jan. 24, 2000); Jacob Weisberg, Ballot Box to Bush: Release the Codes! *Slate Magazine* (Jan. 19, 2000), at www.slate.com. In the initial "money primary" George W. Bush's campaign solicited contributions with the aid of a four-digit code. The code was a kind of private Standard Industrial Classification, with each number representing a different industry group. For example, in January 2000 one of Bush's four hundred "Pioneer" fund-raisers, Tom Kuhn, who heads the Edison Electric Institute, a lobby trade group that represents investor-owned electric utilities, sent a solicitation to group members that read in

part: "As you know, a very important part of the campaign's outreach to the business community is the use of tracking numbers for contributions. Both Don Evans and Jack Oliver [Bush campaign officials] have stressed the importance of having our industry incorporate the #1178 tracking number in your fundraising efforts. Listing your industry's code does not prevent you, any of your individual solicitors or your state from receiving credit for soliciting a contribution. It does ensure that our industry is credited and that your progress is listed among the other business/industry sectors." Id. The Bush campaign reportedly assigned each Pioneer fund-raiser a number that his or her recruits were supposed to write on their contribution checks. Id. Solicitations like these expressly urged donors to write their interest group's code number on their check so that the Bush campaign could keep better track of how much money was coming from, say, the investor-owned electric utilities industry. The Bush campaign dutifully disclosed the names of individual donors and how much each gave, but they refused to release the total amount associated with each code number.

From Bush's perspective, the four-digit code represented an ingenious way of privatizing the PAC-bundling abuse described above. Each distinct four-digit code represents a kind of virtual PAC for distinct interest groups; it allows donors from that group to get credit for much more than the size of their individual $1,000 contributions. But from society's perspective, the fact that the four-digit codes were undisclosed means that Bush ended up knowing substantially more about his contributors' identities than the public—and thus represented a failure of informational parity.

4. We have no particular stake in the $200 threshold. The important consideration is that the number be sufficiently low to make it impossible for politicians to distinguish between givers who have provided relatively trivial gifts and those who have made very big ones.

We should add that *Buckley* gives Congress wide latitude in setting monetary thresholds: "[T]here is little in the legislative history to indicate that Congress focused carefully on the appropriate level at which to require recording and disclosure. Rather, it seems merely to have adopted the thresholds existing in similar disclosure laws since 1910. But we cannot require Congress to establish that it has chosen the highest reasonable threshold. The line is necessarily a judgmental decision, best left in the context of this complex legislation to congressional discretion. We cannot say, on this bare record, that the limits designated are wholly without rationality." *Buckley v. Valeo*, 424 U.S. 1, 83 (1976) (citation omitted).

5. For percentage of donations under $250 see Sidney Verba, Kay Lehman Schlotzman, and Henry E. Brady, *Voice and Equality* 540 (1995).

6. An important limitation to the basic commandment involves political volunteers. Obviously, there is no practicable way to stop candidates from knowing how much they contribute in time and energy—nor should there be—to their own campaigns. As one of us has said: "The point of a political campaign is to inspire lots of Americans to act as conscientious citizens. . . . Volunteers are not in it for the money." Bruce

Ackerman, Crediting the Voters: A New Beginning for Campaign Finance, 13 *Am. Prospect* 71, 76 (1993).

7. We would treat benefit concerts analogously. If Barbara Streisand performs a series of concerts to benefit the Clinton campaign, Clinton could easily estimate how much revenue she generated on his behalf. Allowing benefit concerts would provide an easy end run around the rule mandating that fund-raising dinners must be priced at cost. Many of today's $1,000-a-plate fund-raising dinners could become tomorrow's $1,000-a-seat benefit concerts with only nominal entertainment. Accordingly, we would prohibit an individual or business from dedicating the proceeds from an event to a political campaign. The performer or audience could independently contribute, but the contribution can't be part of the ticket price.

   By the same token, our statute prohibits candidates from "borrowing" money, even if they secure this debt by committing future contributions as collateral. It is entirely too easy for "lenders" to provide covert gifts by extending loans on favorable terms, and administratively impossible to distinguish these covert loans from those which would be made on market rates for comparable risks. The only feasible solution is to ban all loans and require all candidates to proceed on a pay-as-you-go basis.

8. Fred Wertheimer and Susan Weiss Manes, Campaign Finance Reform: A Key to Restoring the Health of Our Democracy, 94 *Colum. L. Rev.* 1126, 1140–41 (1994). The extent to which PACs have used bundling to exceed their $5,000 contribution limit has been staggering at times. For example, in the mid-1980s an insurance PAC bundled more than $168,000 of individual contributions together for a gift to a single member of Congress. See Brooks Jackson, Insurance Industry Boosts Political Contributions as Congress Takes Up Cherished Tax Preferences, *Wall St. J.*, Oct. 10, 1985, at 64. The National Republican Senatorial Committee bundled more than $6 million to 1986 candidates; and EMILY's List, not to be outdone, "used the bundling loophole to become the largest House and Senate PAC contributor in 1992, reportedly bundling some $6 million to congressional candidates." Helen Dewar, EMILY's Lists Falls Prey to PAC Hunt, *Wash. Post*, Mar. 7, 1993, at C1. See also Thomas B. Edsall, Campaign Skirts Rules by "Bundling" Contributions, *Wash. Post*, Oct. 20, 1986, at A8.

9. See Chapter 9. The FEC undertook random audits of 10 percent of House and Senate candidates following the 1976 election. These audits turned up minor but embarrassing inaccuracies in many of the reports of incumbents, leading Congress to strip the FEC of its random audit authority. Brooks Jackson, *Broken Promise: Why the Federal Election Commission Failed* 12 (1990).

10. We are indebted to high-tech gurus Jack Balkin, Larry Lessig, and Silvio Micali for this suggestion. See also Matt Franklin and Tomas Sander, Commital Deniable Proofs and Electronic Campaign Finance, ASIACRYPT 2000, http://citeseer.nj.nec.com/439710.html (proposing algorithm for implementing electronic anonymity).

11. Such a complaint would automatically trigger an intensive audit, but in no event could it trigger a secrecy-destroying lawsuit—although one might imagine employing

special judicial procedures as a last resort, modeled on those used by courts in national security proceedings. Cf. *Alderman v. United States* 394 U.S. 165 (1969) (concerning use of in camera proceeding to protect national security interests).

12. Even after technology comes to the rescue, it may still make sense to continue this practice, though with a longer time lag, because the data will doubtless have historical interest.

13. See Gary S. Becker and George J. Stigler, Law Enforcement, Malfeasance and Compensation of Enforcers, 3 *J. Legal Stud.* 1 (1974).

14. Antifraternization rules have been adopted in a variety of other contexts. For example, the Suffolk County Police Department bars its police officers from fraternizing with "persons known to have been convicted of a misdemeanor or felony under the laws of [New York] or the laws of any other State or Federal Law." See *Morrisette v. Dilworth*, 59 N.Y. 2d 449 (1983).

15. To reduce administrative costs, the trust allows the donor to enclose a note exercising his retraction option at the time he forwards the check. In this case, the trust is acting like a check-cashing agency—after the donor's check clears, the trust immediately sends him the reimbursement check.

16. If corporations could give directly, auditing would be a more serious option—because public corporations do have more stringent accounting obligations. But our model statute continues the current prohibition on corporate giving and demands that all private dollars come from real living persons.

17. The high level of contributions made to incumbents with safe seats is consistent with rent extraction because incumbents have the greatest ability to extort donations. See Frank J. Sorauf, *Inside Campaign Finance: Myths and Realities* 60–97 (1992) (discussing the link between reelection rates and campaign finance); David A. Strauss, Corruption, Equality, and Campaign Finance Reform, 94 *Colum. L. Rev.* 1369, 1380 (1994) ("Some of the data—notably the high levels of contributions to incumbents with safe seats—suggests that [extortion of contributions] is quite common"); cf. Jamin Raskin and John Bonifaz, The Constitutional Imperative and Practical Superiority of Democratically Financed Elections, 94 *Colum. L. Rev.* 1160, 1176–77 (1994) (detailing incumbent's fund-raising advantages).

18. The administrator of the donation booth would verify the potential contributor's identity and give the individual a form indicating that she was authorized to use the donation booth. A contributor would need to include this verification form with her donation—to prove to the commission that she personally had used the booth and not simply had a representative of the campaign donate on her behalf.

19. See Lawrence Lessig, The Regulation of Social Meaning, 62 *U. Chi. L. Rev.* 943, 978 (1995).

20. We have previously described how an electronic signature system might be designed to allow donors to track their previous gifts and make sure that some rogue bureaucrat hasn't misapplied them to the wrong accounts. This procedure also involves a visit to a special facility, and we see no reason why this facility could not function

as the donation booth for large gifts. Doubling up will reduce donor inconvenience: Because big donors will be especially interested in checking against the danger of misappropriation, they will be going to the facility anyway.

21. McCain raised more than $1 million through his Internet Web site in the first forty-eight hours after winning the New Hampshire primary on February 1, 2000. Frank James, E-Campaign Grow Up: McCain Makes Especially Adroit Use of the Internet to Raise Cash and Volunteers, *Chi. Trib.*, Feb. 11, 2000, at 3. McCain raised $2.2 million within a week. John Mintz, McCain Camp Enjoys a Big Net Advantage, *Wash. Post*, Feb. 9, 2000, at A01. By mid-February the McCain campaign had raised $3.7 million online (since the start of the campaign), almost one-fourth of his total contributions. Id.

22. Contributions would be sufficiently concentrated to trigger the algorithm if the ten largest gifts amounted to more than one standard deviation of the contributions for that day.

23. As described in Appendix B, the triggers used by the secrecy algorithm are generally calculated on the basis of a thirty-one-day moving average. At the beginning of campaigns, we suggest that the triggers be based on the first month's average daily contributions of the winning candidate in the previous election.

24. As a further refinement, for example, if small givers gave unexpectedly little on a particular day, we might subject the amount given to randomization.

25. The ratio would be calculated as a moving average of the amounts actually received—so that candidates could not easily decompose the amounts reported into exact Patriot and private components. This would make bombing more complicated because candidates would have to extract information about private contributions from an even noisier signal.

26. We have found a host of prior or independent contemporaneous proponents of the idea. See, e.g., Saul Levmore, The Anonymity Tool, 144 *U. Pa. L. Rev.* 2191, 2222 (1996); James R. Atwood, To End Dollars for Access Make All Campaign Contributions Anonymous, *Legal Times*, Sept. 22, 1997, at 27; Gary Hom, Letter to the Editor, Legislator's Passion Tends to Be Partisan, *N.Y. Times*, Apr. 13, 1997, at A14; Sir Geoffrey Pattie, Letter to the Editor, People's Right to Donate Anonymously, *Fin. Times*, Nov. 19, 1997, at A26; Wayne Rigby, Letter to the Editor, Call Donors' Bluff, *N.Y. Times*, Apr. 13, 1997, at A14. See also Michael W. McConnell, A Constitutional Campaign Finance Plan, *Wall St. J.*, Dec. 11, 1997, at A22.

When Ian Ayres—in collaboration with Jeremy Bulow—originally floated a proposal for a secret donation system (Ian Ayres and Jeremy Bulow, The Donation Booth: Mandating Donor Anonymity to Disrupt the Market for Political Influence, 50 *Stan. L. Rev.* 837 (1998)), newspaper commentary generated the discovery of other preexisting proponents. For example, after Arianna Huffington wrote a syndicated column touting the proposal (see Arianna Huffington, Anonymity Takes Sleaze Out of Fund-Raising, *Chi. Sun-Times*, Oct. 5, 1997, at 42), Sidney J. Goldfarb, a 1997 candidate for the New Jersey State Assembly, wrote Ayres a letter saying that making campaign donations anonymous had been one of his campaign proposals. See Letter from Sidney J. Goldfarb to Ian Ayres (Oct. 21, 1997); see also Fred Hiatt, Campaign Finance: The Anonymous Donor Plan, *Wash. Post*, Nov. 2, 1997, at C7. Paul Carrington also independently proposed mandated anonymity at a Brennan Center Conference on campaign finance in October 1997. See Letter from E. Joshua Rosenkranz, Executive Director, Brennan Center for Justice, to Ian Ayres (Nov. 5, 1997). The anticorruption benefits of donor anonymity were explicitly understood by the Office of Government Ethics in 1993 when it proposed requiring anonymous donations for presidential legal defense funds. See Office of Government Ethics, Advisory Opinion 93x21 (Aug. 30, 1993), and Kathleen Clark, Paying the Price for Heightened Ethics Scrutiny: Legal Defense Funds and Other Ways That Government Officials Pay Their Lawyers, 50 *Stan. L. Rev.* 65 (1997). President Clinton initially considered requiring that defense fund donors be anonymous. Office of Government Ethics Authorization Act of 1994: Hearings on H.R. 2289 before the Subcomm. on Admin. Law and Governmental Relations of the House Comm. on the Judiciary, 103d Cong. 21 (1984) (statement of Michael H. Cardozo, Executive Director, Presidential Legal Defense Trust). But the earliest academic proponent we have discovered seems to have been John Beck, An Alternative Campaign Finance Reform: Public "Laundries" for Secret Cash Contributions, 33 *Public Choice* 125 (1978).

27. The commentary to the 1972 Code of Judicial Conduct (cjc) stated, "[T]he [judicial] candidate should not be informed of the names of his contributors unless he is required by law to file a list of their names. E. Wayne Thode, Reporter's Notes to Code of Judicial Conduct 99 (1973). See Stuart Banner, Note, Disqualifying Elected Judges from Cases Involving Campaign Contributors, 40 *Stan. L. Rev.* 449, 473 n.130 (1988) (identifying ten adopting states as Arkansas, Nebraska, North Dakota, South Carolina, South Dakota, Tennessee, Utah, Washington, West Virginia, and Wyoming). See also 1984 N.Y. St. Comm. on Jud. Conduct Ann. Rep. 77 (1985) (identifying New York's prohibition on judge's attending fund-raisers where attendance fees were charged); Ga. Jud. Qualifications Comm. Op. 7 (1976) (Georgia allows judicial campaign fund-raisers only where the judge is not in attendance); La. Sup. Ct. Comm. on Jud. Ethics Op. 11 (1973) (judges should avoid information regarding contributors to their campaign); Interview with Justice Pamela B. Minzner, New Mexico Supreme Court, in Santa Fe, N.M. (Aug. 20, 1997) (discussing New Mexico's anonymity requirements).

The Colorado Code of Judicial Conduct included a provision that judicial candidates "should not be advised of the source of any campaign contributions." Colo. Rev. Stat., Court Rules ch. 24 app. (Supp. 1984); Leona C. Smoler and Mary A. Stokinger, Note, The Ethical Dilemma of Campaigning for the Judicial Office: A Proposed Solution, 14 *Fordham Urb. L.J.* 353, 378 (1986) (citing Code of Judicial Conduct Canon 7B(2), Colo. Rev. Stat., Court Rules ch. 24 app. (Supp. 1984)).

Of these sixteen jurisdictions, seven leave open the possibility that cjc-like codes continue to operate today (despite other mandatory disclosure laws). See Ark. Code

Ann. Sec. 7(6)(206) (requiring that the candidate, the party, or a person on the candidate's behalf disclose); Colo. Rev. Stat. Ann. Sec. 1(45)(108) (requiring that committees disclose); Fla. Stat. Ch. 106(07) (treasurer must file); Ga. Code. Ann. Sec. 21(5)(34) (committees must disclose); N.M. Stat. Ann. Sec. 1(19)(26) (defining the "reporting individual" as either the candidate or the treasurer); N.Y. Elec. 14(102) (treasurer must file); S.D. Codified Laws 12(25)(13) (candidate or committee must file); Wa. Rev. Code Ann. Sec. 42(17)(080) (candidate or committee must file).

28. See Ayres and Bulow, supra note 26, at 872–73.

29. There are currently two ways to contribute anonymously to elections in Korea. First, "supporters' associations" can contribute amounts "not exceeding one million won [about $750] each time." Political Fund Act, 1 Statutes of the Republic of Korea Art. 6-2(3), 634 (1997). These associations may contribute money only to their central parties—not to any individual candidate. See Arts. 6-3 & 6-4(3). The second method of donation is by nonearmarked gifts directly to the election commission; these are then divided among political parties according to "an allocation ratio of the State subsidy at the time of deposit." Id. Art. 15, 647.

30. Letter from Verena Blechinger (Apr. 2, 2001). See also Tim Beal and Sallie Yea, Corruption, Development and Maturity: A Perspective on South Korea, Paper Presented at the Fifth Asian Forum on Business Education Conference, Rangsit University (June 1997); Soo-Hyun Chon, The Election Process and Informal Politics in South Korea in Informal Politics in East Asia 66–81 (Lowell Dittmer, Haruhiro Fukui, and Peter N. S. Lee eds., 2000); Myoung-Soo Kim, Causes of Corruption and Irregularities, 8 Korea Focus vol. I, (Jan.–Feb. 2000) (downloaded from www.kf.or.kr/koreafocus).

31. See Transparencia y Probidad en el Financiamiento Privado, part 2 in Proposiciones sobre el Financiamento de la Actividad Política (Salvador Valdés-Prieto ed., 2000), and Donaciones Políticas Confidenciales, in Reforma del Estado, vol. 1: Financiamiento Político 361–83, 421–45 (S. Valdés-Prieto ed., 2000).

32. The Neill Report (1998), The Funding of Political Parties in the United Kingdom, Fifth Report of the Committee on Standards in Public Life, appendix 5 at 240 ("There are a number of ways such a body could operate. It could be that parties would only be able to receive donations above a certain figure through the Institute. Alternatively, all anonymous donations would be routed through the PDI"). One motive behind this proposal is to make contributors less reluctant to give: "At the moment a climate has been created in which people feel that nobody who gives money does not have a motive of some kind other than an altruistic or high-minded one, the feeling that there must be something fishy about people who want to give sums of money to political parties. That atmosphere has undoubtedly been created, yet a lot of very honourable people want to give money and do not want the amount to be revealed." Id. vol. 2 at 115 (comment of Lord Parkinson).

Much cruder, privately administered blind trusts were used by the Labour opposition during the 1992–97 Conservative Government and for the 1997 election. But these private blind trusts were discredited after Labour was accused of having changed policy to benefit Bernie Ecclestone, Formula One boss, who had previously given £1 million (Chris Gray, Party Cash Is Still Not Cricket, Suspicions of Sleaze Surrounding Donations to Political Parties Will Not Be Ended by the Radical Measures Suggested Yesterday, *Birmingham Post,* Oct. 14, 1998, at 13).

8. PLUGGING THE GAPS

1. See, e.g., Samuel Issacharoff and Pamela S. Karlan, The Hydraulics of Campaign Finance Reform, 77 *Tex. L. Rev.* 1705 (1999) and Kathleen M. Sullivan, Political Money and Freedom of Speech, 30 *U.C. Davis L. Rev.* 663, 688–89 (1997).
2. The current regulations allow donors to contribute $1,000 each in the primary and general election campaigns. Our model statute treats primaries, general elections, and runoffs as a single campaign to which the contribution caps would apply.
3. We vary the accounting period to take into account the fact that it is easier for a big contribution to stand out early, when overall donations are low. Because serious candidates are soliciting funds a year or more before the primary season, there will be plenty of time for big gifts contributed early to trickle into candidate accounts before costly media buys must occur. (In surveying expenditures of a mixture of sixteen successful candidates in the 2000 election, we found that presidential, senatorial, and House candidates all tend to make more than 90 percent of their expenditures in the year of the election. The data were taken from candidates' FEC Form 3P and Form 3 reports. See herndon1.sdrdc.com/fecimg/index.html).
4. An excellent introduction to event studies can be found in Ronald J. Gilson and Bernard S. Black, *(Some of) The Essentials of Finance and Investment* 188 (1993). See also Sanjai Bhagat and Roberta Romano, Event Studies and the Law (unpublished manuscript, Nov. 2000).
5. Our statute treats spouses as independent individuals for accounting purposes. In framing our contribution limits, however, we assume that spouses are not fooled by the donation booth and have no difficulty coordinating their giving. See Appendix C.
6. Private contributions to a PAC used to fund express independent advocacy would also be filtered through the blind trust. To defend the secrecy, we propose retaining the limits on private dollar contributions flowing into PACs. Individuals could give up to $5,000 in a calendar year to individual PACs for use in independent express advocacy campaigns. PACs would not be allowed either to contribute these private dollars to candidates or to coordinate their expenditure with candidates.
7. See, e.g., Nathaniel Persily and Bruce E. Cain, The Legal Status of Political Parties: A Reassessment of Competing Paradigms, 100 *Colum. L. Rev.* 775, 798 (2000) (minor party candidates can exert disproportionate influence over major parties' agendas).
8. Our $100,000 ceiling contrasts with the current $25,000 limit on annual contributions to all candidates, political committees, and party committees in federal elections. FEC, Supporting Federal Candidates: A Guide for Citizens, $25,000 Annual Limit, www.fec.gov/pages/citn0023.htm (last visited Apr. 9, 2001).

We would subject donations to national party committees to the same contribution limits that apply to presidential candidates: no more than $50,000 in an accounting period, and no more than $100,000 over the course of a presidential election cycle. Our statute allows national parties, unlike PACs, to make unlimited contributions of these private dollars to federal candidates or to coordinate with candidates.

Contributions to the federal fund accounts of state party committees would be subjected to the current contribution limits of $5,000 per calendar year. We would also retain existing regulation of the uses that state and local parties can make of these funds—there is currently a $5,000 limit on contributions from state and local parties to federal candidates and restrictions on coordinated expenditures. See 2 U.S.C. § 441a(d)(3)(B).

9. An individual plutocrat can avoid the donation booth by funding his own express advocacy campaign. But as soon as wealthy individuals join together, the statute requires them to form a political committee. Funds for express advocacy by such committees must go through the donation booth.

10. *Buckley v. Valeo*, 424 U.S. 1, 79 (1976).

11. See Ian Ayres and Jeremy Bulow, The Donation Booth: Mandating Donor Anonymity to Disrupt the Market for Political Influence, 50 *Stan. L. Rev.* 837, 862 (arguing that independent issue advocacy cannot constitutionally be subjected to mandatory anonymity regulation).

12. See Glenn Moramarco, Beyond "Magic Words": Using Self-Disclosure to Regulate Electioneering, 49 *Cath. U. L. Rev.* 107 (1999) (describing the problem, the courts' split, and different ways of expanding the "magic words" test while remaining clear of First Amendment infringement). But see ACLU, Brief on Behalf of the Wisconsin Manufacturers & Commerce, et al. (July 1998), available at www.aclu-wi.org/issues/free-political-speech-acluwi-brief.html ("*Buckley*'s bright-line definition of express advocacy provides the precision and predictability necessary to protect political speech"). The Brennan Center has led an empirical effort to show that the "magic words" test is ineffective in regulating political advertisements. Brennan Center for Justice, Buying Time: Television Advertising in the 1998 Congressional Elections, available at brennancenter.org/programs/cmag_temp/cmag_keyfindings.html (last visited Nov. 13, 2000) (only 4 percent of ads by candidates used the Supreme Court's "magic words" of express advocacy; 99 percent of party ads mentioned a candidate; 93 percent of party ads were seen as primarily generating support for a candidate). See also Phillip Taylor, Reformers Seek Constraints on Election Advocacy, The Freedom Forum Online (May 1, 2000), at freedomforum.org/news/2000/05/2000–05–03.asp (reviewing Brennan Center information: "[T]he Brennan Center had reviewed some 300,000 political ads and found that about 60,000 of these were issue ads from political parties and special interest groups that avoided words of express advocacy").

Lower courts have split on whether there is some elasticity to the *Buckley* "magic words" test. Compare *FEC v. Furgatch*, 807 F.2d 857 (9th Cir. 1987) ("We conclude that speech need not include any of the words listed in Buckley to be express advocacy under the Act, but it must, when read as a whole, and with limited reference to external events, be susceptible of no other reasonable interpretation but as an exhortation to vote for or against a specific candidate") with *Iowa Right to Life Comm. v. Williams,* 187 F.3d 963, 970 (8th Cir. 1999) (declaring that the Supreme Court established a "bright-line rule" in Buckley, and that vaguer standards would "create uncertainty and potentially chill[] discussion of public issues") and *FEC v. Christian Action Network, Inc.,* 110 F.3d 1049, 1049 (4th Cir. 1997) (communications violate FECA "only if the communications employ 'explicit words,' 'express words,' or 'language' advocating the election or defeat of a specifically identified candidate for public office").

13. See Bipartisan Campaign Reform Act of 1997, S. 25, 105th Cong. § 325(b)(1) (1997).

14. See $100 Million in Sham Issue Ads Escaped Disclosure Laws in 2000, Press Release, Brennan Center for Justice (Mar. 14, 2001) available at www.brennancenter.org/presscenter/pressrelease_2001_0314cmag.

15. Our statute requires the commission to calculate a workable estimate of the overall amount of issue advocacy based on mandated disclosure by major broadcast sellers (chiefly television and radio). By requiring only aggregate data, the regulation preserves the constitutional right of speakers/buyers to remain anonymous. The estimate of issue advocacy spending would affect the stabilization algorithm (and hence potentially increase the amount of Patriots distributed) only if the amount of issue advocacy became more than 20 percent of all political speech.

16. *Buckley* itself emphasizes why issue ads are not perfect substitutes for direct donations: "Unlike contributions, such independent expenditures may well provide little assistance to the candidate's campaign and indeed may prove counterproductive. The absence of prearrangement and coordination of an expenditure with the candidate or his agent not only undermines the value of the expenditure to the candidate, but also alleviates the danger that expenditures will be given as quid pro quo for improper commitments from the candidate." *Buckley v. Valeo,* 424 U.S. 1, 47 (1976). More recently, the Supreme Court has recognized that "'the absence of prearrangement and coordination' does not eliminate, but helps 'alleviate' any 'danger' that a candidate will understand the expenditure as an effort to obtain a 'quid pro quo.'" *Colorado Republican Fed. Campaign Comm. v. FEC,* 518 U.S. 604, 616 (1996) (plurality opinion) (quoting *FEC v. National Conservative PAC,* 470 U.S. 480, 498 (1985)).

17. This diminishing-returns argument may not always apply when candidates are competing for an all-or-nothing prize. To use the language of game theory, they are then involved in an "arms race" with discontinuous payoffs, and it is possible to generate pathologic equilibria in which both sides place a very high value on the marginal dollar.

But we do not think that this theoretical possibility will often be a practical reality in a world flooded with 5 billion Patriot dollars and substantial private sums flowing through the donation booth.

18. Under the FEC's new regulation, coordination is defined as speech that is "created,

produced or distributed": "(i) At the request or suggestion of the candidate, the candidate's authorized committee, a party committee, or the agent of any of the foregoing; (ii) After the candidate or the candidate's agent, or a party committee or its agent, has exercised control or decision-making authority over the content, timing, location, mode, intended audience, volume of distribution, or frequency of placement of that communication; or (iii) After substantial discussion or negotiation between the creator, producer or distributor of the communication, or the person paying for the communication, and the candidate, the candidate's authorized committee, a party committee, or the agent of such candidate or committee, regarding the content, timing, location, mode, intended audience, volume of distribution or frequency of placement of that communication, the result of which is collaboration or agreement. Substantial discussion or negotiation may be evidenced by one or more meetings, conversations or conferences regarding the value or importance of the communication for a particular election." 65 Fed. Reg. 76138, codified at 11 C.F.R § 100.23(a)(2)(c)(2) (2000). The McCain-Feingold bill also expands the current definition of coordination. The Bipartisan Campaign Reform Act 2001 passed by the Senate on Apr. 2, 2001, further expands the definition of coordinated communications by inserting in Section 315(a)(7) of the Federal Election Campaign Act of 1971 a new subparagraph (C).

19. The Supreme Court has recently upheld limits on coordinated expenditures of political parties. *FEC v. Colorado Republican Federal Campaign Committee,* 2001 U.S. Lexis 4668 (June 25, 2001).

20. The idea that candidates are the alter egos of their party was at play in the Supreme Court's decision in *Colorado Republican. Colorado Republican Federal Campaign Committee v. Federal Election Commission,* 518 U.S. 604 (1996). At least some of the justices reasoned that a state political party could not corrupt its candidates because it is impossible to corrupt yourself. Justices Stevens and Ginsburg, dissenting, declared that "[a] party shares a unique relationship with the candidate it sponsors because their political fates are inextricably linked. That interdependency creates a special danger that the party—or the persons who control the party—will abuse the influence it has over the candidate by virtue of its power to spend." Id. at 648 (Stevens, J., dissenting). Justices Thomas, Rehnquist, and Scalia, concurring in the judgment but dissenting in the rationale, argued that the anticorruption reasoning in *Buckley* does not apply in the case of campaign expenditures of parties. "As applied in the specific context of campaign funding by political parties, the anticorruption rationale loses its force. . . . What could it mean for a party to 'corrupt' its candidate or to exercise 'coercive' influence over him? The very aim of a political party is to influence its candidate's stance on issues and, if the candidate takes office or is reelected, his votes." Id. at 645.

21. *Buckley v. Valeo,* 424 U.S. 1, 79.

22. Definition of Political Committee, 66 Fed. Reg. 13681 (proposed Mar. 7, 2001) (to be codified at 11 C.F.R. pt. 100).

23. Under existing law, state and local political parties can raise funds for independent advocacy that benefits both state and federal candidates. Our concerns for federalism have lead us to create an exemption from the federal donation booth system for this fund-raising. We require state and local parties only to use the donation booth to cover expenses allocated to their federal account.

    We retain the current rules for state and local parties allocating joint expenses to federal and nonfederal accounts (but we prohibit all transfers of federal monies from the national to the state and local parties). State or local committees are currently allowed to use the more favorable "ballot composition" method of allocation—under which costs "are allocated according to the ratio of federal offices to total federal and non-federal offices expected to be on the ballot in the next federal general election." FEC, *Campaign Guide for Political Party Committees,* at 47–48 and tbl. (1996). National committees, in contrast, must apply the "fixed percentage" method, which allocates as federal expenses 65 percent of both administrative and generic voter drive expenditures. Id. See also 11 C.F.R. § 106.5(b). Although our statute does not overturn the existing allocation rules, we are attracted to a "voter-weighted ballot composition" method that weights the federal and nonfederal offices by the number of potential voters for each office.

24. See 11 C.F.R. § 100.5(g)(2)-(g)(3) (a group of political action committees are affiliated if they are "established, financed, maintained or controlled by the same corporation, labor organization, person, or group of persons").

9. SAFEGUARDING THE GUARDIANS

1. See Bruce Ackerman, *We the People: Foundations,* chaps. 7 and 9 (1991).
2. It would be desirable for the statute to bar FEC members from seeking elected federal office for the rest of their lives, but constitutional problems stand in the way. Although the Supreme Court has upheld legislative restrictions on the political rights of federal employees—see, e.g., *United Public Workers v. Mitchell,* 330 U.S. 75 (1947)—it has also, and more recently, rejected efforts to add qualifications for service in the Congress in addition to those specified by the constitutional text. See *U.S. Term Limits, Inc. v. Thornton,* 514 U.S. 779 (1995).

    Although it is possible to justify restrictions within the reigning precedents, we do not think it worth the trouble. We leave it to the good sense of the president and Congress to refrain from appointing the rare judge who is sufficiently youthful that he can qualify for full retirement and yet hope for a meaningful political career after serving as FEC commissioner.
3. See Douglas Adair, Fame and the Founding Fathers (1974) in an edited volume of his essays, of the same title.
4. The appointment of an outstanding group of founding commissioners is quite probable, because agencies begin their lives in the full glare of public attention, and after a successful burst of reformist zeal. The threats to their integrity come over the long

haul. See Anthony Downs, *Inside Bureaucracy*, chapter 2 (1967) (The Life Cycle of Bureaus).

5. 2 U.S.C. § 437c(a)(1). The members are appointed by the president with advice and consent of the Senate. Id. They serve for a single term of six years. 2 U.S.C. § 437c(a)(2). The commission elects a chairman and a vice chairman from among its members for a term of one year. 2 U.S.C. § 437c(a)(5). The chairman and the vice chairman may not be members of the same political party. Id. All commission decisions are made by majority vote. 2 U.S.C. §437c(c). The commission appoints a staff director and a general counsel, and, with the commission's approval, the staff director appoints and fixes the pay of additional personnel. 2 U.S.C. § 437c(f)(1).

6. The commission has been widely criticized for its poor enforcement. See, e.g., Commission on Campaign Finance Reform, Ass'n of the Bar of the City of New York, *Dollars and Democracy: A Blueprint for Campaign Finance Reform* 75 (2000); James A. Barnes, Wobbly Watchdog, 26 *Nat'l J.* 775 (1994); Kenneth A. Gross, The Enforcement of Campaign Finance Rules: A System in Search of Reform, 9 *Yale L. & Pol'y Rev.* 279 (1991); Federal Election Commission Panel Discussion: Problems and Possibilities, 8 *Admin. L.J. Am. U.* 223, 232 (1994); PricewaterhouseCoopers LLP, *Technology and Performance Audit and Management Review of the Federal Election Commission*, vol. 1, *Final Report*, Jan. 29, 1999, at 4-1. Commentators have also regularly criticized the agency for favoring the two major parties. Comm'n on Campaign Finance Reform, supra, at 149 ("The Commission is too often bipartisan, rather than nonpartisan, winking at violations by the major parties and major party candidates and focusing instead on lesser actors").

7. See Amanda S. La Forge, The Toothless Tiger—Structural, Political and Legal Barriers to Effective FEC Enforcement: An Overview and Recommendations, 10 *Admin. L.J.* 351 (1996); Brooks Jackson, *Broken Promise: Why the Federal Election Commission Failed* (1990). Scholars have often noted that the FEC's distinctive voting system "makes it possibly the weakest of all federal agencies." Jackson, supra, at 63.

8. *Congressional Quarterly*, Campaign Practices Reports, Feb. 11, 1985, at 1.

9. Congress has empowered the current FEC to appoint its inferior officers (see 2 U.S.C. § 437c(f)(1)) and a number of non-Cabinet agencies to appoint inferior officers, following a common practice for independent administrative agencies. See, e.g., 15 U.S.C. § 78d(b)(1) (authorizing the SEC to appoint "such officers . . . as may be necessary to carry out its functions"); 15 U.S.C. § 42 (authorizing the FTC to appoint a secretary); 47 U.S.C. § 155(e) (authorizing the chairman of the FCC to appoint a managing director). For a persuasive justification of this practice as consistent with the Appointments Clause, see Walter Dellinger, Appendix: The Constitutional Separation of Powers Between the President and Congress, 63 *Law & Contemp. Problems* 513 (2000).

10. Alan Greenspan earns $157,000 a year (as of December 2000, when the Senate approved his latest pay raise). CNN Moneyline Newshour (CNN television broadcast, Dec. 7, 2000). The members of the current Federal Election Commission are paid at level IV of the Executive Schedule, making their salaries $122,400 in the year 2000. See 2 U.S.C. § 437c(4), 5 U.S.C. § 5315.

11. Congress has plenary authority to fix the terms of officers of independent agencies. See *Humphrey's Executor v. United States*, 295 U.S. 602, 624 (1935); *Morrison v. Olson* 487 U.S. 654 (1988); *Edmond v. United States*, 520 U.S. 651 (1997).

12. Until the mid-1990s, the Office of Comptroller of the Currency (occ) consistently ran unannounced spot checks on banks in its jurisdictions. Now the banks receive notice, roughly six months in advance of an inspection. See www.occ.treas.gov/ AboutOCC.htm.

13. See Bruce Ackerman, The New Separation of Powers, 113 *Harv. L. Rev.* 642, 716–22 (2000).

14. *Morrison v. Olson*, 487 U.S. 654 (1988).

15. Our statute does not provide for judicial review of the attorney general's countermanding decision. Better to police the countermanding decision through the political process than turn sitting judges into prosecutors.

16. Consider, for example, how Congress clobbered the FTC for considering a requirement that cereals with more than a 50 percent sugar content be labeled as "breakfast candy." The cereal industry responded by persuading Congress to prohibit the agency from spending any money on investigations of cereal labeling. FTC Funds Bill with Legislative Veto Clears, 36 *Cong. Q. Almanac* 233, 235 (1980). See also D. Roderick Kiewiet and Mathew D. McCubbins, *The Logic of Delegation, Congressional Parties, and the Appropriations Process*, 23–24, 206, 229–32 (1991).

17. See Neal E. Devins, Appropriations Redux: A Critical Look at the Fiscal Year 1988 Continuing Resolution, 1988 *Duke L.J.* 389 (1988); Neal E. Devins, Budget Reform and the Balance of Powers, 31 *Wm. & Mary L. Rev.* 993 (1990).

18. See Omnibus Appropriations Act of 1998, Clinton Signs Omnibus Spending Bill, cgi.cnn.com/Allpolitics/stories/1998/10/21/budget (visited February 1, 2001).

19. See, Kate Stith, Congress' Power of the Purse, 97 *Yale. L.J.* 1343, 1379 (1988) ("There exist permanent or indefinite appropriations for a wide range of governmental expenditures. . . . In total, over half of the spending authority in the annual federal budget derives from legislation, including permanent appropriations, enacted by previous Congresses").

20. Once again, there are precedents for insulating costs of administration and oversight. The FAA's operating expense of traffic control centers is currently funded by the airport investment trust fund in ways that parallel the "individual entitlements" like Social Security. See Eric M. Patashnik, *Putting Trust in the U.S. Budget* 146 (2000).

21. American law uses the label *civil* to describe many punitive sanctions that impose heavy financial penalties of one kind or another. We mean to include these punitive penalties within this discussion of "criminalization."

22. See Appendix A. We also propose a crackdown if the ratio moves more slowly but reaches suspicious proportions over time.

10. WHO'S AFRAID OF THE SUPREME COURT?

1. Quotations from, respectively, Elizabeth Drew, Let's Force Politicians to Reform Campaign Finance, *Salt Lake Tribune*, Nov. 10, 1996, at A12; and Scott Turow, The High Court's Twenty-Year-Old Mistake, *N.Y. Times*, Oct. 12, 1997, Section 4, at 15. We have quoted leading liberal journalists whose opinions serve as the best indicator of "respectable" progressive opinion. It is easy to find academic commentary expressing similar views. See, e.g., E. Joshua Rosenkranz, *If Buckley Fell: A First Amendment Blueprint for Regulating Money in Politics* (1999).

2. *Colorado Republican Federal Campaign Committee v. Federal Election Commission*, 518 U.S. 604, 631 (1996) (Thomas, J., dissenting); *Nixon v. Shrink Missouri Government PAC*, 528 U.S. 377, 410 (2000) (Thomas, J., dissenting).

3. *Colorado Republican Federal Campaign Committee v. Federal Election Commission*, 518 U.S. 604 (1996).

4. Consider, for example, the role of the "Pioneers" in George W. Bush's fund-raising campaign. These Bush supporters raised $100,000 from friends and family members, all or most of which came in $1,000 chunks of hard money. The Pioneers themselves were often linked to particular corporations or industries—like Greg Slayton, head of Click Action; Dennis E. Nixon, from International Bank of Commerce; Robert Holland III, from Triton Energy: "The real clout comes when a number of executives in the same company—often together with spouses or other family members—donate a number of $1,000 gifts at the same time," the strategy known as bundling. Dean Calbreath, Corporate Touch: Campaign Money Is Spending More Time Out of Town, *San Diego Union-Tribune*, Oct. 22, 2000, at H1. See also Ellen Miller, The Hard Truth About McCain's Soft Money Ban, *American Prospect*, Mar. 13, 2000, at 12 (criticizing the McCain-Feingold attempt to close the soft money loophole as an ineffective response to bundling).

5. See, e.g., Steve Campbell, Campaign Financing Remains a Hot Topic, *Portland Press Herald*, Jan. 28, 1998, at 1A; Helen Dewar, Constitutional Change to Allow Campaign Fund Limits Rejected, *Wash. Post*, Mar. 19, 1997, at A2; George F. Will, A Pittance for the Pols, *Wash. Post*, Nov. 13, 1997, at A23.

6. On the merits, we think the rise of a voucher alternative to the public school is a most unfortunate development. See Bruce Ackerman, *Social Justice in the Liberal State*, chap. 5 (1980). But this abuse of the voucher concept shouldn't prevent its deployment in other areas where it makes good sense.

7. A presidential candidate is eligible for primary matching payments by showing "broad-based public support"—evidenced by raising $5,000 in twenty states by means of contributions of $250 or less. See Federal Electoral Commission: The FEC and the Federal Campaign Finance Law, www.fec.gov/pages/fecfeca.htm (last visited Sept. 24, 2000). See 26 U.S.C.A. § 9033(b).

8. A candidate accepting a subsidy for his primary campaign must limit his private spending to $10 million (plus an adjustment for cost of living). He must also limit his personal spending to $50,000. See id.

9. See 26 U.S.C.A. § 9003(b)(c). Candidates must also limit their personal spending to $50,000. See 26 U.S.C.A. § 9004(b)(c)(d).

10. Perot also received public funding for the general election in 1996. See 26 U.S.C. §§ 9003, 9004. Maury Taylor, a minor candidate for the Republican presidential nomination, also opted out of public funding for the primaries. See www.fec.gov/pres96/presgen1.htm.

11. See 26 U.S.C. §§ 9003, 9004. In 2000 the private spending limit for candidates accepting subsidy during the primaries was $40.53 million. The public funding for this phase is capped at 50 percent of the national spending limit. See Federal Electoral Commission: The FEC and the Federal Campaign Finance Law, www.fec.gov/pages/pubfund.htm#primary.matchingfunds (last visited Jan. 23, 2001).

12. *Wilkinson v. Jones*, 876 F. Supp. 916 (W.D. Ky. 1995), struck down a section of Kentucky's campaign finance law which limited contributions to privately funded candidates to $100 while permitting $500 contributions to candidates who accepted public financing. Id. at 928. See also *Shrink Missouri Government PAC v. Maupin*, 71 F.3d 1422, 1425 (8th Cir. 1995) (striking down a statute in which nonparticipating candidates could not accept donations from PACs, parties, unions, or corporations).

13. Most lower courts have upheld triggering mechanisms from constitutional challenge. See *Vote Choice v. DiStefano*, 4 F.3d 26 (1st Cir. 1993) (upholding Rhode Island's trigger); *Wilkinson v. Jones*, 876 F. Supp. 916 (W.D. Ky. 1995) (upholding Kentucky's trigger, but not increased contribution limits), aff'd sub nom, *Gable v. Patton*, 142 F.3d 940 (6th Cir. 1998); *Rosential v. Rodriguez*, 101 F.3d 1544 (8th Cir. 1996) (upholding Minnesota's trigger); *Daggett v. Commission on Governmental Ethics and Election Practices*, 205 F.3d 445 (1st Cir. 2000) (upholding Maine's trigger).

14. Candidates who opt for presidential funding can use only $50,000 of their own money if they accept federal subsidies. See 26 U.S.C.A. § 9004 (d). This $50,000 can come from the candidate's personal funds or those of his "spouse, and any child, parent, grandparent, brother, half-brother, sister, or half-sister of the candidate, and the spouses of such persons." See 26 U.S.C.A. § 9004(e).

15. Candidates can make unlimited contributions to their own campaign if they waive their eligibility to receive transfers from Patriot accounts. If they opt into Patriot, they can still self-finance their exploratory funds and also contribute to their subsequent campaigns, subject only to the aggregate annual limit.

16. See, e.g., *Nixon v. Shrink Missouri Government PAC*, 528 U.S. 377, 391 (2000); *Austin v. Michigan Chamber of Commerce*, 494 U.S. 652 (1990); *Buckley v. Valeo*, 424 U.S. 1, 26 (1976).

17. See Charles J. Wichmann III, Ridding FOIA of Those Unanticipated Consequences: Repaving a Necessary Road to Freedom, 47 *Duke L.J.* 1213, 1230–32 (1998); Robert P. Deyling, Judicial Deference and De Novo Review in Litigation over National Security

Information Under the Freedom of Information Act, 37 *Vill. L. Rev.* 67, 67–68 (1992). See generally 5 U.S.C. § 552(b)(1–9) (The Freedom of Information Act contains nine exemptions which exempt nine specific types of information from mandatory disclosure: (1) national security information; (2) internal agency rules; (3) information exempted by other statutes; (4) privileged or confidential business information; (5) interagency and intra-agency memoranda; (6) information that would constitute an invasion of personal privacy; (7) law enforcement records; (8) records of financial institutions; and (9) data concerning oil wells); 10 Md. Code Ann. Section 10–612 (citizens provided with information unless "an unwarranted invasion of the privacy of a person in interest would result").

18. See 5 U.S.C. § 552 (b)(3) taken together with 13 U.S.C. § 9.

19. See *New York Times Co. v. Sullivan,* 376 U.S. 254, 271–72 (1964) ("[e]rroneous statement is inevitable in free debate, and . . . it must be protected if the freedoms of expression are to have the 'breathing space' that they 'need to survive'").

20. Justice Thomas in particular has argued for the superiority of informational over regulatory strategies as anticorruption tools—though the informational strategy he has in mind is full disclosure, not nondisclosure. See *Nixon v. Shrink Missouri Government PAC,* 528 U.S. 377, 428 (2000) (Thomas, J., dissenting); *Colorado Republican Federal Campaign Committee v. FEC,* 518 U.S. 604, 643 (1996) (Thomas, J., concurring in part and dissenting in part).

21. See *Nixon v. Shrink Missouri Gov't PAC,* 528 U.S. 377 (2000) (upholding a Missouri statute imposing campaign contribution limits for state offices between $250 and $1000); *Austin v. Michigan Chamber of Commerce,* 494 U.S. 652 (1990) (upholding a Michigan statute forcing corporations to segregate funds for use as political contributions).

22. The Court endorsed this argument in *Austin v. Michigan Chamber of Commerce,* 494 U.S. 652 (1990), where it justified a diminution of corporations' political advantage (the ability to amass a large treasure chest for political speech) on the ground that it thereby allowed the legislature to embrace the other advantages of the corporate form.

23. There is only one respect in which the appeal to offsetting gains is unpersuasive. Under the existing system, donors of private money can, if they wish, receive a list of all other donors to the same PAC. But when each American walks up to his neighborhood ATM to spend his 50 Patriot dollars, it will be impossible for others to learn where he has sent his money. This means that contributors to a patriotic PAC will be unable to identify one another, and so this aspect of associational freedom will not be realized under the new regime.

As we explained in Chapter 6, only our concern with corruption control requires us to impose this anonymity requirement. And we have carefully limited the scope of this anonymity rule. The National Rifle Association, for example, remains perfectly free to publicize lists of dues-paying members, to encourage them to come to meetings, and so forth. Nevertheless, because this restriction does not obtain at present, we cannot appeal to offsetting gains, and the Court must engage in the full-scale balancing test described below.

24. See *Austin v. Michigan Chamber of Commerce,* 494 U.S. 652 (1990) (upholding state prohibition on use of corporate treasury funds for independent expenditures); *Pipefitters Local Union No. 562 v. U.S.,* 407 U.S. 385, 427 (1972) (upholding restrictions on the political use of funds from the general treasuries of corporations and unions); *U.S. v. Congress of Industrial Organizations,* 335 U.S. 106, 113 (1948) (emphasizing anticorruption rationale for regulation of union and corporate giving). See also *FEC v. National Right to Work Committee,* 459 U.S. 197, 210 (1982) ("we will [not] second guess a legislative determination as to the need for prophylactic measures where corruption is the evil feared"); *First National Bank of Boston v. Bellotti,* 435 U.S. 765, 788 n.26 (1978) ("The overriding concern behind the enactment of statutes such as the Federal Corrupt Practices Act was the problem of corruption of elected representatives through the creation of political debts. The importance of the governmental interest in preventing this occurrence has never been doubted").

25. See *Nixon v. Shrink Missouri Government,* 528 U.S. 377 (2000), upholding contribution limits ranging from $250 to $1,000.

26. Supporting Federal Candidates: A Guide for Citizens, available at www.fec.gov/pages/citn0021.htm (last visited Apr. 4, 2001).

   McCain-Feingold would also increase the total annual amount an individual could contribute from $25,000 to $37,500. See Alison Mitchell, Campaign Finance Bill Passes in Senate, 59–41; House Foes Vow a Fight, *N.Y. Times,* Apr. 3, 2001, at A1.

27. See 2 U.S.C.A. §§ 431(8)(A)(i) and (8)(B)(xii). Soft money is increasingly spent on "issue ads." See Peter H. Stone, The Green Wave, *Nat'l J.,* Nov. 9, 1996, 2410–12; Note, Soft Money: The Current Rules and the Case for Reform, 111 *Harv. L. Rev.* 1323 (1998).

28. See *Buckley v. Valeo,* 424 U.S. 1, 26–28 (1976); *Nixon v. Shrink Missouri Government PAC,* 528 U.S. 377, 392–93 (2000).

29. *Buckley v. Valeo,* 424 U.S. 1, 49 (1976).

30. John R. Lott, Jr., Explaining Challenger's Campaign Expenditures: The Importance of Sunk Nontransferable Brand Name, 17 *Pub. Fin. Q.* 108 (1989) (arguing that spending in previous years builds "brand loyalty" among voters and thus deters challengers from running); John R. Lott, Jr., The Effect of Nontransferable Property Rights on the Efficiency of Political Markets: Some Evidence, 32 *J. Pub. Econ.* 231 (1987) (finding that property rights of incumbency makes successful challenges expensive and unattractive); James M. Snyder, Jr., Long-Term Investing in Politicians, or Give Early, Give Often, 35 *J. Law & Econ.* 15 (1992).

31. See, e.g., *Reynolds v. Sims,* 377 U.S 533, 568 (1964); *Baker v. Carr,* 369 U.S. 186, 187 (1962).

32. Justice Breyer has recently, and rightly, emphasized this theme in *Nixon v. Shrink Missouri Government PAC,* 528 U.S. 377, 403 (2000) (Breyer, J., concurring).

33. See John Ely, *Democracy and Distrust* (1980). Although Ely's account has been criticized from a wide variety of angles, few deny the importance of his emphasis on the
problem of incumbency advantage. They merely insist that other problems are also
important and that Ely's concerns are too narrow to motivate all major doctrinal
developments.

34. *Buckley v. Valeo*, 424 U.S. 1, 16–17 (1976).

35. For a classic statement of the extreme position, see J. Skelly Wright, Politics and the
Constitution: Is Money Speech? 85 *Yale L.J.* 1001, 1012 (1976). Many other reformers
recognize the existence of First Amendment problems but minimize their practical
significance. See, e.g., Vincent Blasi, Free Speech and the Widening Gyre of Fund-
Raising: Why Campaign Spending Limits May Not Violate the First Amendment
After All, 94 *Colum. L. Rev.* 1281 (1994) (justifying campaign spending limits as a
legitimate way of limiting the amount of time candidates spend fund-raising); Burt
Neuborne, Toward a Democracy-Centered Reading of the First Amendment, 93 *Nw.
U. L. Rev.* 1055 (1999) (offering a variety of rationales for sustaining comprehensive
legislation); Daniel Hays Lowenstein, On Campaign Finance Reform: The Root of
All Evil Is Deeply Rooted, 18 *Hofstra L. Rev.* 301, 335, 348–66; Cass R. Sunstein, Political Equality and Unintended Consequences, 94 *Colum. L. Rev.* 1390, 1392 (1994) (political equality as a justification).

36. See *Buckley v. Valeo*, 424 U.S. 1, 48–49 (1976). We deny, for example, that plutocrats
have a constitutional right to spend their own money in their own campaigns without
any limits.

11. PATRIOTIC POLITICS

1. See Bruce Ackerman, *Social Justice in the Liberal State*, chap. 6 (1980).

2. See Moisei Ostrogorski, The Rise and Fall of the Nominating Caucus, Legislative and
Congressional, 5 *Am. Hist. Rev.* 253 (1899); James Sterling Young, *The Washington
Community, 1800–1828*, 114, 147–48 (1966).

3. See David R. Mayhew, *Placing Parties in American Politics* (1986) (providing a state-
by-state assessment of the vitality of party organizations in contemporary politics).

4. The term *money primary* was first used in 1987 in an article in the *Los Angeles Times
Magazine*. See Ronald Brownstein, The Money Machine, *L.A. Times*, Nov. 15, 1987,
at 14.

5. The very name of the influential Democratic women's political action committee,
EMILY's list, emphasizes this point: "EMILY is an acronym for 'Early Money Is Like
Yeast,' it raises the dough," *Houston Chronicle*, Nov. 16, 2000, at YO 7.

6. John Sawyer, Gephardt's Decision Wins Clinton's Praise, *St. Louis Post-Dispatch*, Feb.
4, 1999, at A1.

7. Dan Balz, Kerry Won't Run Against Gore; Senator Cites Fund-Raising; Bradley Remains the Challenger, *Wash. Post*, Feb. 27, 1999, at A4.

8. Leading Wall Street investment banks accounted for the top six sources of income

for Bradley's presidential campaign. See John Broder, Bradley Relies on Wall Street to Raise Funds, *N.Y. Times*, Oct. 24, 1999, at A1.

9. Our list comes from Voter Guide, *Des Moines Register*, Nov. 1, 1998, at 15, which enumerated the number of days spent by potential candidates for president in Iowa from January 1997 to November 1, 1998. Also included were (then) House Speaker Newt Gingrich, New York City Mayor Rudolph Giuliani, Senator Fred Thompson, and Representative J. C. Watts—but we have omitted them because they didn't do more than visit Iowa for a couple of days.

   Conspicuously absent was Texas Governor George W. Bush, who had not yet begun to campaign in Iowa, and was months away from declaring even his exploratory committee.

10. Nicholas D. Kristof, The 2000 Campaign: The Decision; For Bush, His Toughest Call Was the Choice to Run at All, *N.Y. Times*, Oct. 29, 2000, at A1.

11. See Federal Electoral Commission: The FEC and the Federal Campaign Finance Law, www.fec.gov/pages/pubfund.htm#primary.matchingfunds (last visited Jan. 23, 2001).

12. Receipts of 1999–2000 Presidential Campaigns Through July 31, 2000, www.fec.gov/finance/precm8.htm (last visited Feb. 10, 2001). By this point, Bill Bradley had raised $11 million, while Al Gore claimed $18 million. Marc Lacey, Bush Beats All Others in Checkbook Primary, *L.A. Times*, June 30, 1999, at A4.

13. Before he had even announced his exploratory committee, Bush had garnered the support of numerous Republican governors, senators, and representatives. Ronald Brownstein, Big Guns Ready, Bush Makes a Move, *L.A. Times*, Mar. 8, 1999, at A12 ("At the news conference, Bush aides released a list showing he has been endorsed by a dozen Republican governors, 72 Republicans in the House, five GOP senators and delegations of state legislators and other local officials from . . . such pivotal early primary states as Iowa, California and South Carolina").

14. Scott Montgomery, Kasich Out of Running for President, Congress, *Dayton Daily News*, July 14, 1999.

15. Receipts of 1999–2000 Presidential Campaigns Through July 31, 2000, www.fec.gov/finance/precm8.htm (last visited Feb. 10, 2001).

16. Elizabeth Dole: "It's More Important to Raise Issues Than to Raise Campaign Funds," CNN Live Event/Special, Oct. 20, 1999.

17. Other opponents included the free-spending plutocrat Steve Forbes and a couple of hard-right ideologues operating on a shoestring: Gary Bauer and Alan Keyes. Forbes, Bauer, and Keyes obtained 13, 1, and 6 percent of the vote, respectively, in the New Hampshire primary.

18. Receipts of 1999–2000 Presidential Campaigns Through July 31, 2000, www.fec.gov/finance/precm8.htm (last visited Feb. 10, 2001). See Jim Drinkard, McCain, Far Behind Bush in Funds, Hopes for Boost, *USA Today*, Feb. 1, 2000, at 4A; Dan Balz, McCain Trounces Bush by 18 Points; Gore Deals Bradley His Second Defeat, *Wash. Post*, Feb. 2, 2000, at A1.

19. FEC Disclosure Form 3P (Feb. 10, 2001), http://herndon2.sdrdc.com/cgi-bin/dcdev/

forms/C00342154/4594 (last visited Feb. 10, 2001). McCain-Bush Finance Gap Closing; Both Candidates Go for TV Laughs, *Seattle Post-Intelligencer,* Mar. 1, 2000, at
A12.

20. Receipts of 1999–2000 Presidential Campaigns Through July 31, 2000, www.fec.gov/
finance/precm8.htm (last visited Feb. 10, 2001).

21. Financial Conditions of the Different Campaigns After the Release of Information
Regarding Fund-Raising and Spending, National Public Radio, Morning Edition,
Feb. 21, 2000. Bush spent roughly $5 million in South Carolina (Don Van Natta Jr.
and John M. Broder, The 2000 Campaign: The Money, *N.Y. Times,* Feb. 21, 2000,
at A12), while McCain spent only $1.5 million (Receipts of 1999–2000 Presidential
Campaigns Through July 31, 2000, www.fec.gov/finance/precm8.htm [last visited
Feb. 10, 2001]).

22. Bush even outspent his rival $2 million to $1 million in McCain's home state
of Arizona. Edward Walsh, McCain Bounces Back in Michigan; Non-GOP Votes
Crucial; Arizonan Wins Home State, *Wash. Post,* Feb. 23, 2000, at A1. In Michigan, McCain spent $3.2 million on campaigning, but it is unclear whether or
(more likely) by how much he was outspent by Bush. See Robert Cohen, Democrats
Hoping Lighter Wallet Will Slow Bush, Newshouse News Service, Feb. 17, 2000.
McCain commanded 50 percent of the Michigan vote, while Bush received 43 percent.

23. Fifteen states held Democratic primaries on Super Tuesday (Mar. 7, 2000). See Dan
Balz, Gore Seals Nomination, *Wash. Post,* Mar. 8, 2000, at A1.

24. Through February 2000 Bush outspent McCain by a margin of $63 million to $36
million. And through March, Bush outspent him by $73 million to $43 million. See
Expenditures of 1999–2000 Presidential Campaigns, www.fec.gov/finance/
precm8.htm (last visited Feb. 10, 2001).

25. See 2 U.S.C. § 9004(a)(2). Moreover, if the Greens had successfully leaped over the
5 percent threshold, they would have been entitled to recover from the treasury a
variety of expenses incurred during the 2000 election. See 2 U.S.C. § 9004(a)(3).

26. As it turns out, Gore and Nader might have cut a deal to avoid this result. If Gore
had withdrawn from the ballot and directed his supporters to vote for Nader in
the eight states (Alaska, Idaho, Kansas, Nebraska, South Dakota, Texas, Utah, and
Wyoming) where Gore was more than 20 percent behind in the polls, and if Nader
had withdrawn from the polls in the twelve states (Arkansas, Arizona, Colorado,
Florida, Minnesota, Missouri, Nevada, New Mexico, Oregon, Pennsylvania, Washington, and Wisconsin) in which the Bush-Gore race was within 10 percentage points,
Nader might have doubled his vote and qualified for federal funding, while Gore
would have picked up Florida and won the election.

More broadly, Gore could afford to give up four votes in the states where he
was sure to lose for every one Nader vote he picked up in the states where he had
a chance of victory. This vote-trading possibility is not simply the result of ex post
analysis. One of us proposed just such a swap two weeks before the elections (in an

unsuccessfully marketed op-ed piece). Ian Ayres, Vote Trading Writ Large (unpublished manuscript, Oct. 22, 2000).

27. Frank James, E-Campaign Grow Up: McCain Makes Especially Adroit Use of the Internet to Raise Cash and Volunteers, *Chi. Tribune,* Feb. 11, 2000, at 3.

28. According to data compiled by the Center for Responsive Politics, Elizabeth Dole raised 40.6 percent of her individual donations from women—second only to Gary Bauer, who raised 45.5 percent. George W. Bush raised 35.3 percent from women. Sheryl Fred, Gender Politics: Women Donors Making a Financial Statement, Center for Responsive Politics (July 1999), www.opensecrets.org/newsletter/ce64/01gender. htm; Presidential Fund-raising by Gender, Center for Responsive Politics (July, 1999) www.opensecrets.org/newsletter/ce64/01gender_side2.htm.

29. See Amy Holmes, Nader Campaign Stymies Feminists, *USA Today,* Nov. 10, 2000, at 15A.

30. For an analysis, see Bruce Ackerman, Anatomy of a Constitutional Coup, *London Review of Books* 3–7 (Feb. 8, 2000); Bruce Ackerman ed., *Bush v. Gore: Crisis of Legitimacy?* (forthcoming).

31. For a more complex appreciation of the values of equal citizenship, see Bruce Ackerman, *Social Justice in the Liberal State* (1980) and *We the People* (vol. 1: *Foundations* 1991; vol. 2: *Transformations* 1998).

32. See www.fec.gov/press/pac1800text.htm.

33. See James Buchanan and Gordon Tullock, *The Calculus of Consent* (1965); John Ferejohn, *Pork-Barrel Politics* (1974); Kenneth A. Shepsle and Barry R. Weingast, Political Preferences for the Pork Barrel: A Generalization, 25 *Am. J. Pol. Sci.* 96–111 (1981); David P. Baron, Majoritarian Incentives, Pork Barrel Programs, and Procedural Control, 35 *Am. J. Pol. Sci.* 57–90 (1991).

34. See Robert M. Stein and Kenneth N. Bickers, Congressional Elections and the Pork Barrel, 56 *Journal of Politics* 377–99 (1994) (the distribution of pork is likely to depend on the attentiveness of voters to politics, their interest group affiliations, and their sources of political information).

35. Of course, gun manufacturers' contributions to the NRA are easier to explain in narrowly self-interested terms.

36. See Paul E. Johnson, Interest Group Recruiting: Finding Members and Keeping Them, in *Interest Group Politics* 35–62 (Allan J. Ciglar and Burdett A. Loomis eds., 5th ed. 1998). Theda Skocpol, Advocates Without Members: The Recent Transformation of American Civic Life, in *Civic Engagement in American Democracy* 461–509 (Theda Skocpol and Morris Fiorina eds., 1999).

37. It will be illegal for any group to lower transaction costs too much. For example, the leader of a labor union or church group cannot end a meeting by "passing the hat" to collect his members' Patriot or private dollars and then send them onward on their behalf. As we have emphasized, each citizen must go to his ATM and vote his Patriot dollars individually; similarly, he is the only one who may send his check to the blind trust administering the secret donation booth.

38. See David Mayhew, *Placing Parties in American Politics* (1986) (analyzing different forms of party organization prevailing in different states and regions). Alan Ware, *The Breakdown of Democratic Party Organization, 1940–1980* (1985).

39. See Russell J. Dalton, *Parties Without Partisans: The Decline of Party Identifications Among Democratic Publics* (1998); Warren E. Miller and J. Merrill Shanks, *The New American Voter* (1996) (especially chap. 7, updating the classic, Angus Campbell et al., *The American Voter* (1960)); Steven Rosenstone and John Mark Hansen, *Mobilization, Participation, and Democracy in America* (1993) (especially chap. 5).

40. See Paul S. Herrnson, National Party Organizations at the Century's End, in *The Parties Respond: Changes in American Parties and Campaigns* 59 (L. Sandy Maisel ed., 3d ed. 1998).

41. Alan S. Gerber and Donald P. Green, The Effects of Canvassing, Direct Mail, and Telephone Contact on Voter Turnout: A Field Experiment, 94 *Am. Pol. Sci. Rev.* 653–64 (2000) (face-to-face visits substantially increase voter turnout).

42. See Gary C. Jacobson, Party Organization and Distribution of Campaign Resources: Republicans and Democrats in 1982, 100 *Pol. Sci. Q.* 603 (1986); Web Helping with Presidential Run-off, *National Journal's Technology Daily*, Nov. 21, 2000 (stating that "Republicans [were] making more aggressive use of the technology" than were Democrats).

43. See *Encyclopedia of Associations* (Patricia Tsune Ballard ed., 37th ed. 2001). Other ideological groups on the left have much smaller memberships: the Audubon Society (600,000), the Sierra Club (550,000), the NAACP (400,000), the ACLU (275,000), NOW (250,000), and NARAL (400,000). On the conservative side, the National Federation of Independent Businesses has 607,000 members. Id. We do not know how many people are members of more than one of these groups. But the great unknown is how many will send their Patriot dollars to an ideological group's PAC rather than to candidates, political parties, or sociological groups.

Last but not least: As we shall discuss, the eight hundred–pound gorilla is the 32 million–member American Association of Retired Persons. See Charles R. Morris, *The AARP: America's Most Powerful Lobby* 44 (1996). From 1990 to 2000, labor unions gave $308,017,332 to Democrats and $20,841,837 to Republicans—representing a 94 to 6 split (see Center for Responsive Politics, PAC Contributions, www.opensecrets.org/industries/indus.asp?Ind=Q14). It is harder to assess the partisan breakdown of contributions made by religiously inspired groups. On one narrow issue, the pattern of giving by pro-life PACs was the mirror image of labor PACs—with 91 percent to Republicans and 8 percent to Democrats. But this issue has generated a much smaller sum of money—$2,791,332 (see Center for Responsive Politics, PAC Contributions, www.opensecrets.org/industries/indus.asp?Ind=Q14). We have not tried to construct an estimate of overall financial flows on all issues generated by religiously inspired groups—let alone assess how these might change under patriotic conditions. See Steven Peterson, Church Participation and Political Participation: The Spillover Effect, 20 *Am. Pol. Q.* 123–39 (1992).

45. See Herbert Alexander, Spending in the 1996 Election, in *Financing the 1996 Election* 11, 27–28 (John C. Green ed., 1999) (about 6 percent of the adult population made contributions in 1996 to political parties, PACs, or other interest groups). There were 193 million Americans of voting age in 1996, so a 6 percent contribution rate translates into 11.6 million contributors. See Census Population Reports: 1996, www.census.gov/prod/3/98pubs/p20–504.pdf (detailing voting age population).

46. A November 1998 Census reported that 54 percent of citizens with incomes of less than $35,000 were registered to vote, compared with 72 percent of citizens earning more. Moreover, only 63 percent of lower-income registered voters actually voted, compared to 71 percent for others. This means that poorer Americans go to the polls at only two-thirds the rate of those earning more than $35,000. See Reported Voting and Registration of Family Members, by Age and Family Income, U.S. Census Bureau, July 19, 2000, (www.census.gov/population/socdemo/voting/cps1998/tab08.txt). See also Raymond E. Wolfinger and Steven J. Rosenstone, *Who Votes?* 90–91 (1980); Frances Fox Piven and Richard A. Cloward, *Why Americans Still Don't Vote* 39–44 (2000); Rodolfo O. de la Garza and Louis DeSipio, Save the Baby, Change the Bathwater, and Scrub the Tub: Latino Electoral Participation After Seventeen Years of Voting Rights Act Coverage, 71 *Tex. L. Rev.* 1479, 1511 (1993) (with similar data concerning the Latino population).

47. See Ian Shapiro, Why the Poor Don't Soak the Rich: Notes on Democracy and Distribution, 130 *Daedalus* (forthcoming, fall 2001), available at pantheon.yale.edu/7Eianshap/soakrich.doc; John Roemer, Does Democracy Engender Justice? in *Democracy's Value* 56–68 (Ian Shapiro and Casiano Hacker-Cordón, eds., 1999); John Roemer, Why the Poor Do Not Expropriate the Rich, 70 *J. Pub. Econ.* 399–424 (1998). For philosophically sophisticated empirical studies, see Jennifer Hochschild, *Facing Up to the American Dream* (1995); Jennifer Hochschild, *What's Fair?* (1981); Douglas W. Rae et al., *Equalities* (1981).

48. For such an effort, see Bruce Ackerman and Anne Alstott, *The Stakeholder Society* (1999).

49. John Rawls, *A Theory of Justice* (1971). See also Douglas W. Rae, The Limits of Consensual Decision, 69 *Am. Pol. Sci. Rev.* 1270–94 (1975); Douglas Rae, Decision-Rules and Individual Values in Constitutional Choice 63 *Am. Pol. Sci. Rev.* 40–56 (1969).

THE MODEL STATUTE

1. The provision is broader than analogous sections of the McCain-Feingold bill (which is limited to communication that "refers to a clearly identified candidate for Federal office" and is made within sixty days of a general election or thirty days of a primary election), S. 27, 107th Cong., Sec. 201. In contrast to McCain-Feingold, we narrowly regulate expenses for such communications for only two purposes: (1) to require that gifts be made though the donation booth (if they are coordinated with the activities of a regulated speaker), and (2) for use as a potential trigger of larger Patriot disburse-

ments if private contributions of political communication dollars begin to swamp the system. In setting the outer contours of the definition of political communication, the commission should seek to capture "sham" issue advocacy while excluding non-political speech that innocuously refers to political issues ("Some people like elephants, others like donkeys, but everyone likes Coke!").

2. There is, of course, a potential problem here. If the commission had a widely circulated list of large contributors, it could undermine the anonymity regime. To satisfy this provision, the Enforcement Division should instead maintain a confidential list of contributors of $10,000 or more. Upon receiving an offer for private employment, past or present commission employees with inside knowledge would submit the name of the potential employer to the Enforcement Division and would then be told whether accepting the offer is permissible.

This procedure is similar to the "restricted securities list" maintained by many law firms. Before trading in a security, employees must inquire whether it is on the restricted list. But the list is not widely circulated because this would unnecessarily disclose the identities of corporations whose stock might be "in play."

3. Our statute does not change the treatment of private dollars that remain unspent at the end of a particular candidacy.

4. We remain faithful to *Buckley* by safeguarding each candidate's right to spend an unlimited amount from his own bank account. But we do not endorse this aspect of existing law and would provide an alternative statutory provision if the Court ever reversed its decision in this regard.

5. Subsections 13(b) and (c) have the combined effect of barring transfers of funds from national to state or local parties. The statute does not change the existing allocation rules governing how state and local parties must treat expenditures that benefit both federal and nonfederal candidates. It therefore allows continued use of the more lenient "ballot composition" method, which allocates costs "according to the ratio of federal offices to total federal and non-federal offices expected to be on the ballot in the next federal general election." FEC, *Campaign Guide for Political Party Committees*, at 47–48 and tbl. (1996). The Commission might well consider strengthening its allocation rules to dampen the hydraulic shift of fund-raising away from national party accounts. One way requires state and local parties to use a "Voter-Weighted Ballot Composition" method that weights the federal and nonfederal offices by the number of potential voters for each office. Under this system, a state party could not allocate more expenses to its nonfederal accounts merely because it has many candidates for small districts (i.e., for the state legislature) and only one candidate for the United States Senate.

6. Appendix A discusses the details of the algorithm needed to implement these adjustments.

7. Appendix D estimates the annual cost of administration as approximately $300 million. To cover the inevitable start-up expenses the act appropriates $4 billion to the commission for the first four years. It appropriates $1 billion every two years thereaf-

ter—almost double expected costs, but it is wiser to avoid any risk of starving the commission. Section 29 provides for a review of appropriation levels by the GAO eight years after the act is adopted. This should be sufficiently timely to prevent the accumulation of unacceptably large surpluses in the Patriot Fund.

APPENDIX A. THE STABILIZATION ALGORITHM

1. The commission will also calculate an analogous amount for total contributions in the previous three off years. There will be an analogously lagged response for off-year elections, with the commission comparing status quo off-year contributions to the previous off-year result under our Voting with Dollars regime to see whether an increase in the Patriot amount is necessary. But for simplicity, our analysis only works through the formulae relevant to presidential elections. In all that follows, the parallel off-year analysis proceeds solely on the basis of a comparison of off-year data, while the presidential analysis is based solely on a comparison of presidential-year data. We also assume for simplicity that all dollar amounts are expressed in today's dollars.

2. As mentioned in Chapter 8, we would include in VC_L the total amount that broadcast sellers report has been spent on issue advocacy ads which mention candidates or parties by name in the last year before the election, if such expenditures represent more than 20 percent of VC_L.

APPENDIX B. THE SECRECY ALGORITHMS

1. Because of the recission period, we define a contribution as being "actually" contributed only on the fifth day after its receipt by the blind trust.

2. The total amount of anonymously contributed dollars that a candidate (or political intermediary) would have available to spend on day t would be:

$$\sum_{i=1}^{t} [R(i) - S(i)]$$

where $S(i)$ would equal the amount that the candidate could spend on the ith day. Reporting of nonanonymous contributions would not affect the secrecy algorithm.

3. To allow these calculations to be made at the beginning of a campaign (for all $1 < t < 30$), we define:

$$A(t - 30) = WR(t) \quad \forall \ 1 \leq t \leq 30$$

where $WR(t)$ equals the reported total private dollar receipts for the winning candidate in the previous election on the tth day of her campaign. For purposes of the simulations reported below, the two values on day 31 were simply imputed to the first thirty days of each campaign.

4. This figure, like those reported below, is in addition to the five-day delay created by the recission period.

5. We gratefully thank Douglas Weber of the Center for Responsive Politics for providing these data.

APPENDIX C. DESIGNING CONTRIBUTION LIMITS

1. To reject the null hypothesis of randomness does not mean, however, that a candidate would accept any alternative hypothesis. For example, if a contributor claimed to give a candidate $100,000 on a particular day but the trust balance displayed a statistically significant abnormal increase of only $60,000, a candidate would tend to infer that the contributor probably gave $60,000 instead of the higher figure.

2. For the purposes of this appendix, we have assumed that the blind trust accepts contributions only on five business days per week—so that ten-day limits are synonymous with two-week limits.

3. For sufficiently large contributions, some of the amounts randomly attributed during the latter parts of the two-week period may be large enough to trigger a second round of randomization. Under these circumstances, some of the contribution will be reported during the next two-week period. If Bill Gates gives a million dollars to a House candidate, it would take our algorithm several weeks to deliver all the money to the happy recipient's account. But under the contribution caps that we ultimately shall propose, this possibility is much reduced.

4. See Ronald J. Gilson and Bernard S. Black, *(Some of) The Essentials of Finance and Investment* 204 (1993).

5. The ten-day standard deviation is 3.16 larger than the one-day standard deviation because $10^{1/2} = 3.16$. This can also be seen in table 2 in that the ten-day standard deviation ($31,623) is 3.16 times as great than the one-day standard deviation ($10,000).

6. We choose a low confidence level of 20 percent in part because many donors will have the opportunity to coordinate donations with spouses. Table 3 shows that if spouses simultaneously give a contribution equaling a quarter of a standard deviation, the candidate would still have only a 38 percent confidence that a claimed gift had in fact been made. Although this number may seem high to some, it will be greatly reduced once it is recalled that serious candidates will be hearing many big donors make big promises and claims. As we shall see, severe attribution problems result later on, and once they are taken into account, we believe that coordinated bombing by spouses will not defeat the system under the contribution limits we propose.

7. Once again, we thank Douglas Weber of the Center for Responsive Politics for graciously providing us with data on daily contributions.

8. By daily standard deviation, we mean the standard deviation of daily contributions over the prior thirty-day period.

9. Our model statute ties these (and all other) numbers to an inflation-adjusted index so that they remain constant in real terms over time.

10. More precisely, we recommend that the periodic contribution limit for a particular state's Senate candidates be $5,000 plus $40 per 100,000 members of that state's adult population. This formula was tailored by regressing the Senate standard deviations on the individual state populations.

11. Two hundred thousand dollars (two-year overall cap) divided by $5,000 (candidate-specific house cap) equals forty, and $600,000 (four-year overall cap) divided by $15,000 (average candidate-specific Senate cap) equals forty.

12. Consider, for example, the problem of "endogenous volatility." The foregoing examples assumed a uniform standard deviation in daily contributions (of $10,000), but the volatility in contributions varies widely across different types of elections. The standard deviation in daily contributions for House campaigns is much smaller than for Senate or presidential campaigns. This heterogeneity opens the possibility for contributors to exploit the low-volatility (House) campaigns as a mechanism for signaling that they gave to high-volatility (Senate or presidential) campaigns. Because large gifts are likely to stick out more in low-volatility campaigns, a contributor might give $5,000 to ten House candidates as a way of signaling that she had given $100,000 to a particular presidential candidate. Given the higher volatility of presidential campaigns, the $100,000 contribution might not allow a presidential candidate to infer an abnormally large gift, but when combined with $50,000 in contributions spread among low volatility campaigns, it may enhance the credibility of the presidential gift.

But even here, the presidential candidate will have to worry about chiseling. The savvy contributor may establish that she has given to the ten House races, but knowing that this is enough to send a credible signal, she could refrain from making good on her promise of the $100,000 to the presidential campaign.

INDEX